Praise for *DISSENT: Voices of Conscience*

When the actions of government become dangerous to the security of the nation and the liberties of the people, it takes a special courage and makes a special contribution for men and women inside the government to speak out, to sound the alarm, to keep alive the spirit of dissent. If we care about keeping democracy alive, we must welcome this book.

–**Howard Zinn**, author of *A People's History of the United States*

Ann Wright is a burr under the saddle of the Bush White House. She is, without question, one of the most honest and ethical individuals I have been privileged to know. As a soldier and a diplomat, Wright always placed her country, its direction and its welfare at the top of her priority list. When she resigned her State Department Foreign Service Officer position in protest over the unprincipled actions of the Bush administration in preemptively attacking Iraq, she did the right thing. I salute Ann Wright and all whose voices are heard in Dissent. *These are powerful voices of truth in an ocean of government deception.*

–**Brigadier General (Ret.) Pat Foote,**
   Former Commanding General, Fort Belvoir, Virginia

Voices of conscience are usually smothered in spin. That the stories of these heroes are recorded here gives me great hope—even more so, since I know many of them personally. Their examples show that in midst of the banality of war, it is still possible to do the right thing. Good news indeed!

–**Ray McGovern**, retired CIA Analyst
   and Presidential Briefer for George H.W. Bush

Ann Wright is an American hero. She has shown immense bravery and resolve in her quest for peace and her efforts to restore the reputation of the United States around the world. For her energy and commitment to peace, justice, and strengthening democratic principles, Ann Wright has earned the first annual Truthout Freedom and Democracy Award.

–**Victoria Harper**, truthout.org

Listen to Ann Wright. Her clear thinking will help us get out of this war.
   –**Maxine Hong Kingston**, author of *The Fifth Book of Peace,*
   and editor of *Veterans of War, Veterans of Peace*

Ann Wright is not one to be silenced.
   –**Ms. Magazine**

D0898292

DISSENT

Voices of Conscience

Colonel (Ret.) Ann Wright
and Susan Dixon

koa books

Koa Books
P.O. Box 822
Kihei, Hawai'i 96753
www.koabooks.com

Copyright © 2008 by Ann Wright and Susan Dixon
Edited by Arnie Kotler
Cover and book design © 2008, by Ayelet Maida, A/M Studios
Cover photograph by Dragan Trifunovic
Photo of Ann Wright © Alexis Ibarra
Photo of Susan Dixon © Shelley Hartling
Index by Madge Walls, All Sky Indexing

Printed in the United States of America
Koa Books are distributed to the trade by SCB Distributors

The opinions and characterizations in this book are those of the authors and do not necessarily represent official positions of the United States Government.

For more about Ann Wright and Susan Dixon's work, visit www.voicesofconscience.com

Publisher's Cataloging-in-Publication

Wright, Ann, 1946–

Dissent : voices of conscience / Ann Wright and Susan Dixon.
1st ed.—Kihei, Hawai'i : Koa Books, ©2008.

p. ; cm.

ISBN: 978-0-9773338-4-4
Includes bibliographical references and index.

1. Iraq War, 2003– 2. Bush, George W. (George Walker), 1946– 3. War on Terrorism, 2001– 4. United States—Foreign relations—2001– 5. Intervention (International law) 6. Unilateral acts (International law) 7. Whistle blowing. 8. Conscientious objectors I. Dixon, Susan L. I. Title. II. Title: Voices of conscience.

DS79.76 .W75 2008
956.7044/3—dc22   0801

1 2 3 4 5 6 7 8 9 / 12 11 10 09 08

Contents

Foreword

Daniel Ellsberg

This is a book that should be leaked into the government. I would like to see it, in digital form, hacked in its entirety into every personal computer in the Pentagon, the White House, State Department, NSA, CIA, and FBI. Is there someone out there who could do that?

That would be a marvelously subversive act. Nothing could be more subversive of the shameful silence to the Congress and American public within those institutions, the tolerance of dishonesty and manipulation, the complicity by those who know better with wrongful policies that endanger lives and our Constitutional order. We might even avoid a repetition, in Iran, of the horrors those public servants saw coming in Iraq and did their very best to avert.

If you who are fortunate to hold this book in your hands do not yourself hold office in the "national security" apparatus—if you lack guilty national secrets, if you have no safe in your office filled with documentary evidence of governmental crimes and lies (like the Pentagon Papers I belatedly revealed)—do you know someone, a friend or relative, who does? I urge you to share this book with them, your own copy after you have read it or a new one; I don't count on their choosing to pick it out themselves. And, then, keep after them to read it. It's not for their coffee table or their overstuffed shelves. It should be by their bedside or in their bathroom. (It's very readable, and each brief story stands alone, though the cumulative effect is overwhelming).

These suggestions are not rhetorical. Even someone like me, who has lived through the same trajectory of official experience, disillusion, and new choices as those in this book, will find this account illuminating and remarkably impressive. For one thing, though I have made it a point to come to know personally many of these individuals whose actions I so much admire, I didn't realize, till reading their resignation letters and interviews here, how amazingly *prescient* they had been about the course in Iraq they were criticizing internally before they left office.

Were there others in their agencies who foresaw what lay ahead so clearly? Almost surely so; some of those here mention it. It's a credit to their departments that such good officers, so conscientious and knowledgeable and candid as these, were on the inside, having risen through the ranks; and, of course, discreditable to these departments that they were so little listened to or influential, and in effect compelled to leave as the current catastrophe approached. Congress should hold investigative hearings that call them, and others like them then and now, to testify as to what was knowable at the time; and call their superiors as well to explain, along with them, how what they knew was suppressed within the bureaucracy, concealed from the public, and lied about at highest levels, and how those superiors came to participate in disastrous illegalities and cover-up.

The object of these hearings would be not punishment but enlightenment and reform. Is there any reason to suppose that this process of lying the country into new aggression is not being repeated right now, with respect to Iran and perhaps other target-areas of which Congress and public are still ignorant? Such hearings could provide a forum, which did not exist in Congress for those described here under Republican leadership as the war approached—and still does not exist under Democrat-chaired committees!—for potential truth-tellers like these still on the inside or recently resigned to educate Congress, in public hearings, under oath. Readers, press your representatives to hold such hearings now, before the onset of the next war, and perhaps we will be able to avert it.

If you're at all like me, you will have a whole set of new heroes when you finish reading this. Who has too many of those—people you'd like to know, to be like, to act as they did? Most of the individuals depicted here would probably dissent from their description as heroes. It's not a title one gives oneself. In any case, they would probably point out, they just did what anyone in their position, with their knowledge, should have done. And that is true. But how many of their colleagues and others in the same position, knowing pretty much what they did and, many of them, feeling about it much the same way, actually did do what they should, what these people did—withdraw their complicity and their silence, tell the truth to those outside their own organizations, at cost to their own clearances and careers?

Whistleblowers are few and isolated in any walk of life, but there have been, until very recently, many more of them outside the national security establishment than within it, though remarkably, this book has gathered together more of the latter than would have been possible even a few years ago. No doubt that is because whistleblowers in industry or civilian agencies, though they generally suffer greatly in their advancement, careers, and personal lives, do not have to face the possibility of prosecution or the almost-certain charge, however misdirected and unfounded, that they have hurt national security, allegedly endangered troops, shown disloyalty and lack of patriotism, or (more factually) broken promises to keep secrets on which their clearances and access were based.

Most of those national security officials who do *not* blow the whistle when they should, are not even conscious of the conflict with the oath of office they all took, which was not to the President or Commander-in-Chief, not to their agencies or the secrecy system, but solely *to uphold and defend the Constitution.* They fail to see a conflict between their complicity with unconstitutional or illegal policies and their oath of office simply because they have never reflected on what the latter obligation—which, in fact, many of them violate every day they keep silent—might actually entail. The rare exception like Lt. Ehren Watada (pp. 161–167), who testifies here that he did perceive this contradiction and did act to resolve it by disobeying illegal orders, is perhaps the single officer in the U.S. Armed Forces today who has actually been faithful to his oath of office.

Yet the very same oath has been taken by every officeholder in the government and by every member of Congress, most of whom are in actual practice no more loyal to the Constitution than I was—having taken that oath to defend it as a Marine, an official in the Department of Defense, and a Foreign Service Officer (FSR-1) in Vietnam —before I revealed the Pentagon Papers and started telling the truth I knew to Congress and others. When British diplomat Carne Ross says (p. 54), "I am ashamed that I didn't speak up earlier," and former FSO

John Brady Kiesling, the first U.S. diplomat to resign in opposition to the coming war in Iraq, says (p. 25), "Because we were loyal to the President and our careers, we failed the American people," they speak for me.

Katharine Gun of Britain (pp. 39–43), 28 years old at the time, is the *single* civil servant known to me who did what I have been urging others to do for the past two years with respect to Iran: release an incriminating classified document to the public *before* the war. Her success in helping deny the U.S. the votes of support it sought in the UN Security Council—though it did not prevent, as she had reasonably hoped, the U.S. or even the UK from going ahead without Security Council authorization—did deny them any cloak of legitimacy for what was, thereby, clear-cut aggression (triggering the resignations and later revelations of Elizabeth Wilmshurst and Robin Cook, pp. 43–48). Gun's own fidelity to international obligations and its effects may yet preserve the possibility, in the future, of a world of law.

This book in the hands of current, future, or recently resigned officials, with its examples of moral courage in people like their own colleagues, like themselves, could awaken them to do likewise, to do better than they have done so far. This country will not escape further human, legal, and moral catastrophes, or preserve itself as a democratic, constitutional republic, if that does not happen. It is for the rest of us to hold our officials—and ourselves, in whatever groups and organizations we participate—to that standard.

This book can change your life.

Prologue

Ann Wright

*It's a dog day in our nation when high-level
authorities will seek to use every method to silence
dissent.... I say that those who are seeking to make it
appear that anyone who opposes the war... is a fool or
a traitor or an enemy of our soldiers is a person who
has taken a stand against the best in our tradition.*[1]

   –Dr. Martin Luther King, Jr.

I
n December 2001, I volunteered to be part of the team that re-
opened the U.S. Embassy in Afghanistan. A month later, a few of
us went to Bagram Air Base in Kabul to wish Afghanistan's interim
leader, Hamid Karzai, good luck as he left for Washington to attend
the State of the Union address. We encouraged him to secure commitments for military and development funds, knowing that America's
attention seldom stays on any one country for long.

Three days later, I was sitting in a bunker outside Kabul's old Chan-
cery building, watching President Bush's State of the Union address on
a TV our team had connected to a satellite dish made from flattened
Coke cans and activated with a Pakistani computer chip. We were awaiting news of the President's plans for Afghanistan, but after he said a
few words about Afghanistan, he began talking about Iran, Iraq, and
North Korea, calling them the "Axis of Evil." The TV cameras focused
on Hamid Karzai, in the gallery, and I could almost see him wince.

Like many other Americans, I'd felt that the U.S. needed to respond
to the attacks of 9/11, and going after al Qaeda in Afghanistan seemed
sensible and appropriate. Countries around the world supported our
action as a legitimate response to the attacks. But as I stayed in Afghanistan longer, I began to wonder when the full strength of the United

States would be brought to bear. Why was it was taking so long to clear out the Taliban, capture al Qaeda, and help the Afghan people rebuild their country? Washington kept telling us we couldn't expand our presence to all the major cities or begin economic development too quickly. Why? We were in an extremely dangerous situation without enough military, but instead of deploying additional troops, President Bush started threatening other countries, the so-called Axis of Evil. I sat there stunned.

Half a year later, I was Deputy Chief of Mission (Deputy Ambassador) in the U.S. Embassy in Mongolia and followed developments in Afghanistan and the buildup to war in Iraq. By then, the U.S. had deployed tens of thousands troops to the Middle East. When the Bush administration's mushroom-cloud rhetoric began, it was obvious that Bush, Cheney, Rumsfeld, and Rice were not waiting for UN authorization, that they intended to go to war. For the first time in my thirty-five years of government service—military and diplomatic—I was unable to represent a position of the United States. I'd disagreed with policies of many administrations, but none seemed as fundamentally dangerous and morally wrong as the imminent invasion of Iraq.

Much of my military background concerns the law of warfare. The U.S.'s action in Afghanistan, it seemed to me, had met the criteria for engagement under international law as a direct response to the September 11th attacks. But going to war in Iraq was entirely different. Iraq had not done anything to us. Therefore, under international law—the Nuremberg Principles and the Geneva Conventions—this would be a war of aggression, a war crime.

I felt the claim that America and the world were in imminent danger from Iraq's weapons of mass destruction (WMD) was misleading. Although I had no specific knowledge of Iraq's weapons of mass destruction, I felt that Saddam would not use them because he knew the response of the U.S. would be massive. During the decade following the first Gulf War, the United States and our allies flew 400,000 missions over two no-fly zones, taking photos the whole time. If there had been WMD in Iraq, we would have seen evidence of it, as would the UN weapons inspectors, many of whom were U.S. intelligence officials. Ten years after the rout of Saddam's forces and the destruction of much of his military hardware—reinforced by a ten-year embargo on replacement military equipment—Iraq did not pose a challenge to the best-equipped, best-trained military on earth. A "preemptive strike" in that part of the world could easily incite individuals and groups to attack the United States and American citizens.

This was the first time I ever thought about resigning. I loved my job and serving my country, and wanted to continue. But a foreign service officer's assignment is to implement the policies of the administration in power, and if one disagrees strongly with an administration's policy and wants to speak out publicly, the only option is to resign. It was winter in Mongolia, and I was waking up at three or four o'clock most mornings, freezing cold. So I developed a ritual to try to make sense of my government's actions and what I might do about them: I wrapped myself in blankets, went to the kitchen table, and wrote page after page on the Bush administration's intentions and my responses.

I'd also begun to study Buddhist texts to try to understand the cultural and spiritual foundations of Mongolian society.

One commentary stated that all actions have consequences, and nations, like individuals, are ultimately accountable for their actions. Another text, the Dalai Lama's statement on the first anniversary of 9/11, declared, "Conflicts do not arise out of the blue. They occur as a result of causes and conditions, many of which are within the antagonists' control. This is where leadership is important. Terrorism cannot be overcome by the use of force, because force does not address the complex, underlying problems. In fact, the use of force can exacerbate the problems and frequently leaves destruction and suffering in its wake."[2] On March 19, 2003, the day before the bombing began, I cabled my letter of resignation to Secretary of State Colin Powell. The moment I did, I felt a huge weight lift from my shoulders. I was taking a stand, joining two other American diplomats who had already resigned in protest. In the days that followed, I received nearly 400 emails from State Department colleagues saying, in effect, We're sad you are not going to be with us, but we're proud of the three of you who resigned, because we think going to war in Iraq will have terrible consequences.

Each letter writer then described the growing anti-American sentiment in the country where he or she was serving.

Because of the Bush administration's highly successful propaganda campaigns and a huge media failure in the United States, most Americans didn't realize until recently how often the Bush administration has violated domestic and international law. The lack of independent, credible information in America's mainstream media came about, in part, by the administration's punitive stance toward those who disagree with or criticize its policies. Since 9/11, the Bush administration has treated speaking out as unpatriotic, if not treasonous. Many of those who have dissented have faced the administration's wrath and retribution.

Despite this, people within our government did speak out. Susan Dixon and I wrote *Dissent: Voices of Conscience* as a tribute to these government insiders and active-duty military personnel who exposed our leaders' illegal actions, or resigned rather than accede to the actions, or refused to fight in what they considered an illegal war. Their loyalty to the Constitution and the American people transcended partisan politics.

Most Americans don't know about these courageous men and women —American and coalition insiders—who spoke out. These are patriots of our democracy, who stayed loyal to what is right, risking their own security. President Bush said that "questioning his actions . . . is a betrayal of the troops in battle today."[3] For those we profile in this book, the real betrayal would have been to stand by silently while our leaders were implementing policies destructive to our country and the world. They dared to dissent, dared to risk everything for the sake of *real* national security. We honor their courage, integrity, and patriotism by sharing their stories.

We must learn to welcome and not to fear the voices of dissent.

    –James William Fulbright,
      The Arrogance of Power

How We Got Into Iraq

In a time of universal deceit,
telling the truth becomes a revolutionary act.
    –George Orwell

On May 1, 2003, six weeks after U.S.-led forces invaded Iraq, President Bush landed on the *USS Abraham Lincoln* and announced, "Major combat operations in Iraq have ended." On a tower behind the President, a banner celebrated "Mission Accomplished" as Bush emphasized, "In this battle, we have fought for the cause of liberty and for the peace of the world.... Iraq is free."[1]

Nearly four years later, longer than the time than it took to defeat the Axis powers in World War II, President Bush declared, "Victory will not look like the ones our fathers and grandfathers achieved. There will be no surrender ceremony on the deck of a battleship."[2] Several months after that, in May 2007, the White House issued this statement: "President George W. Bush would like to see a lengthy U.S. troop presence in Iraq like the one in South Korea to provide stability but not in a frontline combat role."[3]

As we go to press, four and a half years after the invasion of Iraq, violence and bloodshed continue to spiral out of control. Thousands of American and coalition forces have been killed; many more have sustained physical and psychological injuries; and, according to a November 2006 Johns Hopkins University study, more than 655,000 Iraqis have been killed during this war—a figure ten times higher than U.S. government estimates.[4] Poverty, hunger, and public health in Iraq continue to worsen. According to Oxfam International, as many as four million Iraqis, many of them children, are in dire need of food; 70 percent of the country now lacks access to adequate water supplies; and 90 percent of the country's hospitals lack basic medical and surgical supplies.[5] Public frustration in the U.S. is at an all-time high, as the deaths increase, costs skyrocket, and America's reputation around the world plummets. Yet, President Bush has rejected calls from retired generals, active-duty soldiers, the Iraq Study Group, members of Congress, and 70 percent of the American public for a phased withdrawal of U.S. troops from this disastrous quagmire.[6]

Why *are* we in Iraq? In 1991, at the end of the first Gulf War,[7] then-President George H. W. Bush decided not to invade Baghdad or try to capture Saddam Hussein. He explained in his 1998 book, *A World Transformed,* that such action "would have incurred incalculable human and political costs . . . There was no viable 'exit strategy' we could see . . . Had we gone the invasion route, the United States could conceivably still be an occupying power in a bitterly hostile land."[8]

Why, then, did his son, George W. Bush, choose the opposite policy when he became President? According to many sources, the Bush administration was single-mindedly obsessed with removing Saddam Hussein from power. U.S. Treasury Secretary Paul O'Neill participated in a National Security Council meeting with President Bush on January 30, 2001, just ten days after the inauguration. O'Neill was stunned that the focus of the administration was regime change in Iraq.[9]

Former White House counterterrorism adviser Richard Clarke says that after September 11, "President Bush and senior administration officials wanted to bomb Iraq . . . even though they knew that it had no connection to al Qaeda, and that al Qaeda was responsible for the attacks."[10]

Before the U.S.-led invasion of Iraq, the Bush administration told our soldiers that they had "to fight—to die, if necessary—for a particular reason. That reason was a threat to the American homeland."[11] Bush, Cheney, Rumsfeld, and Rice warned, week after week, that Iraq had weapons of mass destruction and posed an imminent threat because Saddam "is seeking the means to strike the U.S., our friends and allies with weapons of mass destruction."[12]

In September 2002, Condoleezza Rice said, on CNN, "There will always be some uncertainty about how quickly [Saddam] can acquire a nuclear weapon. But we don't want the smoking gun to be a mushroom cloud."[13] The next month, Bush echoed Rice, "Facing clear evidence of peril, we cannot wait for the final proof—the smoking gun

—that could come in the form of a mushroom cloud."[14] Therefore, in order to protect America's national security, we needed to depose Saddam as quickly as possible.

The Bush administration deliberately blurred the threat that Iraq posed, lumping together biological, chemical, and nuclear weapons as weapons of mass destruction. Their campaign was so successful that, in March 2003, more than 90 percent of Americans believed Saddam Hussein had WMD.[15]

The administration also suggested, by repeatedly talking about 9/11 and Iraq "in the same breath,"[16] that Saddam had a role in the World Trade Center attacks, and this campaign was equally effective. Polls showed that, soon after 9/11, when Americans were asked "open-ended questions about who was behind the attacks, only 3 percent mentioned Iraq or Hussein.[17] By February 2003, "72 percent [of Americans] said it was either very or somewhat likely" that Saddam was "personally involved in the September 11th attacks.[18] In January 2003, nearly half of all Americans said "either 'most' or 'some' of the September 11th hijackers were Iraqi citizens," when, in fact, none of them were from Iraq.[19] Several months after the war started, one in four Americans "wrongly believed that Iraq had actually used its weapons of mass destruction against American forces during the fighting in March and April 2003.[20]

Since these claims were all proven false, why was the Bush administration so focused on regime change in Iraq? In the 1990s, Dick Cheney, Donald Rumsfeld, Paul Wolfowitz, I. Lewis ("Scooter") Libby, Jeb Bush, John Bolton, Richard Perle, William Kristol, Grover Norquist, and other influential neoconservatives formed the Project for a New American Century (PNAC). They had felt it was a mistake not to remove Saddam from power in 1991 at the end of the first Gulf War, and they were already planning a military strategy and logistics for a war to topple Saddam Hussein.[21] Shortly before the 2000 elections, PNAC released a report, *Rebuilding America's Defenses,* calling for a more aggressive policy in the Middle East, including the use of force to remove Saddam from power. In September 2001, President Bush announced a new *National Security Strategy of the United States of America.* It was "an ideological match" to *Rebuilding America's Defenses.*[22]

PNAC felt that a preemptive attack on Iraq would "dissuade" other countries from creating "asymmetrical threats" to U.S. power in the Middle East, provide the U.S. with the chance to build permanent bases in the region, and maintain access to the world's second-largest oil reserve, located in Iraq.[23]

In addition to this neoconservative drive for hegemony, other likely reasons for the U.S. invading Iraq include the political capital gained from being "a war president"; war profiteering for administration friends; and the opportunity to reverse Saddam's decision to sell oil for euros rather than dollars, a shift that could have devastated the American economy.[24] In addition, invading Iraq also gave George W. Bush the chance to eliminate an enemy who had haunted his family for more than a decade,[25] and possibly an opportunity to prove himself vis-à-vis his father.

While the Bush administration has repeatedly told us they acted to protect national security, in fact, their obsession with Saddam Hussein diverted attention from the real threat of al Qaeda. According to White House counterterrorism adviser Richard Clarke, CIA Director George Tenet repeatedly warned the President prior to 9/11 that "a major al Qaeda attack is going to happen against the United States somewhere in the world in the weeks and months ahead."[26] These warnings were ignored. Since 9/11, the Bush administration has denied allegations that American intelligence agencies had identified the hijackers. Yet, more than a year before the attacks of September 11, a secret military intelligence team identified Mohamed Atta and three other hijackers as probable members of an al Qaeda cell operating in the U.S.[27]

By early 2002, George W. Bush and his team were already diverting U.S. military and financial resources from going after Osama bin Laden and other al Qaeda operatives in Afghanistan—who were almost certainly the planners and perpetrators of the 9/11 attacks—to invading Iraq. Richard Clarke later revealed, "President Bush and senior administration officials wanted to bomb Iraq after 9/11 even though they knew that it had no connection to al Qaeda, and that al Qaeda was responsible for the attacks."[28] Clarke told Secretary of State Colin Powell, "Having been attacked by al Qaeda, for us to go bombing Iraq in response would be like our invading Mexico after the Japanese attacked Pearl Harbor."[29] The CIA knew that Iraq had no past or present contact with bin Laden, who was, in fact, a "longtime enemy of Iraq."[30] Michael Scheuer, a CIA analyst and former Chief of the bin Laden Issue Station, says that prior to the Iraq War, George Tenet was "briefed repeatedly by the head of the bin Laden department that—any invasion of Iraq would break the back of our counterterrorism program."[31]

Leaked documents reveal that Bush and his colleagues deliberately withheld information from Congress and the American public to inspire fear and create support for a war with Iraq—a country that had not attacked us and had no links to al Qaeda. It was not a failure of intelligence that led to invading Iraq. It was a war of choice.

In his mission-accomplished speech, President Bush said, "The use of force has been—and remains—our last resort."[32] In fact, veteran CIA officials confirm that by spring 2002, "it was almost taken for granted that we were going to go to war with Iraq," because the Vice President was giving them the clear message to find evidence showing "that Iraq was a threat."[33] The Downing Street Memos (DSM), leaked to the London *Times* in 2005, reveal that the Bush administration had already decided to use force and then fixed the intelligence to support this decision.[34]

PBS's *Frontline* documented Dick Cheney's role "as the chief architect of the war on terror," turning questionable intelligence—all later proven false—into "facts" delivered to Congress, the UN, and the American public. *Frontline* described Cheney as "the most powerful vice president in the nation's history," who, after the September 11th attacks, "seized the initiative. He pushed to expand executive power, transform America's intelligence agencies, and bring the war on terror to Iraq."[35] He consistently discounted findings of UN weapons inspectors that there were no WMD there.[36]

The Bush administration's campaign, supported by mainstream media, was so effective that in March 2003, 90 percent of Americans believed Saddam had weapons of mass destruction.[37] Even today, Bush and Cheney insist there was a link between Saddam Hussein's regime and al Qaeda, noting that Abu Musab al-Zarqawi was leading al Qaeda's operations in Iraq prior to the U.S. invasion. Although Zarqawi was in Iraq before the U.S. invaded, it was in an area of Iraq outside of Saddam Hussein's control, and in any case, Zarqawi didn't join forces with al Qaeda until late 2004.[38] The CIA has stated clearly that Saddam's regime "did not have a relationship [with], harbor, or turn a blind eye toward Zarqawi and his associates." The Senate Select Committee on Intelligence added that "far from aligning himself with al Qaeda and ... Zarqawi, Hussein repeatedly rebuffed al Qaeda's overtures and tried to capture Zarqawi." Saddam was a secular nationalist who, according to a classified CIA report from January 2003, "viewed Islamic extremists operating inside Iraq as a threat."[39]

We may never know exactly *why* Bush, Cheney, and other key players in the administration were obsessed with Iraq, why they chose not to pursue bin Laden and al Qaeda vigorously, or why the mainstream media failed to investigate the administration's claims, including Saddam's stockpile of WMD and his 9/11 connection. But we do know *how* the Bush White House, with the help of overseas allies, especially British Prime Minister Tony Blair, did deceive the Congress and the American public to get us into the present quagmire. It is a story of secrecy and deceit, known to us primarily because of leaked British documents.

While George Bush was assuring Congress and the public that he was doing everything possible to avoid war, invasion plans were well under way as early as April 2002. By this time, Tony Blair had already secretly committed the United Kingdom to joining the efforts to oust Saddam Hussein.

Tony Blair first spoke to his Cabinet about taking military action in Iraq in February 2002, and the level of internal dissent was described as "near mutiny."[40] Robin Cook, Leader of the House of Commons, later told the press that Blair ignored "the large number of ministers who spoke up against the war."[41] In addition to Cook, Home Secretary David Blunkett, Trade Secretary Patricia Hewitt, and International Development Secretary Clare Short spoke out.[42] One minister asked Blair, "What has changed that suddenly gives us the legal right to take military action that we didn't have a few months ago?"[43] Cabinet members feared that Blair's position on Iraq was motivated more by his loyalty to the American President than by his desire to protect the UK from terrorist attacks.[44]

The following month, in March 2002, the United States and its closest ally, the UK, secretly held high-level meetings to discuss their mutual commitment to remove Saddam Hussein from power. When top British officials met with their American counterparts, they left a paper trail in the form of classified meeting notes and memos between President Bush, Prime Minister Blair, and their aides. A number of these memos were leaked in the UK, and help us understand the Bush administration's obsession in early 2002 with overthrowing Saddam Hussein, while publicly claiming to focus on Osama bin Laden and al Qaeda.

In May 2005, the London *Times* printed the first of what turned out to be a series of leaked memos, now known as the Downing Street Memos (DSM). The earliest meetings described in the DSM took place in March 2002 in Washington between high-level members of the Bush and Blair administrations to discuss the invasion of Iraq.[45] David Manning, Blair's foreign policy adviser, told Condoleezza Rice that Blair was committed to working with the Americans to remove Saddam from power.[46] Christopher Meyer, British ambassador to the U.S., suggested to Paul Wolfowitz that their two countries use the UN and its weapons inspectors to require Saddam to adhere to standards he would likely violate, giving them legal justification to attack.

Tony Blair was scheduled to meet with President Bush on April 8, 2002, in Texas. To prepare his boss for that meeting, British Foreign Secretary Jack Straw drafted a memo in which he noted that the U.S. had already "assumed regime change,"[47] and Straw added a warning that "a stable post-war government would be impossible without keeping large numbers of troops there for 'many years.'"[48] Despite this warning and the Cabinet's near mutiny, Blair gave President Bush his country's commitment to help the U.S. oust Saddam Hussein.[49] This was months before Blair consulted Parliament about this.

Blair knew it would take time to convince Parliament and the British public that invading Iraq was necessary, and there wasn't much time, as U.S. plans for war were already in full swing. Two Downing Street Memos describe meetings of Blair's "inner circle" in July 2002.[50] On

July 21, the ministers were told to meet without him. According to Michael Smith, the London *Times* reporter who broke the story, these senior ministers were warned "that Britain was committed to taking part in an American-led invasion of Iraq and they had no choice but to find a way of making it legal."[51] The leaked memo describing that meeting said that "since regime change was illegal it was 'necessary to create the conditions' which would make it legal."[52] Blair was desperate to find legal grounds for this invasion, because even if the UK did not actively join in the military action, the U.S. had plans to use British bases in Cyprus and Diego Garcia; and the UK would therefore be complicit in any military actions.

Two days later, on July 23, 2002, Blair met with his senior ministers to hear their findings. The most damaging revelation from that meeting comes from Sir Richard Dearlove, chief of the British Secret Intelligence Service (MI6), who described his earlier meeting with CIA Director George Tenet:[53] Dearlove warned Blair that for the Bush administration "military action was now seen as inevitable. Bush wanted to remove Saddam, through military action, justified by the conjunction of terrorism and WMD. But the intelligence and facts were being fixed around the policy." At the same meeting, Foreign Secretary Jack Straw admitted that the case for war "was thin. Saddam was not threatening his neighbors, and his WMD capability was less than that of Libya, North Korea, or Iran." Additionally, American officials had given little thought to how to handle Iraq after the military action ended.[54]

Although President Bush continued to maintain publicly that "the use of force has been and remains our last resort,"[55] the Downing Street Memo of July 23 reveals that the U.S. had *already* begun bombing Iraq secretly to bait Saddam Hussein into retaliating. According to the British government, an average of ten tons of bombs were dropped on southern Iraq every month between May and August 2002, but these "spikes of activity," as the memo describes the bombing, did not goad Saddam into reacting.[56] In yet another leaked document, this one attached to the DSM, top British Foreign Office lawyers stated that the bombing campaign to put pressure on Saddam's regime "was illegal under international law, despite U.S. claims to the contrary."[57]

The Downing Street Memos, leaked to the British press in the spring of 2005, contain what authors Robert McChesney and John Nichols have called a "classic 'smoking gun' revelation."[58] London *Times* reporter Michael Smith, the first to report on the memos, argued that they were as important and revealing as the Pentagon Papers.

> This was the equivalent of an NSC [National Security Council] meeting, with President [Bush], Donald Rumsfeld, Colin Powell, Condi Rice, George Tenet, and Tommy Franks all there. They say the evidence against Saddam Hussein is thin, the Brits think regime change is illegal under international law so we are going to have to go to the UN to get an ultimatum, not as a way of averting war but as an excuse to make the war legal, and oh, by the way, we aren't preparing for what happens after and no one has the faintest idea what Iraq will be like after a war.[59]

The European media treated the memo as a smoking gun when it was leaked in the spring of 2005. "What more could journalists ask for than evidence that the big boss of British intelligence had secretly acknowledged that the president and his aides had faked the case" for the war in Iraq?[60] Yet most of the American media ignored the story for over a month. When they finally did cover it, they dismissed it as "old news."[61] The *Washington Post* further demeaned the memos by referring to the chief of British intelligence as simply "a British official."[62]

Soon after Blair's July 23 meeting with his ministers, the UK joined the U.S.'s extensive bombing of Iraq. The war against Saddam began "not in March 2003, as most believed, but in August 2002."[63] By late August, "the allies dramatically intensified the bombing into what was effectively the initial air war. The number of bombs dropped on southern Iraq by allied aircraft shot up to 54.6 tons in September alone" and continued to increase into 2003. Bush started his secret war six weeks before receiving congressional backing and two months before the UN passed Resolution 1441, "which the allies claim authorized military action."[64] In October 2002, when Congress did give Bush the authorization to use force in Iraq, he stated, "I have not ordered the use of force. I hope the use of force will not become necessary."[65]

On September 24, 2002, Tony Blair presented an intelligence dossier to the British government and public with purported evidence that

Saddam Hussein could launch WMD within forty-five minutes, thus posing an urgent threat to the UK and the world. The dossier was filled with inaccuracies, and it presented claims that were, at best, tentative as though they were certain. British intelligence analysts found Blair's claims to be distorted "for political purposes" to exaggerate the threat posed by Saddam.[66] Months later, it was discovered that parts of the dossier were plagiarized via the Internet from an Iraqi-American student's 1991 Ph.D. dissertation. Blair's closest adviser apologized to MI6 Chief Dearlove "for discrediting the service."[67]

Carne Ross, Britain's Iraq expert at the UN from 1998 to 2002, had read all the British and American intelligence on Iraq's weapons and was in constant contact with weapons inspectors.[68] He had worked on early drafts of this dossier and was deeply troubled to realize that the Blair administration was presenting "totally implausible" evidence about Iraq's WMD.[69] Ross later testified that Britain's "conduct at the UN Security Council in the run-up to the invasion amounted to deceit" and that the invasion was illegal.[70]

Senior intelligence officers within the British Defence Ministry, it was later revealed, had deep concerns about this intelligence report, especially the forty-five-minute claim.[71] Dr. David Kelly, an expert on chemical and biological warfare and a former UN weapons inspector in Iraq, was also troubled.[72] A senior official in the Defence Intelligence Staff said that he and his staff found three things troubling: the lack of detail, the lack of supporting evidence, and the questionable credibility of the source.[73]

Still, in November 2002, the UN passed Resolution 1441, demanding that Iraq disarm or there would be "serious consequences."[74] Lawyers in the British Foreign Office "were crystal clear in advising that Resolution 1441 did not authorize the use of force and that without a further resolution the UK could not lawfully use force against Iraq to ensure compliance with Iraq's WMD obligations."[75]

The British had more at stake than the U.S. in securing international approval. Unlike the U.S., the UK is a signatory to the International Criminal Court (ICC), established in 2002 as "the first permanent international war-crimes tribunal."[76] The British government and individuals acting under its authority—civilian and military—could be found guilty by the ICC of war crimes. During the run-up to the Iraq War, the British "government was so concerned that it might be prosecuted, it set up a team of lawyers to prepare for legal action in an international court."[77]

As Attorney General, Lord Peter Goldsmith was chief legal adviser to the British government. Because this was a case involving international law and Lord Goldsmith's expertise was in financial law, he had to rely on the Foreign Office for guidance in these matters. At first, he agreed with the Foreign Office "that the threat posed by Saddam Hussein did not warrant a pre-emptive strike" and that military action in Iraq would be legal only with a new UN resolution.[78] This was not what Tony Blair wanted to hear, and he asked the Attorney General not to declare his position "formally, . . . [rather] to stay silent until he could guarantee that his advice was helpful in justifying war."[79]

Foreign Secretary Jack Straw, who had previously expressed concerns about invading Iraq, was now among the few British government officials who felt a second UN resolution would not be necessary. In autumn 2002, Foreign Office legal chief Michael Wood and his deputy Elizabeth Wilmshurst confronted Straw about this, and Straw said, "I am a lawyer. I have negotiated every dot and comma of this. Thank you for your advice, but I am not going to take it."[80] He "flatly overruled" Wood and Wilmshurst, "causing them to appeal to Goldsmith to act as an arbiter." In early 2003, Lord Goldsmith told the Foreign Office lawyers, "The prime minister has told me that I cannot give advice, but you know what my views are."[81]

Despite having told the Foreign Office that war with Iraq would be legal even without a new UN resolution, in a January 2003 note to Tony Blair, Jack Straw "expressed his private concerns about the absence of a smoking gun." He said he hoped that Hans Blix, the UN's chief weapons inspector, "would come up with enough evidence to report a breach by Iraq of its UN obligations."[82] By the end of January, however, UN inspectors had spent six weeks searching for weapons throughout Iraq as part of UN Security Council Resolution 1441, and their searches had turned up no evidence of WMD.

On January 31, 2003, Tony Blair met with George Bush in the White House. A top secret memo detailing this meeting, leaked to the British press in 2006, revealed that both leaders "candidly express[ed] their doubts that chemical, biological, or nuclear weapons would be found in Iraq in the coming weeks."[83] Bush suggested additional ways they might provoke Saddam Hussein, to provide an excuse for war. He even proposed painting a U.S. drone plane with UN colors to incite Saddam to shoot the plane down.

Blair insisted they needed to lobby for a new UN resolution for Iraq, one that clearly spelled out the conditions under which an invasion would be regarded as legal. Bush reluctantly agreed, saying that "the U.S. would put its full weight behind efforts to get another resolution and would twist arms and even threaten." Then he told Blair that "military action would follow"[84] no matter what decision the Security Council made and "even if UN inspectors found no evidence of a banned Iraqi weapons program."[85] He reminded Blair that "the diplomatic strategy has to be arranged around the military planning." Blair confirmed that he was solidly behind U.S. plans to invade Iraq.[86] In public, both leaders continued to assure their governments and citizens that no decision had been made.

On January 31, while Bush and Blair were meeting in Washington, Katharine Gun, a translator for the Government Communications Headquarters (GCHQ), the British counterpart to the U.S. National Security Agency (NSA), read a top secret email from a senior NSA official. The email asked the British intelligence services to join the U.S. in spying on members of the United Nations Security Council "as part of the U.S. effort to win Security Council support for an invasion of Iraq."[87] Throughout the month of January, the U.S. had been preparing to present to the UN Security Council its case that Saddam posed an urgent threat to the international community because he had weapons of mass destruction. Most of the world believed this case was built on faulty intelligence and wanted UN inspections to continue. Knowing it was facing a difficult challenge, the U.S. government wanted every advantage. The email that Gun read exposed "for the first time the scope and scale of U.S. communications intercepts targeted against" UN delegates, including Secretary General Kofi Annan.[88] It was part of the Bush administration's effort to "twist arms and even threaten" countries to secure UN support for war.[89]

Gun was convinced that invading Iraq was morally and legally wrong[90] and thought the U.S. and UK might not start a war if they didn't receive the UN's approval. So she leaked a copy of this highly classified email to the *Observer*, which printed it on the front page.[91] Gun then confessed to being the source, and she was arrested and fired.

At the same time as the U.S. was spying on UN Security Council delegates, President Bush told a White House press conference, "I've not made up our mind [*sic*] about military action. Hopefully, this can be done peacefully." In his weekly radio address, he added, "We are doing everything we can to avoid war in Iraq."[92] Tony Blair told his country that no decision had been made yet about Iraq.[93] Three weeks after meeting with Bush in Washington, Blair told the House of Commons that "the government was giving Saddam 'one further, final chance to disarm voluntarily.'"[94]

On February 5, 2003, Secretary of State Colin Powell presented the U.S. government's case against Iraq to the United Nations. Powell used satellite photos as evidence of Iraq's weapons programs. When he spoke of Saddam Hussein's mobile facilities for making biological, chemical, and nuclear weapons, he quoted an "eyewitness account" of an Iraqi chemical engineer who had supervised the facilities.[95] In fact, the Defense Intelligence Agency and the CIA had already identified the source as "a liar" and "a con artist who drove a taxi in Iraq."[96]

Before the speech, CIA Director George Tenet had assured Powell that the information was "ironclad." He did not tell Powell that no American had ever talked to the source, code-named "Curveball," or that Curveball was the only source for that information. Curveball's accusations became a key part of the October 2002 National Intelligence Estimate (NIE). Soon after Powell gave his speech, Tenet informed him that the evidence he had presented to the UN turned out to be untrue.[97] Three years later, Powell admitted that he and "his department's top experts never believed that Iraq posed an imminent nuclear threat, but that the President followed the misleading advice of Vice President Dick Cheney and the CIA in making the claim."[98] In July 2007, Powell said that he'd spent two hours trying to persuade President George Bush not to invade Iraq: "I tried to avoid this war, I took

him through the consequences of going into an Arab country and becoming the occupiers."[99]

Leaked documents also indicate that Tony Blair pressured Attorney General Lord Goldsmith to declare British participation in the
invasion of Iraq to be legal. Goldsmith felt uneasy about this and, in
late January 2003, wrote a memo to Blair expressing his concerns.[100]
Knowing that the Attorney General felt that war would be illegal, Blair
sent him to Washington in February 2003 to meet with senior members of the Bush administration.[101] According to Lord Goldsmith's classified testimony, recorded in a 2004 inquiry, he met with Attorney
General John Ashcroft and a "senior associate counsel to the President
and legal adviser to the National Security Council,"[102] John Bellinger.
Bellinger, now legal adviser to the U.S. Department of State, later
boasted, "We had a problem with your Attorney General, who was
telling us it was legally doubtful under international law. We straight-
ened him out."[103] At this point, Goldsmith told lawyer friends that his
position was "impossible" and questioned whether he should stay in
his job.[104]

Leaked documents confirm that at the beginning March 2003, Lord
Goldsmith continued to believe that military action in Iraq would be
illegal without a new Security Council resolution. Blair was desperate
for a new resolution to "provide political, diplomatic, and even legal
authority for a military conflict," one which Blair had already committed to.[105] When passage of a second UN resolution began to seem unlikely, Blair pressured Lord Goldsmith to change his opinion about the
legality of the war. On March 7, 2003, Goldsmith wrote a thirteen-
page memo carefully considering whether war with Iraq could be legal
without a second resolution, and he concluded that a reasonable case
could be made that a war would be legal, although the case would likely
be challenged.

This memo did not satisfy Britain's military leaders, who "were wary
of being accused of war crimes in the aftermath of the conflict."[106] General Sir Mike Jackson, head of the British Army, said privately, "I have
spent a good deal of time in the Balkans to make sure [Serbian President Slobodan] Milosevic was put behind bars. I have no intention
of ending up in the cell next to him in The Hague."[107] The UK's Chief

of Defence Staff, Admiral Sir Michael Boyce, said he "needed a more definitive declaration if he was to commit his forces."[108] The military chiefs were being asked to wage a "new kind of pre-emptive war, in which it was far from clear that Britain itself was under imminent threat."[109]

It was "a crisis of monumental proportions" for Tony Blair when he learned that his military leaders would refuse to send troops without a ruling that the war was legal.[110] British troops were already on Iraq's border. He had to find a way to gain government approval for the war, and his last chance was for the Attorney General to declare unequivocally that war would be legal. Under this intense pressure, Lord Goldsmith again considered resigning, because he couldn't give this definitive response. But if Britain's Attorney General "resigned in circumstances that suggested he thought Mr. Blair was flouting international law," the damage to Blair's reputation would be "immense."[111] The Bush administration told Blair to find a new lawyer.[112]

Days before the war in Iraq was to begin, Lord Goldsmith was ordered to find any means necessary to declare the war legal. On March 13, 2003, he asked Professor Christopher Greenwood of the London School of Economics for advice, knowing that Greenwood was one of the few British lawyers who believed that war with Iraq would be legal even without a new UN resolution.[113] It was later revealed that Greenwood "received more than £50,000 from Lord Goldsmith for his services, a fact never revealed in his media appearances."[114]

The day he met with Greenwood, Lord Goldsmith was also summoned to Downing Street to meet with Prime Minister Blair's closest aides—Baroness Sally Morgan, Director of Political and Government Relations, and Lord Charles Falconer, Secretary of State for Constitutional Affairs. During their meeting, Goldsmith told Baroness Morgan and Lord Falconer that he now felt that war in Iraq would be legal without a second UN resolution. He had chosen to rely on Blair's assertion that Iraq was in material breaches of several UN resolutions. When asked during a later inquiry about this decision, Lord Goldsmith "suggested it was the Prime Minister's call to make the final determination on WMD." Never before had an Attorney General felt unable to give legal direction on his own.[115]

By March 17, 2003, it had become clear that the UN would not support military action in Iraq, and Bush and Blair announced their intention to invade Iraq anyway. The same day, Attorney General Goldsmith stood in front of Tony Blair's Cabinet, and then before Parliament, and declared that invading Iraq would be legal *without* a second UN resolution. The Cabinet and Parliament were told, falsely, that the single sheet of paper they had been given was the full extent of the Attorney General's legal advice on the war. This was in violation of the official ministerial code of conduct, requiring "the full text of any advice to be made available."[116] When asked in a 2004 inquiry why Lord Goldsmith's full advice had not been circulated to the Cabinet or Parliament, Blair indicated that "he could not trust some members of his cabinet with such papers."[117]

In fact, it was Blair who couldn't be trusted. By March 2003, "intelligence and legal advice were being stretched beyond breaking," a fact later confirmed by top spymaster Sir Richard Dearlove, Blair's European adviser Sir Stephen Wall, and two other former government officials.[118]

The single page published on March 17 as the Attorney General's legal opinion was not his legal advice or even a summary of his advice.[119] Testifying at an inquiry in 2004, the Attorney General admitted that Baroness Morgan and Lord Falconer "shortly, of course, set out my view in a Parliamentary Question,"[120] giving clear legal support to the Iraq War. When this testimony was leaked to the press in 2005, it revealed that Lord Goldsmith did not actually write his March 17 memo. It had been written by Morgan and Falconer. The problem was not just that Lord Goldsmith had changed his mind. It was that Members of Parliament "were not made aware of—to put it politely—the progression of his thinking."[121] The Attorney General's authorization paved the way for Britain to take part in the Iraq War. Members of Parliament voted, based on what they believed was the Attorney General's unequivocal counsel, to approve the use of military force in Iraq.[122]

In response, a number of high-ranking British officials resigned. Robin Cook, Leader of the House of Commons, had served the British government for nearly thirty years. In his March 17 resignation speech to Parliament, he argued that invading Iraq without a new UN resolution would be illegal and immoral, and he received the first standing ovation in the 700-year history of the House of Commons.[123]

The next day, Elizabeth Wilmshurst, a government attorney with three decades of experience and an expert on crimes of aggression, also resigned in protest.[124] She was deeply concerned, because invading Iraq without a new UN resolution would constitute a crime of aggression.[125] To initiate such a war would be "the supreme international crime," according to the Nuremberg Tribunal convened after World War II. It would be the same crime for which the Allied powers sentenced Nazi leaders to death.[126]

Unlike Cook, Wilmshurst went out quietly, but her letter of resignation made her position on the illegality of the war clear. She wrote that the Attorney General had given Blair more advice than the one-page March 17 memo and, even worse, that Lord Goldsmith's view of the legality of the war had changed dramatically in the two weeks leading up to the invasion. Hoping to prevent the public and Parliament from knowing this explosive information, the Blair administration sealed Wilmshurst's letter of resignation, and it remained classified for two years, until a Freedom of Information request forced the government to release it.

On March 18, 2003, the day Elizabeth Wilmshurst resigned, Tony Blair used the Attorney General's declaration and the September 2002 intelligence dossier—subsequently debunked—to persuade Parliament to authorize military action in Iraq *without* the support of the UN or the international community. He warned Parliament that Saddam Hussein posed a serious threat to Britain and the world because "Iraq has WMD it can deploy on as little as forty-five minutes' notice,"[127] thus violating UN Security Council Resolution 1441.[128] Late that evening, following nine hours of debate, Parliament voted to authorize military action in Iraq, based on the Prime Minister's claims. More than one-third of the MPs voted to oppose the government's stance,[129] declaring in an amendment that "the case for war on Iraq was 'not proven'"[130] and that "there was no moral justification for war without a new UN resolution."[131] On March 20, the war began.

To get the authorization he wanted, Tony Blair had given Parliament false information. Robin Cook later revealed that at the time Parliament was being asked to vote on war, Blair admitted to him that Saddam did not have the capacity to pose a serious threat to British interests. Blair's comment "appeared to contradict directly the assertion in the September [2002] Iraq dossier that Saddam could make his WMD ready for use in forty-five minutes."[132] Cook said that Blair also misled the public about a third justification for war—that there were links between Saddam Hussein, al Qaeda, and the September 11, 2001, attacks on New York and Washington.[133]

In addition to Cook and Wilmshurst, at least eight other British officials resigned in protest:

- Junior Health Minister Lord Philip Hunt
- Home Office Minister John Denham
- Shadow Environment Minister Jonathan Sayeed
- Shadow Home Affairs Minister Humfrey Malins
- Shadow Health Minister John Baron
- Conservative Junior Whip John Randall
- Anne Campbell, Labour MP for Cambridge, resigned as parliamentary private secretary to Patricia Hewitt, the Trade and Industry Secretary.
- Bob Blizzard resigned as parliamentary private secretary to Work and Pensions Minister Nick Brown.[134]

Two months later, in May 2003, Cabinet member and Secretary of State for International Development Clare Short also resigned in protest. She viewed war in Iraq not only as illegal but also as a distraction from more serious threats to U.S. and British safety and security.

At the same time, "the UK's top scientific adviser on Iraq," Dr. David Kelly, leaked information to the BBC that Tony Blair had distorted prewar intelligence, especially the forty-five-minute claim, to exaggerate the threat and justify the war.[135] This story of Blair's deception "appeared on the *BBC News* once and never again. The BBC's Director of News said the company faced 'an unprecedented level of pressure from Downing Street' to drop the story and to apologize for the allegations." The BBC complied.[136]

By July 2003, the administration had identified David Kelly as the source of the leak, and Blair ordered Kelly to testify in front of the Ministry of Defence (MOD) and the Foreign Affairs Committee (FAC).[137] The Prime Minister's involvement and the pressure put on the BBC indicate the effort to silence Dr. Kelly and discredit his allegations. On July 18, two days after Kelly testified, he was found dead in the woods near his home.[138] David Kelly's death triggered the Hutton Inquiry that eventually ruled the cause of death as suicide, even though the evidence was far from conclusive. By January 2004, the Hutton Inquiry also declared Blair innocent of deliberately manipulating the 2002 intelligence assessment on Iraq's WMD.[139]

Two weeks after David Kelly's death, Britain's top spymaster, Sir Richard Dearlove, retired early, dealing yet another "blow to the government's credibility over its presentation of intelligence on Iraq."[140]

In February 2004, Katharine Gun's case came to trial. Even though she had confessed to leaking the classified spying memo, the British government waited eight months before charging her with violating the Official Secrets Act. The Bush administration wanted Gun severely punished to discourage future whistleblowers, but the Blair administration struggled with whether to take her case to trial at all. Gun's lawyers had made it clear they would use the opportunity to challenge whether Britain's involvement in the war in Iraq was legal. The government was concerned that Gun's lawyers had evidence that the entire Foreign Office legal team believed that the war in Iraq violated international law.[141] The day before Gun's trial, her defense team asked the government for all the advice it had received from Attorney General Goldsmith prior to the invasion about the legality of the Iraq War.

The morning the trial was to begin, the government dropped all charges, despite Gun's confession.[142] Government prosecutors realized that if they prosecuted Gun, the Attorney General's wavering would be revealed, so they dropped the case to keep that information secret, insisting instead, that it was because of lack of evidence.[143]

Gun's lawyers had intended to call Elizabeth Wilmshurst as a witness for the defense. When the press caught wind of this, Wilmshurst publicly confirmed that she had resigned because she believed the war in Iraq was illegal. This led to a public debate about how the Attorney

General could have come to the conclusion that war would be legal if the government's top international lawyers thought otherwise. Then it was revealed that Lord Goldsmith had changed his mind twice during the ten days before the war, and more questions arose. Why did he waiver? Had he been pressured or manipulated to say the war was legal?[144] The revelation that Lord Goldsmith's decision went against the entire legal team at the Foreign Office was devastating to the Blair administration.[145]

Dr. David Kay, head of the U.S.'s WMD search in Iraq, testified to the Senate in January 2004 that, after spending nine months in Iraq searching for weapons of mass destruction, he didn't think they ever existed.[146] Kay then resigned and called for a full investigation into this huge intelligence failure. Kay's conclusion was more damaging for Blair than for Bush and "stampeded" Blair into another governmental inquiry.[147] The Butler Inquiry, which began in February 2004, scrutinized how the prewar intelligence could have been so wrong about Iraq's WMD. After testifying that Blair's WMD claims were "totally implausible," Carne Ross, the UK's expert on Iraq at the UN, resigned in protest over his government's deception.[148]

Attorney General Goldsmith told the Butler Inquiry he could not show them "the contentious legal advice he provided to Blair on March 7, 2003.... The five-person committee was flabbergasted. Goldsmith gave in to their demand only after they told him they would abandon their inquiry and announce why they had done so."[149]

In the end, this inquiry, like the Hutton Inquiry, cleared Blair of deliberate deception, a verdict many government officials reject. A senior official in the Defence Intelligence Staff argued publicly that his department "got it mostly right on Iraq's WMD, but was ignored by its chief and the joint intelligence committee."[150] While the investigation ruled that Blair had not lied, it was still damaging to the government. It rejected one of Blair's justifications for the war—Iraq's links to al Qaeda.[151]

The Blair administration faced yet another challenge when Craig Murray, British ambassador to the central Asian country of Uzbekistan, complained about the use of information gained through torture. Murray was deeply concerned about American and British support for Islam

Karimov, Uzbekistan's brutal dictator, who was America's ally in the war on terror. Murray understood that the U.S. wanted to use Uzbekistan's strategic air base near Afghanistan's border, but he warned, "The U.S. is misconceived. In the short term, it may help fight terror, but in the medium term it will promote it."[152] The British government ordered Murray to stop talking about these issues and threatened him with lawsuits and jail. When he didn't comply, they accused him of trading sex for visas and other crimes he hadn't committed. In October 2004, Craig Murray was fired for "bad management."[153]

In February 2005, nearly a year after Attorney General Lord Goldsmith had testified privately to the Butler Inquiry, a transcript of his testimony was leaked to the *Guardian*. Goldsmith said the transcript was "inaccurate,"[154] that his statement regarding the legality of war had been "genuinely my own view, and I was not leaned on to give that view."[155] The Butler Inquiry agreed to rewrite the transcript.[156]

In March 2005, forced by the Freedom of Information Act, the British government released Elizabeth Wilmshurst's letter of resignation, but only after blanking out "a key passage," stating that it was not in the "public interest" to release the deleted section.[157] That night, an anonymous source leaked the blanked-out paragraph, revealing Wilmshurst's assertion that the Attorney General's view of the war had changed dramatically. MPs from all parties demanded that Blair publish the full advice of the Attorney General.[158] John Major, the former Prime Minister who had led his country in the first Gulf War, said "there was no logical or credible reason why full transcripts of Lord Goldsmith's opinions could not be published."[159]

Tony Blair was gearing up for the May 5, 2005, national elections, trying to focus on domestic issues and not on the Iraq War. But under pressure, on April 28, 2005, a week before the elections, Blair declassified and published "the full legal advice given to him by the Attorney General."[160] Upon the release of the memos, Lord Goldsmith declared that they were, in fact, consistent. The memo of March 7, 2003, he said, simply explored the complex legal possibilities, while the memo of March 17 was more definite because he had received information from the Prime Minister two days earlier that Iraq was in breach of its responsibilities as detailed in the UN Security Council resolutions.[161]

Goldsmith never explained how this "breach of responsibilities" gave the U.S. and UK the authorization to go to war.

British leaders have faced much more pressure about the war than American leaders have. The fact that so many top secret documents were leaked to the British press indicates the frustration felt throughout the British government. The Blair administration was subject to several Inquiries into deception and misconduct. While the verdicts cleared Blair of wrongdoing, British officials continue to criticize the findings of the Inquiries. Because British government insiders spoke out and leaked documents, we now have a nearly complete picture of how U.S. and UK leaders deceived Congress, Parliament, and the public into an illegal war that continues to devastate Iraq, the Middle East, and the world.

2

Diplomats Who Resigned

A very few... serve the state with their consciences,
and so necessarily resist it...
    –Henry David Thoreau

W hen a government employee opposes an administration's position, his first effort is usually to work from within. Sometimes one *is* able to influence policy. Career employees in the Justice, State, and Defense Departments, the military, and the CIA made valiant efforts to effect change from within to temper the Bush administration's war policies. When John Yoo, a junior attorney in the Justice Department's Office of Legal Counsel, advanced legal theories that denied minimal Geneva convention protection for detainees and subjected them to interrogation techniques that amounted to torture, State and Justice employees and some senior military legal officers argued against him.[1] Ultimately, they failed, but their efforts are an example of the courage some insiders have shown trying to contest policies of the Bush administration. We don't usually hear about efforts like these until those involved have left government service. Although the war on Iraq was not supported by many—perhaps most—career federal employees, they were unable to slow down, much less stop, the momentum of the war.

Institutional encouragement of dissent within the State Department began in the 1960s when Foreign Service officers and other policy officials felt their views on the war in Vietnam were not being heard. Some feared reprisals if they spoke out, and a task force was formed to look into these concerns. As a result, in 1971 the State Department created a "dissent channel" for contrary viewpoints to be transmitted privately and directly to the Secretary of State. It has been used sparingly; an average of fewer than ten messages per year have been sent.[2]

A foreign service officer's job is traditionally understood to be the implementation of the policies of the administration in power, and if an officer disagrees strongly with a policy and wants to speak out, her only option is to resign. But in the May 2007 edition of *Foreign Service Journal*, Steve Kashkett, vice president of the American Foreign Service Association, challenges this understanding: "What does a professional Foreign Service member do if he or she reaches a point of insurmountable personal disagreement with a major component of U.S. foreign policy?" Kashkett says that questions like these are being "whispered in the hallways by career employees in the Pentagon, the CIA, and other parts of the federal government," even though "the ethic of our profession is to keep one's personal opinions to oneself and to carry out faithfully the policies of the present administration." He continues:

> But what happens, if a once-in-a-lifetime crisis arises in which we see our government pursuing a course of action which, we cannot help but conclude, threatens the very security of our nation and its standing in the world? What if it is a matter of war and peace? If our sense of patriotism impels us to speak out, do we not have an obligation to bring our unique perspective to the public debate over this course of action—whatever the risk to our careers? Is it acceptable, for reasons of conscience, to refuse to accept assignments in the area directly affected by this particular foreign policy issue? Can we allow "conscientious objectors" to pursue their careers in other areas of foreign policy and reward them for excellence in those areas, rather than punishing them for their principled refusal to work on something they felt is deeply wrong?

> These days, we often hear certain colleagues declare self-righteously that anyone who refuses to embrace and carry out, without question, the administration's policies should be considered disloyal and should be removed from the Service. I would respectfully suggest that true patriotism is something broader than loyalty to one administration's policies, and that honorable, conscientious people in the Foreign Service may well feel that they are being patriotic by expressing dissent or choosing to avoid working on certain issues at a time of crisis so as not to advance policies they see as dangerously misguided.[3]

In February and March 2003, during the run-up to the invasion of Iraq, three career Foreign Service officers—John Brady Kiesling, John Brown, and coauthor Ann Wright—resigned in protest of the Bush administration's decision to go to war. We were all seasoned diplomats who agonized over this decision, ultimately resigning because our differences with the Bush administration were so great that we could see no alternative.[4] Shane Harris, in *Government Executive* magazine, wrote, "Those who know [these] former diplomats describe them as modest, patient, serious, and not prone to acting rashly. If these career diplomats were troubled enough to quit, it tells me something is wrong."[5]

↪ John Brady Kiesling
Diplomat

> *Because we were loyal to the President*
> *and our careers, we failed the American people.*
> –John Brady Kiesling

The first U.S. diplomat to resign in opposition to the war in Iraq was John Brady Kiesling. Kiesling had entered the Foreign Service in 1983 and served in Tel Aviv, Casablanca, Yerevan, Athens, and Washington, DC. He was no stranger to dissent. In the early 1990s, he and eleven colleagues used the dissent channel to press for military intervention to save Bosnian Muslims from Serbian genocide. They won an award from the American Foreign Service Association for their efforts.[6] When he resigned, he was political counselor at the U.S. Embassy in Greece. The political counselor promotes U.S. policies to government officials, journalists, diplomats, and other citizens and organizations the State Department wants to influence.

Kiesling tried to persuade increasingly skeptical diplomats in Greece that it was wise for the U.S. to invade Iraq, but he found the Bush administration's rationale increasingly difficult to explain. After Bush's September 12, 2002, speech to the UN General Assembly in which he linked al Qaeda to Iraq, convincing longtime contacts in Greece became impossible. With war in Iraq on the horizon, Kiesling resigned. His position had become untenable: "Until this administration, it had been possible to believe that by upholding the policies of my President I was also upholding the interests of the American people and the world," he wrote to Secretary of State Powell on February 23, 2003. "I believe it no longer."[7]

Eight months after resigning, Kiesling wrote that the decision to go to war—against the advice of Army Chief of Staff Eric Shinseki, who warned about troop levels needed to maintain security, and against the State Department's predictions concerning the negative reactions of Iraqis—"suggested that the people who ordered the war put their own political or bureaucratic interests above the interest of the American people they were sworn to serve."[8] In response to former House Speaker Newt Gingrich's complaint that U.S. diplomacy failed to convince our allies because we were disloyal to President Bush, Kiesling said the opposite was true: "Because we were loyal to the President and our careers, we failed the American people," adding that "...humiliation and powerlessness are a cause of terrorism, not its cure. Global threats require global alliances. Sacrificing allies to domestic politics is bad policy."[9]

Kiesling urged an honest assessment:

> By admitting the obvious about Iraq, we make ourselves stronger. We cannot adopt Saddam's methods, or even Sharon's, at a price America is willing to pay. Let us learn from history that no one will successfully govern Iraq until they are armed with the legitimacy that comes from driving us out ...When the protection of speaking the truth fails us, the most we can hope is that some of the cost of misusing U.S. diplomacy will be borne by those responsible for it. But there is no valid option of ceding our expert judgment to others less qualified, or speaking less than the truth about the planet.[10]

John Brady Kiesling's book about his experiences as a diplomat, *Diplomacy Lessons: Realism for an Unloved Superpower*, was published in 2006.

John Brady Kiesling's Letter of Resignation

February 27, 2003

Dear Mr. Secretary:

I am writing you to submit my resignation from the Foreign Service of the United States and from my position as Political Counselor in U.S. Embassy Athens, effective March 7. I do so with a heavy heart. The baggage of my upbringing included a felt obligation to give something back to my country. Service as a U.S. diplomat was a dream job. I was paid to understand foreign languages and cultures, to seek out diplomats, politicians, scholars, and journalists, and to persuade them that U.S. interests and theirs fundamentally coincided. My faith in my country and its values was the most powerful weapon in my diplomatic arsenal.

It is inevitable that during twenty years with the State Department I would become more sophisticated and cynical about the narrow and selfish bureaucratic motives that sometimes shaped our policies. Human nature is what it is, and I was rewarded and promoted for understanding human nature. But until this administration it had been possible to believe that by upholding the policies of my President I was also upholding the interests of the American people and the world. I believe it no longer.

The policies we are now asked to advance are incompatible not only with American values but also with American interests. Our fervent pursuit of war with Iraq is driving us to squander the international legitimacy that has been America's most potent weapon of both offense and defense since the days of Woodrow Wilson. We have begun to dismantle the largest and most effective web of international relationships the world has ever known. Our current course will bring instability and danger, not security.

The sacrifice of global interests to domestic politics and to bureaucratic self-interest is nothing new, and it is certainly not a uniquely American problem. Still, we have not seen such systematic distortion of intelligence, such systematic manipulation of American opinion, since the war in Vietnam. The September 11th tragedy left us stronger than before, rallying around us a vast international coalition to cooperate for the first time in a systematic way against the threat of terrorism. But rather than take credit for those successes and build on them, this administration has chosen to make terrorism a domestic political tool, enlisting a scattered and largely defeated al Qaeda as its bureaucratic ally. We spread disproportionate terror and confusion in the public mind, arbitrarily linking the unrelated problems of terrorism and Iraq. The result, and perhaps the motive, is to justify a vast misallocation of shrinking public wealth to the military and to weaken the safeguards that protect American citizens from the heavy hand of government. September 11th did not do as much damage to the fabric of American society as we seem determined to do to ourselves. Is the Russia of the late Romanovs really our model, a selfish, superstitious empire thrashing toward self-destruction in the name of a doomed status quo?

We should ask ourselves why we have failed to persuade more of the world that a war with Iraq is necessary. We have over the past two years done too much to assert to our world partners that narrow and mercenary U.S. interests override the cherished values of our partners. Even where our aims were not in question, our consistency is at issue. The model of Afghanistan is little comfort to allies wondering on what basis we plan to rebuild the Middle East, and in whose image and interests. Have we indeed become blind, as Russia is blind in Chechnya, as Israel is blind in the Occupied Territories, to our own advice, that overwhelming military power is not the answer to terrorism? After the shambles of postwar Iraq joins the shambles in Grozny and Ramallah, it will be a brave foreigner who forms ranks with Micronesia to follow where we lead.

We have a coalition still, a good one. The loyalty of many of our friends is impressive, a tribute to American moral capital built up over a century. But our closest allies are persuaded less that war is justified than that it would be perilous to allow the U.S. to drift into complete solipsism. Loyalty should be reciprocal. Why does our President condone the swaggering and contemptuous approach to our friends and allies this administration is fostering, including among its most senior officials? Has *oderint dum metuant* ("Let them hate us, as long as they fear us") really become our motto?

I urge you to listen to America's friends around the world. Even here in Greece, purported hotbed of European anti-Americanism, we have more and closer friends than the American newspaper reader can possibly imagine. Even when they complain about American arrogance, Greeks know that the world is a difficult and dangerous place, and they want a strong international system, with the U.S. and EU in close partnership. When our friends are afraid of us rather than for us, it is time to worry. And now they are afraid. Who will tell them convincingly that the United States is as it was, a beacon of liberty, security, and justice for the planet?

Mr. Secretary, I have enormous respect for your character and ability. You have preserved more international credibility for us than our policy deserves, and salvaged something positive from the excesses of an ideological and self-serving administration. But your loyalty to the president goes too far. We are straining beyond its limits an international system we built with such toil and treasure, a web of laws, treaties, organizations, and shared values that sets limits on our foes far more effectively than it ever constrained America's ability to defend its interests.

I am resigning because I have tried and failed to reconcile my conscience with my ability to represent the current U.S. administration. I have confidence that our democratic process is ultimately self-correcting, and hope that in a small way I can contribute from outside to shaping policies that better serve the security and prosperity of the American people and the world we share.

Signed
John Brady Kiesling
Political Counselor
U.S. Embassy
Athens, Greece

∾ John Brown
Diplomat

The second U.S. diplomat to resign in opposition to the Bush administration's decision to wage war on Iraq was John Brown, who had served in the diplomatic corps for twenty-two years. Brown has a Ph.D. in Russian history and had served in the Foreign Service in London, Prague, Krakow, Kiev, Belgrade, Moscow, and Washington. He was senior Cultural Affairs officer to Russia from 1992 through 2001.[11]

Brown described the administration's arguments for the war as crudely presented propaganda, with the constant repetition of words and slogans, the demonization of opponents of the war, and the appeal to fear of outsiders and shadowy enemies, all disrespectful of the sensitivities of foreign audiences.

President Bush's March 6, 2003, press conference, in the wake of the administration's failure to win the UN support, was

> the straw that broke the camel's back in making me decide to resign. Speaking to a docile media in a faux-imperial White House setting, red carpet and all, his scripted performance was a disastrous effort to explain why the United States should attack Iraq at this time ... After that debacle, I could not see myself continuing to work for the State Department.
>
> For most of my twenty-two-year career, I served in Eastern Europe and Russia, and I've had the privilege to meet extraordinary persons who stood up for cultural freedom and human rights at great personal risk (and with the encouragement of the embassies for which I worked). My resignation, of course, in no way can be compared to their struggle for truth and justice, but as I think about my decision to leave the State Department, I now realize that I was influenced by the example of those dissidents more than I was aware at the time.[12]

Following his resignation, Brown became research associate at the Institute for the Study of Diplomacy and adjunct professor at Georgetown University. He is also senior fellow at the University of Southern California Center on Public Diplomacy and editor of the Center's Public Diplomacy Press and Blog Review.

John Brown's Letter of Resignation

March 10, 2003
To: Secretary of State Colin Powell

Dear Mr. Secretary:

I am joining my colleague John Brady Kiesling in submitting my resignation from the Foreign Service (effective immediately) because I cannot in good conscience support President Bush's war plans against Iraq.

The president has failed:

- To explain clearly why our brave men and women in uniform should be ready to sacrifice their lives in a war on Iraq at this time;
- To lay out the full ramifications of this war, including the extent of innocent civilian casualties;
- To specify the economic costs of the war for ordinary Americans;
- To clarify how the war would help rid the world of terror;
- To take international public opinion against the war into serious consideration.

Throughout the globe the United States is becoming associated with the unjustified use of force. The President's disregard for views in other nations, borne out by his neglect of public diplomacy, is giving birth to an anti-American century.

I joined the Foreign Service because I love our country. Respectfully, Mr. Secretary, I am now bringing this calling to a close, with a heavy heart but for the same reason that I embraced it.

✑ Ann Wright
Diplomat

I was the third U.S. diplomat to resign during the run-up to war. I was troubled not only about the imminent invasion of Iraq, but also the administration's failure to address the North Korean nuclear crisis or engage in the Israeli–Palestinian peace process. And I was concerned about the unnecessary curtailments of civil rights in the U.S. following September 11.[13]

I had served in the Army and Army Reserves for twenty-nine years, taking part in civil reconstruction following U.S. military operations in Grenada and Somalia, and as a diplomat for sixteen years as Deputy Chief of Mission to Sierra Leone, Micronesia, Afghanistan (briefly in 2002), and Mongolia, and in Nicaragua, Grenada, Uzbekistan, Somalia (U.S. Liaison office), and Kyrgyzstan. I received the State Department's Award for Heroism for leading the evacuation of a large part of the international community from Sierra Leone in 1997.

Before resigning, I tried using the dissent channel to raise concerns, especially about possible reactions in the Middle East. I didn't expect my input to change policy, considering how the Bush administration's Iraq decisions were dominated by the Defense Department, but I wanted State Department policymakers to know there was at least one more Foreign Service officer who disagreed with the rush to war. The response from senior levels of the department broke no new ground regarding the need for immediate military action and did not lessen my disagreement.[14]

Following my dissent cable, I continued to hope the administration would not take military action without explicit Security Council authorization. But once President Bush gave Saddam Hussein forty-eight hours to get out of Iraq, it was obvious the administration had no intention of working further within the international community—including traditional allies—to address their legitimate concerns and broaden the base of support for actions in Iraq. Once that sunk in, I could no longer defend or represent this administration, and I cabled my letter of resignation to Secretary of State Powell.[15]

Like Kiesling and Brown before me, I received hundreds of emails and telephone calls from Foreign Service colleagues, employees of other U.S. and international agencies, and people I had never met from around the world expressing respect for the decision and frustration about the impending war.[16]

A few others let me know that they found any disagreement, even a call for continued discussion, to be insubordinate, even unpatriotic. To me, our country is stronger precisely because it stands for free speech, dialogue, and the protection of the rights of all, and becomes weaker when we discourage the diversity of ideas and opinions, particularly when we're talking about military action and the resultant loss of life and the destiny of a nation, or perhaps two.[17]

Since resigning, using my background in military and foreign affairs, I speak at colleges and universities, civic groups, and peace rallies throughout the U.S. about the necessity of ending the Iraq War and stopping future wars.

♥

Ann Wright's Letter of Resignation

March 19, 2003
Secretary of State Colin Powell
U.S. Department of State
Washington, DC 20521

Dear Secretary Powell:

When I last saw you in Kabul in January 2002, you arrived to officially open the U.S. Embassy that I had helped reestablish in December 2001 as the first political officer. At that time, I could not have imagined that I would be writing a year later to resign from the Foreign Service because of U.S. policies. All my adult life I have been in service to the United States. I have been a diplomat for fifteen years and the Deputy Chief of Mission in our Embassies in Sierra Leone, Micronesia, Afghanistan (briefly), and Mongolia. I have also had assignments in Somalia, Uzbekistan, Kyrgyzstan, Grenada, and Nicaragua. I received the State Department's Award for Heroism as chargé d'affaires during the evacuation of Sierra Leone in 1997. I was twenty-six years in the U.S. Army/Army Reserves and participated in civil reconstruction projects after military operations in Grenada, Panama, and Somalia. I attained the rank of Colonel during my military service.

This is the only time in my many years serving America that I have felt I cannot represent the policies of an administration of the United States. I disagree with the administration's policies on Iraq, the Israeli–Palestinian conflict, North Korea, and curtailment of civil liberties in the U.S. itself. I believe the administration's policies are making the world a more dangerous, not a safer, place. I feel obligated morally and professionally to set out my very deep and firm concerns on these policies and to resign from government service, as I cannot defend or implement them.

I hope you will bear with my explanation of why I must resign. After thirty years of service to my country, my decision to resign is a huge step and I want to be clear in my reasons for why I must do so.

I disagree with the administration's policies on Iraq
I wrote this letter five weeks ago and held it hoping that the administration would not go to war against Iraq at this time without United Nations Security Council agreement. I strongly believe that going to war now will make the world more dangerous, not safer.

There is no doubt that Saddam Hussein is a despicable dictator and has done incredible damage to the Iraqi people and others of the region. I totally support the international community's demand that Saddam's regime destroy weapons of mass destruction.

However, I believe we should not use U.S. military force without UNSC agreement to ensure compliance. In our press for military action now, we have created deep chasms in the international community and in important international organizations. Our policies have alienated many of our allies and created ill will in much of the world.

Countries of the world supported America's action in Afghanistan as a response to the September 11th al Qaeda attacks on America. Since then, America has lost the incredible sympathy of most of the world because of our policy toward Iraq. Much of the world considers our statements about Iraq as arrogant, untruthful, and masking a hidden agenda. Leaders of moderate Muslim/Arab countries warn us about the predictable outrage and anger of the youth of their countries if

America enters an Arab country with the purpose of attacking Muslims/Arabs, not defending them. Attacking the Saddam regime in Iraq now is very different than expelling the same regime from Kuwait, as we did ten years ago.

I strongly believe the probable response of many Arabs of the region and Muslims of the world if the U.S. enters Iraq without UNSC agreement will result in actions extraordinarily dangerous to America and Americans. Military action now without UNSC agreement is much more dangerous for America and the world than allowing the UN weapons inspections to proceed and subsequently taking UNSC-authorized action if warranted.

I firmly believe the probability of Saddam using weapons of mass destruction is low, as he knows that using those weapons will trigger an immediate, strong, and justified international response. There will be no question of action against Saddam in that case. I strongly disagree with the use of a "preemptive attack" against Iraq and believe that this preemptive attack policy will be used against us and provide justification for individuals and groups to "preemptively attack" America and American citizens.

The international military buildup is providing pressure on the regime that is resulting in a slow but steady disclosure of weapons of mass destruction (WMD). We should give the weapons inspectors time to do their job. We should not give extremist Muslims/Arabs a further cause to hate America, or give moderate Muslims a reason to join the extremists. Additionally, we must reevaluate keeping our military forces in the Middle East, particularly in Saudi Arabia. Their presence on the Islamic "holy soil" of Saudi Arabia will be an anti-American rally cry for Muslims as long as the U.S. military remains and a strong reason, in their opinion, for actions against the U.S. government and American citizens.

Although I strongly believe the time is not yet right for military action in Iraq, as a soldier who has been in several military operations, I hope that General Franks, U.S., and coalition forces can accomplish the missions they will be ordered to do without loss of civilian or military life and without destruction of the Iraqi people's homes and livelihood.

I strongly urge the Department of State to attempt again to stop the policy that is leading us to military action in Iraq without UNSC agreement. Timing is everything, and this is not yet the time for military action.

I disagree with the administration's lack of effort in resolving the Israeli–Palestinian conflict

Likewise, I cannot support the lack of effort by the administration to use its influence to resurrect the Israeli–Palestinian peace process. As Palestinian suicide bombers kill Israelis and Israeli military operations kill Palestinians and destroy Palestinian towns and cities, the administration has done little to end the violence. We must exert our considerable financial influence on the Israelis to stop destroying cities and on the Palestinians to curb their youth suicide bombers. I hope the administration's long-needed "Road Map for Peace" will have the human resources and political capital needed to finally make some progress toward peace.

I disagree with the administration's lack of policy on North Korea

Additionally, I cannot support the administration's position on North Korea. With weapons, bombs, and missiles, the risks that North Korea poses are too great to ignore. I strongly believe the administration's lack of substantive discussion, dialogue, and engagement over the last two years has jeopardized security on the Korean Peninsula and in the region. The situation with North Korea is dangerous for us to continue to neglect.

I disagree with the administration's policies on unnecessary curtailment of rights in America

Further, I cannot support the administration's unnecessary curtailment of civil rights following September 11. The investigation of those suspected of ties with terrorist organizations is critical, but the legal system of America for 200 years has been based on standards that provide protections for persons during the investigation period. Solitary confinement without access to legal counsel cuts the heart out of the legal foundation on which our country stands. Additionally, I believe the administration's secrecy in the judicial process has created an atmosphere of fear to speak out against the gutting of the protections on which America was built and the protections we encourage other countries to provide to their citizens.

Resignation

I want to continue to serve America. However, I do not believe in the policies of this administration and cannot defend or implement them. It is with heavy heart that I must end my service to America and therefore resign due to the administration's policies.

Mr. Secretary, to end on a personal note, under your leadership, we have made great progress in improving the organization and administration of the Foreign Service and the Department of State. I want to thank you for your extraordinary efforts to that end. I hate to leave the Foreign Service, and I wish you and our colleagues well.

Very Respectfully,
Mary A. Wright, FO-01
Deputy Chief of Mission
U.S. Embassy
Ulaanbaatar, Mongolia

3

Coalition-of-the-Willing Dissenters—British, Australian, and Danish

*The statesman who yields to war fever must
realize that once the signal is given, he is no longer
the master of policy but the slave of unforeseeable
and uncontrollable events.*[1]
　　–Winston Churchill

I f it weren't for outspoken British government insiders, we would
　know far less today about the machinations of U.S. and UK lead-
　ers during the run-up to war. Following are the stories of insiders from Great Britain, Denmark, and Australia.

✎ Katharine Gun
Translator, Government Communications Headquarters

> *Katharine Gun has a much better grasp of the true
> spirit of democracy than Tony Blair.*
> 　　–Editorial, *New York Times,* January 19, 2004

In early 2003, 28-year-old Katharine Gun, a translator for the British
Government Communications Headquarters (GCHQ), leaked a top
secret email revealing U.S. eavesdropping on UN Security Council
members to gather information that might help the U.S. pressure them
to vote in favor of authorizing the use of force in Iraq. While much
of the world was rocked by the news of "U.S. dirty tricks to win the
UN vote,"[2] White House Press Secretary Ari Fleischer refused to comment.[3] The British media didn't pursue the story for almost a year,[4] and
it took another year, until 2005, for the *New York Times* to break the

"silence shared with almost all major U.S. media outlets."[5] The biggest reaction in the U.S. came from the conservative online Drudge Report, which "suggested that the memo was a fake and invited readers to send 'flame' email messages to the British newspaper that actually printed the memo."[6]

Katharine Gun describes herself as "a very ordinary, concerned individual who could not sit back in silence while the leaders of the UK and the U.S. plotted about 'shock and awe.'"[7] She had worked at the GCHQ for two years when, on January 31, 2003, she read a top secret email from Frank Koza, a senior official at the U.S. National Security Agency (NSA), GCHQ's U.S. counterpart, revealing "that the [NSA] had started a 'surge' of spying on diplomats at the United Nations in New York, including wiretaps of home and office telephones along with reading of emails."[8] The 1961 Vienna Convention on Diplomatic Relations "strictly outlaws espionage at the UN missions in New York."[9]

Koza was asking the British intelligence services to help spy on members of the UN Security Council "as part of the U.S. effort to win Security Council support for an invasion of Iraq."[10] The U.S. government was specifically interested in the six countries that held the rotating (nonpermanent) seats on the Security Council—Angola, Bulgaria, Cameroon, Chile, Guinea, and Pakistan—to obtain "the whole gamut of information that could give U.S. policymakers an edge."[11] This email was sent six days before Secretary of State Colin Powell would present, on February 5, 2003, on the floor of the UN, the Bush administration's evidence that Iraq had weapons of mass destruction.[12]

Even though Gun was not being asked to participate in the spying, she was horrified by what she read, because it "would undermine the whole UN democratic process."[13] Gun still believed the U.S. and UK "might not launch the war" without the Security Council's approval. She wrestled with her conscience and decided she had to act in the hope that it might help save lives.[14] Although she was bound by the British Official Secrets Act not to disclose classified information without authorization, she felt the contents of this email "overrode her obligations" to secrecy. She leaked a copy to a friend, who passed it on to a journalist.[15]

Gun later explained, "I was very angry at first and very saddened that it had come to this, and that despite all of the talk from both Tony Blair and George Bush about how important it was to get the UN on board and to legitimize any kind of aggression, that they were actually going around it in such a low-handed manner. I decided that the risk to my career was minute compared to the upcoming war in Iraq."[16]

One month later, on March 2, 2003, the highly classified NSA email was published on the front page of the *Observer*. It had taken that long for journalists to authenticate it. Almost immediately, Gun confessed to leaking the memo, saying "her actions were justified"[17] because she was trying to prevent an illegal war "in which thousands of Iraqi civilians and British soldiers would be killed or maimed."[18]

Katharine Gun was arrested on March 5, under suspicion of breaching the Official Secrets Act. She spent one night at a local police station and was released on bail the next day.[19] In June, she was fired, but she wasn't charged with a crime until November 2003. The Bush administration had been pressuring the British to prosecute her to the full extent of the law in order to discourage other whistleblowers, but Gun's lawyers had made it clear that if the case went to court, they would challenge the legality of Britain's involvement in the war. The Blair administration did not want to publicly debate the legality of a war that had little domestic support. In the end, the government did file charges, and Gun's trial was set for February 2004. Gun faced up to two years in prison for violating the Official Secrets Act.[20]

Members of Parliament and others urged the British government to drop the charges. Five U.S. congressmembers also sent Tony Blair a letter in support of Katharine Gun, stating, "The British and American public deserve to know all the elements involved in the build-up to the war."[21] Rep. Lynn Woolsey (D-CA) commented, "Katharine Gun shouldn't be facing two years in jail when she deserves a hero's welcome. We have the right to know what our government is doing in our name, and it appears we must count on people like Katharine to tell the real story."[22]

Daniel Ellsberg wrote, in the *Guardian*, that Gun's "revelation of a classified document urging British intelligence to help the U.S. bug the phones of all the members of the UN Security Council to manipulate their votes on the war may have been critical in denying the invasion a false cloak of legitimacy."[23] Ellsberg, Jesse Jackson, Ron Kovic, and the American Civil Liberties Union wrote a joint statement in support of Katharine Gun, asking, "Should this woman go to prison for the 'crime' of telling the truth?"[24] Tony Benn, who served in the British Parliament for over fifty years, argued, "Gun's conscience fully intersected with the needs of democracy and a free press."[25]

On February 25, 2004, the day the trial was to begin, the British government dropped the charges, even though Gun had confessed. The process took thirty minutes: Gun entered her plea of 'not guilty' and the government prosecutor announced he would not present any evidence. When asked by the judge why he was dropping the case, the prosecutor said, "It would not be appropriate to go into the reasons for this decision."[26] Attorney General Lord Goldsmith said that "although they believed they could prove the Official Secrets Act had been breached, they had concluded they could not disprove Ms. Gun's defense 'of necessity'... that she felt a duty to do something to save lives in an unlawful war."[27] Although his government chose not to prosecute Katharine Gun, Prime Minister Blair warned potential whistleblowers that "it would be a very dangerous situation if people thought they could just spill out allegations, whether false or true... and get away with it."[28]

Katharine Gun's story gathered increasing attention in Britain but received almost no coverage in the U.S.[29] She's been called a woman of "fierce principle,"[30] "a genuine heroine,"[31] and "a whistleblower who bravely risked [everything] to inform the public about illegal spying in support of a war based on deception."[32]

Gun joined the Truth-Telling Coalition, founded by Daniel Ellsberg and made up of former government employees who, Gun says, "have spoken out about the abuses, cover-ups, and lies that [their] respective governments have peddled before and after the invasion of Iraq."[33] Its members are urging "federal employees... to come forward with information exposing government wrongdoing,"[34] especially about the war in Iraq and now the threats to Iran. Gun stresses that the members of the Truth-Telling Coalition "felt that in order to encourage more of our former colleagues to 'speak truth to power,' we had to show that we were united and willing to support them."[35] The group argues that whistleblowers should not be made scapegoats for revealing illegal acts committed by their governments. Gun insists that we need "to distinguish between espionage breaches which genuinely endanger national security and public-spirited whistle-blowing."[36]

In an open letter written March 20, 2006, Gun warned the public about U.S. plans to use "mini-nukes" to attack Iran, noting the irony in threatening to use nuclear weapons to punish a country for its nuclear ambitions. She then made a public appeal to people working for the American and British governments to leak any information "which relates to this planned aggression," because "we cannot . . . rely on others to speak truth to power." Gun stressed that "truth telling and whistle-blowing are crucial after a war as ill-advised as Iraq—at least it allows us to piece together the facts—but it's too late to save lives. Where are the memos and emails about Iran now?" Gun pleaded to government officials to follow their consciences: "Don't put your loyalty above truth and the law; help us avoid this unnecessary evil."[37]

✎ Robin Cook
Leader, House of Commons

On March 17, 2003, Robin Cook learned that Tony Blair had committed the UK to invading Iraq without UN approval, and he submitted his resignation from his Cabinet post as Leader of the House of Commons. On the floor of Parliament, Cook argued that Iraq did *not* pose an urgent threat to Britain and asked the MPs point-blank, "Why is it now so urgent that we disarm a military capacity that has been there for twenty years and which we helped to create?" Cook then reprimanded Blair for working to obtain a Security Council resolution to authorize the use of force and, when he didn't get it, deciding that UN approval didn't matter. Cook said that invading Iraq without UN support was wrong in principle and on practical grounds.[38] His resignation speech received the first standing ovation in the nearly 700-year history of the House of Commons.[39]

Robin Cook had served the British government for nearly thirty years. In 1997, Tony Blair appointed Cook as Foreign Secretary, one of the four most senior and prestigious positions in the British government. During his five years in this position, Cook attempted to add an "ethical dimension" to Britain's foreign policy.[40] He created a human rights department and published reports on human rights abuses even in countries that were Britain's allies.[41]

After the June 2001 British elections, Blair demoted Cook to Leader of the House of Commons.[42] Even prior to 9/11, Cook had strongly disagreed with the new U.S. foreign policy that flouted international law. It appears that the Bush administration pressured Blair to replace Cook as Foreign Secretary, because they did not want someone so vigorously opposed to them in a such a high position in the British government.[43] Cook's successor, Jack Straw, was much more willing to support Bush's aggressive strategies. Cook probably would not have agreed to go to war with Iraq, and had he remained Foreign Secretary and resigned from that position on the brink of war, it would have been difficult for Tony Blair to commit British troops to Iraq or possibly even to stay in office.[44]

In response to Cook's resignation as Leader of the House of Commons, Blair wrote a letter justifying his stance on Iraq. He laid blame on the French for unreasonably blocking the Security Council vote. Blair then argued that his administration's position was not *defying* the UN, but rather "staying true to resolution 1441," which demanded the immediate disarmament of Iraq. He insisted that "others, in the face of continuing Iraqi non-compliance, are walking away from it."[45]

Robin Cook's book, *The Point of Departure: Why One of Britain's Leading Politicians Resigned over Tony Blair's Decision to Go to War in Iraq*, elaborates on Blair's manipulation of intelligence to win support for the war. Until his untimely death, Cook continued to criticize Blair's deceptions and to press the administration for accountability. While hiking in the Scottish highlands in August 2005, Robin Cook collapsed and died of a heart attack.[46] "His principled resignation as Leader of the House of Commons on the eve of the Iraq War elevated him to the ranks of those for whom statues are cast," wrote Torcuil Crichton in the Scotland *Sunday Herald*, "and earned him a reputation as the greatest parliamentarian of his generation—a consensus that nobody across the political spectrum departed from on the news of his death."[47] He is remembered as a champion of human rights, an advocate of international law, and a man of principle.

~

Robin Cook's Letter of Resignation

March 17, 2003

At cabinet for some weeks I have been frank about my concern over embarking on military action in the absence of multilateral support. I applaud the heroic efforts that you and Jack [Straw] have put into the attempt to secure a second resolution at the UN.

It is not your fault that those attempts have failed. However, the evident importance that we attached to a second resolution makes it all the more difficult now to proceed without one, and without agreement in any other international forum.

As I cannot give my support to military action in these circumstances, I write with regret to resign.

You and I have both made the case over the years for an international order based on multilateral decisions through the UN and other forums. In principle I believe it is wrong to embark on military action without broad international support. In practice I believe it is against Britain's interests to create a precedent for unilateral military action.

As our foreign secretary I was impressed by the energy and skill with which you ended Britain's isolation in Europe and achieved for our country equal status and influence to Germany or France. I am dismayed that once again Britain is divided from our major European neighbours. As president of the party of European socialists, of which the Labour party is a member, it troubles me that I know of no sister party within the European Union that shares our position.

I regret leaving my post as leader of the House of Commons, in which I have had two fulfilling years modernising the procedures of a parliament for which I have a deep affection. I also am proud of the real achievement of your government. Among those many achievements, I take particular satisfaction from our record on delivering devolution, investing in hospitals and tackling poverty among children.

All of these have only been made possible by your successful leadership and two record election victories which were your personal achievement. You will continue to have my personal support as leader of our party. I am only too sorry that our differences on the present crisis mean that I can no longer continue to serve you in cabinet.

Yours sincerely,
Robin

✎ Elizabeth Wilmshurst
Deputy Legal Adviser for the Foreign Office

Elizabeth Wilmshurst, a government attorney and one of the UK's top authorities in international law, was shocked when she learned that Attorney General Lord Goldsmith had declared that a new UN resolution would not be necessary for war with Iraq to be legal. This was the opposite of the judgment of the government's legal team at the Foreign Office and most other experts in international law.[48]

Lord Goldsmith's opinion went against everything Wilmshurst believed in. As Deputy Legal Adviser for the Foreign Office, Wilmshurst had been Britain's representative in negotiations with the International Criminal Court regarding crimes of aggression. On March 18, 2003, she quietly submitted her letter of resignation, saying she saw no ambiguity: that military action in Iraq would be illegal without a second UN resolution. She viewed invading Iraq as a crime of aggression that would damage the very system of international law and order. She wrote that she could not "in conscience go along with" an invasion.[49]

In 2004, Wilmshurst made her position public when lawyers for Katharine Gun said they intended to call as a witness a former government lawyer who had resigned over the war. When the British press attempted to identify this lawyer, Wilmshurst revealed her name with this short statement: "I left my job as a deputy legal adviser in the Foreign and Commonwealth Office because I did not agree that the use of force against Iraq was lawful, and in all the circumstances, I did not want to continue as a legal adviser."[50]

Shortly after she released her statement, British Parliamentarians and other officials learned that, in fact, the entire Foreign Office legal team agreed with Wilmshurst.[51] She was simply the only one who resigned.[52] This revelation undermined Blair's contention that the British government was solidly in favor of the war. Two weeks after the Gun case was dropped, Greenpeace attorneys announced that they would call Wilmshurst to testify in a case defending antiwar activists, because the defendants had acted to stop what they felt was an illegal war.[53]

Elizabeth Wilmshurst is now head of the International Law Program at Chatham House, Britain's leading foreign-affairs think tank, where she specializes in the laws of military intervention.[54] She continues to write about the use of force in international law and specifically about the illegal war the U.S. and UK are waging in Iraq. In an article in the *Guardian* titled "Rules of Engagement," she wrote, "The UN charter prohibits a state from using force in another country without the latter's consent. There are, however, two well-established exceptions: if force is used in self-defence and if force is authorized by a Security Council resolution under Chapter VII of the Charter.... Regarding the Iraq conflict in 2003, it would not have been possible to claim . . . that force was the last reasonable option."[55]

In 2003, both Elizabeth Wilmshurst and her Foreign Office boss Michael Wood firmly believed that the Iraq War was illegal. When Blair took the country to war, Wilmshurst resigned in protest. Michael Wood stayed on as the Foreign Office's chief legal adviser and was rewarded with knighthood in 2004.

✍

Elizabeth Wilmshurst's Letter of Resignation

March 18, 2003

1. I regret that I cannot agree that it is lawful to use force against Iraq without a second Security Council resolution to revive the authorisation given in SCR 678. I do not need to set out my reasoning; you are aware of it.

The following paragraph was blacked out when this letter was first released:

> My views accord with the advice that has been given consistently in this office before and after the adoption of UN security council resolution 1441 and with what the attorney general gave us to understand was his view prior to his letter of 7 March. (The view expressed in that letter has of course changed again into what is now the official line.)
>
> I cannot in conscience go along with advice—within the Office or to the public or Parliament—which asserts the legitimacy of military action without such a resolution, particularly since an unlawful use of force on such a scale amounts to the crime of aggression; nor can I agree with such action in circumstances which are so detrimental to the international order and the rule of law.

2. I therefore need to leave the Office: my views on the legitimacy of the action in Iraq would not make it possible for me to continue my role as a Deputy Legal Adviser or my work more generally.

   For example in the context of the International Criminal Court, negotiations on the crime of aggression begin again this year.

   I am therefore discussing with Alan Charlton whether I may take approved early retirement. In case that is not possible this letter should be taken as constituting notice of my resignation.

3. I joined the Office in 1974. It has been a privilege to work here. I leave with very great sadness.

✑ Clare Short
Secretary of State for International Development

As Tony Blair's Secretary of State for International Development, Clare Short had seen the Iraq people suffer "very terribly" under UN-imposed economic sanctions.[56] By 1995, the UN estimated that more than half a million children under five had died as a result of the sanctions.[57] People lacked food and medicine and contracted fatal diseases through contaminated water. The chlorine needed to disinfect water was one of the items banned by the embargo. The UN's Humanitarian Coordinator in Iraq, Assistant Secretary General Denis Halliday, called the sanctions genocide and resigned in protest.

Short was solidly against going to war in Iraq because "a lot of people were going to die unnecessarily." She believed the UN should end the sanctions, bring Saddam to trial as a war criminal, and provide the Iraqi people with the resources to build their own future.[58] On March 9, 2003, she announced she would resign if Blair took the country to war without a new UN resolution, calling Blair "reckless."[59]

Tony Blair was desperate to keep Clare Short from resigning to stop the hemorrhaging from his Cabinet after "a series of ministerial resignations over his Iraq policy."[60] Blair asked what would change her mind, and Short replied she would be willing to stay on if the reconstruction of Iraq would be led by the UN rather than the U.S.-led coalition. She later explained, "I still felt, even though the rush to war had been wrong, if we internationalized the reconstruction, if the people of Iraq got a better future out of it, that rush might be forgiven."[61] Blair said he would see to it.[62]

Less than two months later, Short was stunned to learn that Blair and Jack Straw were secretly negotiating a UN resolution whereby the U.S.-led coalition would lead the reconstruction of Iraq. After six years as Secretary of State for International Development, Clare Short resigned, accusing Blair of breaking his promise.[63] Like Robin Cook, she used her resignation speech to Parliament to criticize Blair's decision to invade Iraq, warning that the military actions in Iraq were "undermining international law and the authority of the UN [and creating] the risk of instability, bitterness, and growing terrorism that will threaten the future for all of us." She reminded Members of Parliament that coalition forces were an occupying power and therefore bound by law to limit their actions to maintaining stability, meeting humanitarian needs, and operating the civil administration. Instead, the coalition was making "major political, economic, and constitutional changes," including establishing an interim government, a process for creating a constitution, and electing a government. Only the UN Security Council has the legal authority to make such changes.[64] She also pointed out that waging war in Iraq was diverting attention from "the biggest threat to the safety and security of the world": high levels of poverty and inequality. Clare Short was filled with regret as she told members of Parliament that she had made promises, out of a misplaced trust in Tony Blair, that she could no longer keep.

Since leaving government, Short has continued to criticize Blair, even demanding his resignation. In February 2004, she revealed that during the run-up to war, British secret intelligence agents had eavesdropped on UN Secretary General Kofi Annan. Blair's response was to call her "totally irresponsible."[65]

In a 2005 interview, Short said, "The failure to prepare for afterward, the chaos, the criminality, the looting, the continuing death, the unemployment, the lack of electricity and water, is a complete disaster. And it's criminally incompetent."[66] In her book, *An Honorable Deception?: New Labour, Iraq and the Misuse of Power,* Clare Short spells out Blair's duplicity. Not only did he engineer the Attorney General's opinion that the war was legal, he led his country into war under false pretenses by cherry-picking intelligence reports to support his conclusions. Short was stunned that Blair would act in such a manipulative way, especially "over a matter of war, fighting for human life and taking it."[67]

Short reported being present during the emergency Cabinet meeting that Tony Blair called just days before the invasion. The Attorney General announced to the Cabinet his opinion that the war was legal without a second UN resolution, without mentioning any of his doubts, an omission that violated the ministerial code. When Short spoke up to discuss the matter, she was cut off. Most unusually, the Cabinet was not allowed to ask any questions. When the *Guardian* leaked part of a transcript in which the Attorney General admitted under oath during the Butler Inquiry that he did not actually write the memo stating war was legal, Short demanded that Parliament officially investigate the Attorney General's advice.[68]

Clare Short says she doesn't feel bitter toward Blair. "It's too big for that. Far too big to be personal. I think it's desperately sad. What I feel most deeply about is the state of Iraq and the people who have lost their lives and suffered. I feel almost guilty about it. We're all part of it. We're guilty of it."[69]

✑

Clare Short's Letter of Resignation

May 12, 2003

Dear Tony

I have decided I must leave the government.

As you know, I thought the run-up to the conflict in Iraq was mishandled, but I agreed to stay in the government to help support the reconstruction effort for the people of Iraq.

I am afraid that the assurances you gave me about the need for a UN mandate to establish a legitimate Iraqi government have been breached.

The Security Council resolution that you and Jack have so secretly negotiated contradicts the assurances I have given in the House of Commons and elsewhere about the legal authority of the occupying powers and the need for a UN-led process to establish a legitimate Iraqi government. This makes my position impossible.

It has been a great honour for me to have led the establishment and development of the Department for International Development over the past six years.

I am proud of what we have achieved and much else that the government has done.

I am sad and sorry that it has ended like this.

Yours
Clare

∽ **Carne Ross**
Diplomat

As Britain's Iraq expert at the United Nations from 1998 to 2002,[70] Carne Ross was his country's key negotiator with UN weapons inspectors and the Iraqi government.[71] For four years, he read the intelligence on Iraq's weapons program, later revealing, "All the time I worked on Iraq as a British diplomat, our assessment, both inside the British government and inside the U.S. government, was that Iraq was not a threat."[72]

On September 24, 2002, Tony Blair presented the intelligence dossier that Saddam Hussein had the capacity to launch WMD within forty-five minutes and therefore posed a serious threat to British interests. Ross was stunned. He had worked on earlier versions of this same dossier and realized there was no way the intelligence "could sustain the case that the government was presenting."[73]

Angry and frustrated, he thought about resigning but decided that resigning would be like "standing up in front of a runaway train."[74] Instead, he took a yearlong sabbatical to earn a graduate degree in international affairs at the New School in New York.[75] At the end of his sabbatical, he requested a position at the UK mission in Kosovo.

In 2004, Carne Ross secretly submitted evidence to the Butler Inquiry that Tony Blair had manipulated intelligence on Iraq's WMD.[76] Ross told the inquiry that at no point during his time at the UN did the British government "assess that Iraq's WMD . . . posed a threat to the UK or its interests."[77] To the contrary, all assessments showed Saddam had been effectively contained, and no new evidence had surfaced to change that evaluation.[78] For several months after giving evidence to the Butler Inquiry, Ross "wrestled with his conscience" and finally decided to resign.[79] The Blair administration warned Ross that if the information in his testimony became public, he would likely be prosecuted under the Official Secrets Act.[80]

In November 2006, Ross told the British Parliament's Foreign Affairs Committee that he had given evidence to the Butler Inquiry that was still being kept secret.[81] He testified "that the UK's conduct at the UN Security Council in the run-up to the invasion amounted to deceit."[82] Ross also told the Committee that Prime Minister Blair had

been warned that invading Iraq would lead to chaos and would fuel terrorist acts against Britain. When a member of the Committee requested
Ross' Butler Inquiry testimony, it sparked a constitutional row.

Ross made it clear that he wanted to provide the evidence—it had
been on his conscience for a very long time[83]—yet he still feared prosecution under the Official Secrets Act.[84] The MP who requested the
testimony assured Ross that "he would be protected from prosecution
by parliamentary privilege."[85] But the British Foreign Office threatened
legal action against him if he disclosed this information and demanded
that he "return any confidential material in his possession."[86] They also
forced him to delete portions of his book, *Independent Diplomat: Dispatches from an Unaccountable Elite*, "on the grounds of national security."[87]

The Parliamentary committee prevailed, and Ross' testimony was
made public in late 2006. His revelation that the Prime Minister had
manipulated intelligence on Iraq's WMD dealt a devastating blow to
the Blair administration.[88] The *Independent* reported, "The Government's case for going to war in Iraq has been torn apart by the publication of previously suppressed evidence that Tony Blair lied over
Saddam Hussein's weapons of mass destruction."[89] Ross argued, "It's
not an honest mistake." For the U.S. and British governments to pretend now "that it was the intelligence that misled them is false."[90]

Ross also told the committee that he had served briefly in Afghanistan following the 2001 invasion and that "the Afghans and the British
and American military who were there were clear that we needed to
devote a lot more forces to stabilizing the country… The senior British
officers in the International Security Assistance Force, which I helped
to set up in the UN Security Council, said that their equipment and
men were being held back in order to prepare for the invasion of Iraq.
That was in early 2002."[91] In a strategy often used against whistleblowers, the Blair administration downplayed Ross' position, stating that he
"has exaggerated his role on Iraq policy and his access to intelligence
about unconventional weapons."[92]

Carne Ross had been a diplomat for fifteen years. He slowly came
to realize that the priorities of diplomacy, based on national interest
more than morality, often neglect the people they affect the most.
"At the Foreign Office you are taught to think that trade and market

share and security are the most important things, and that human suffering is not important if it's nothing to do with Britain. I disagree with
that analysis. The best way to a safer and more peaceful world is through
alleviating suffering."[93] Ross founded Independent Diplomat, a non-
profit diplomatic advisory group, to provide counsel to inexperienced
governments and marginalized groups.[94] In 2005, he was named one
of seven "visionaries for a just and peaceful world" by the Joseph Rown-
tree Charitable Trust.[95] In a 2007 interview with Wolf Blitzer, Ross
confessed, "I am ashamed that I didn't speak up earlier . . . I was too
attached to my career."[96]

✍

Carne Ross' Submission to the Butler Inquiry

Submitted June 9, 2004
Published December 15, 2006

I am in the Senior Management Structure of the Foreign and Commonwealth Office (FCO), currently seconded to the UN in Kosovo.
I was First Secretary in the UK Mission to the United Nations in New
York from December 1997 until June 2002. I was responsible for Iraq
policy in the mission, including policy on sanctions, weapons inspections, and liaison with the United Nations Special Commission (for
weapons' inspections in Iraq—UNSCOM) and later the United Nations
Monitoring, Verification, and Inspection Commission (UNMOVIC).

During that time, I helped negotiate several UN Security Council
resolutions on Iraq, including resolution 1284, which, *inter alia*, established UNMOVIC (an acronym I coined late one New York night during the year-long negotiation). I took part in policy debates within Her
Majesty's Government (HMG) and in particular with the U.S. government. I attended many policy discussions on Iraq with the U.S. State
Department in Washington, New York, and London.

My concerns about the policy on Iraq divide into three:

1. The Alleged Threat
    I read the available UK and U.S. intelligence on Iraq every working
day for the four and a half years of my posting. This daily briefing would

often comprise a thick folder of material, both Human Intelligence (HUMINT) and Signals Intelligence (SIGINT). I also talked often and at length about Iraq's WMD to the international experts who comprised the inspectors of UNSCOM/UNMOVIC, whose views I would report to London. In addition, I was on many occasions asked to offer views in contribution to Cabinet Office assessments, including the famous WMD dossier (whose preparation began some time before my departure in June 2002).

During my posting, at no time did HMG assess that Iraq's WMD (or any other capability) posed a threat to the UK or its interests. On the contrary, it was the commonly held view among the officials dealing with Iraq that any threat had been effectively contained. I remember on several occasions the UK team stating this view in terms during our discussions with the U.S. (who agreed). (At the same time, we would frequently argue, when the U.S. raised the subject, that "regime change" was inadvisable, primarily on the grounds that Iraq would collapse into chaos.)

Any assessment of threat has to include both capabilities and intent. Iraq's *capabilities* in WMD were moot: many of the UN's weapons inspectors (who, contrary to popular depiction, were impressive and professional) would tell me that they believed Iraq had no significant matériel. With the exception of some unaccounted-for Scud missiles, there was no intelligence evidence of significant holdings of conventional weapons (CW), biological weapons (BW), or nuclear material. Aerial or satellite surveillance was unable to get under the roofs of Iraqi facilities. We therefore had to rely on inherently unreliable human sources (who, for obvious reasons, were prone to exaggerate).

Without substantial evidence of current holdings of WMD, the key concern we pursued was that Iraq had not provided any convincing or coherent *account* of its past holdings. When I was briefed in London at the end of 1997 in preparation for my posting, I was told that we did not believe that Iraq had any significant WMD. The key argument therefore to maintain sanctions was that Iraq had failed to provide convincing evidence of destruction of its past stocks.

Iraq's ability to *launch* a WMD or any form of attack was very limited. There were approx 12 or so unaccounted-for Scud missiles; Iraq's air force was depleted to the point of total ineffectiveness; its army was but a pale shadow of its earlier might; there was no evidence of any connection between Iraq and any terrorist organisation that might have planned an attack using Iraqi WMD (I do not recall any occasion when the question of a terrorist connection was even raised in UK/U.S. discussions or UK internal debates).

There was moreover no intelligence or assessment during my time in the job that Iraq had any *intention* to launch an attack against its neighbours or the UK or U.S. I had many conversations with diplomats representing Iraq's neighbours. With the exception of the Israelis, none expressed any concern that they might be attacked. Instead, their concern was that sanctions, which they and we viewed as an effective means to contain Iraq, were being delegitimised by evidence of their damaging humanitarian effect.

I quizzed my colleagues in the FCO and MOD working on Iraq on several occasions about the threat assessment in the run-up to the war. None told me that any new evidence had emerged to change our assessment; what had changed was the government's determination to present available evidence in a different light. I discussed this at some length with David Kelly in late 2002, who agreed that the Number 10 WMD dossier was overstated.

2. Legality

The legality of the war is framed by the relevant Security Council resolutions, the negotiation and drafting of which was usually led by the UK.

During the negotiation of resolution 1284 (which we drafted), which established UNMOVIC, the question was discussed among the key Security Council members in great detail how long the inspectors would need in Iraq in order to form a judgement of Iraq's capabilities.

The UK and U.S. pushed for the longest period we could get, on the grounds that the inspectors would need an extensive period in order to visit, inspect, and establish monitoring at the many hundreds of possible WMD-related sites. The French and Russians wanted the shortest duration. After long negotiation, we agreed the periods specified in 1284. These require some explanation. The resolution states that the head of UNMOVIC should report on Iraq's performance 120 days once the full system of ongoing monitoring and verification had been established (OMV, in the jargon). OMV amounts to the "baseline" of knowledge of Iraq's capabilities and sites; we expected OMV to take up to six months to establish. In other words, inspectors would have to be on the ground for approximately ten months before offering an assessment. (Resolution 1441, though it requested Blix to "update" the Council 60 days after beginning inspections, did not alter the inspection periods established in 1284.) As is well known, the inspectors were allowed to operate in Iraq for a much shorter period before the U.S. and UK declared that Iraq's cooperation was insufficient.

Resolution 1441 did not alter the basic framework for inspections established by 1284. In particular, it did not amend the crucial premise of 1284 that any judgement of cooperation or noncooperation by Iraq with the inspectors was to be made by the Council not UNMOVIC. Blix at no time stated unequivocally that Iraq was not cooperating with the inspectors. The Council reached no such judgement either.

Resolution 1441 did not authorise the use of force in case of noncooperation with weapons inspectors. I was in New York, but not part of the mission, during the negotiation of that resolution (I was on Special Unpaid Leave from the FCO). My friends in other delegations told me that the UK sold 1441 in the Council explicitly on the grounds that it did not represent authorisation for war and that it "gave inspections a chance."

Later, after claiming that Iraq was not cooperating, the UK presented a draft resolution which offered the odd formulation that Iraq had failed to seize the opportunity of 1441. In negotiation, the UK conceded that the resolution amounted to authority to use force (there are few public records of this, but I was told by many former colleagues involved in the negotiation that this was the case). The resolution failed to attract support.

The UN charter states that only the Security Council can authorise the use of force (except in cases of self-defence). Reviewing these points, it is clear that in terms of the resolutions presented by the UK itself, the subsequent invasion was not authorised by the Security Council and was thus illegal. The clearest evidence of this is the fact that the UK sought an authorising resolution and failed to get it.

There is another subsidiary point on the legality question. During my spell at the UN, the UK and U.S. would frequently have to defend in the Security Council attacks made by our aircraft in the No-Fly Zones (NFZs) in northern and southern Iraq. The NFZs were never authorised by the Security Council, but we would justify them on the grounds (as I recall it, this may be incorrect) that we were monitoring compliance with resolution 688 which called for the Iraqi government to respect the human rights of its people. If our aircraft bombed Iraqi targets, we were acting in self-defence (which was in fact the case, as the Iraqis would try to shoot down our aircraft).

Reading the press in the months leading up to the war, I noticed that the volume and frequency of the attacks in the NFZs considerably increased, including during the period when UNMOVIC was in country inspecting sites (i.e., before even the UK/U.S. declared that Iraq was not complying). I suspected at the time that these attacks were not in self-defence but that they were part of a planned air campaign to prepare for a ground invasion. There were one or two questions in Parliament about this when the Defence Secretary claimed that the NFZ attacks were, as before, self-defence. His account was refuted at the time by quotations by U.S. officials in the press and by later accounts, including Bob Woodward's *Plan of Attack,* which confirmed that the attacks did indeed comprise a softening-up campaign, of which the UK was an active part.

3. Alternatives to War

I was responsible at the UK Mission for sanctions policy as well as weapons inspections. I had extensive contacts with those in the UN responsible for the Oil-for-Food Programme, with NGOs active in Iraq, with experts in the oil industry and with many others who visited Iraq (I tried to visit on several occasions but was denied a visa by the Iraqi government). I read and analysed a great deal of material on Iraq's exports, both legal and illegal, sanctions and related subjects, such as the oil industry.

Much of my work and that of my close colleagues was devoted to attempting to stop countries breaching Iraqi sanctions. These breaches were many and took various forms.

The most serious was the illegal export of oil by Iraq through Turkey, Syria, and Iranian waters in the Gulf. These exports were a substantial and crucial source of hard currency for the Iraqi regime; without them the regime could not have sustained itself or its key pillars, such as the Republican Guard. Estimates of the value of these exports ranged around $2 billion a year.

In addition, there were different breaches, such as Iraq's illegal and secret surcharge on its legal sales of oil through the UN. Iraq would levy illegal charges on oil-for-food contracts. The regime also had substantial financial assets held in secret overseas accounts. The details of these breaches and our work to combat them are complicated.

On repeated occasions, I and my colleagues at the mission (backed by some but not all of the responsible officials in London) attempted to get the UK and U.S. to act more vigorously on the breaches. We believed that determined and coordinated action, led by us and the U.S., would have had a substantial effect in particular to pressure Iraq to accept the weapons inspections and would have helped undermine the Iraqi regime.

I proposed on several occasions the establishment of a multinational body (a UN body, if we could get the Security Council to agree it) to police sanctions busting. I proposed coordinated action with Iraq's neighbours to pressure them to help, including by controlling imports into Iraq. I held talks with a U.S. Treasury expert on financial sanctions, an official who had helped trace and seize Milosevic's illegal financial assets. He assured me that, given the green light, he could quickly set up a team to target Saddam's illegal accounts.

These proposals went nowhere. Inertia in the FCO and the inattention of key ministers combined to the effect that the UK never made any coordinated and sustained attempt to address sanctions busting. There were sporadic and half-hearted initiatives. Bilateral embassies in Iraq's neighbours would always find a reason to let their hosts off the hook (the most egregious example was the Embassy in Ankara). Official visitors to the neighbours always placed other issues higher on the agenda. The Prime Minister, for example, visited Syria in early 2002.

If I remember correctly, the mission sent a telegram beforehand urging him to press Assad on the illegal pipeline carrying Iraqi oil through Syria. I have seen no evidence that the subject was mentioned. Whenever I taxed ministers on the issue, I would find them sympathetic but uninformed.

Coordinated, determined and sustained action to prevent illegal exports and target Saddam's illegal monies would have consumed a tiny proportion of the effort and resources of the war (and fewer lives), but could have provided a real alternative. It was never attempted.

Carne Ross
Pristina, Kosovo

✎ Craig Murray
Ambassador

Shortly after arriving in Uzbekistan to serve as UK ambassador, Craig Murray was horrified to learn that two Muslim prisoners had been murdered in one of the grisliest ways possible: they had been boiled alive.[97] He soon discovered that these gruesome murders were part of a policy of ruthless suppression by the Uzbek government, and the Bush administration was supporting the regime financially and politically.

Before the attacks of September 11, the U.S. State Department described Uzbekistan as "an authoritarian state" whose security services used torture "as a routine investigation technique."[98] But after September 11, the U.S. sought Uzbekistan as an ally in the war on terror. Uzbek President Islam Karimov was willing to provide the U.S. access to K2, a huge military base near the Afghan border, in exchange for a good-sized U.S. aid package and the U.S. government's silence about Uzbekistan's terrible human rights abuses.[99] In a sudden reversal of policy, the Bush administration then financed "much of the regime's security apparatus"[100] and welcomed Karimov as an official guest at the White House.[101]

Craig Murray understood Uzbekistan's strategic value: the country borders Afghanistan and lies right in the middle of Central Asia, a region with the largest untapped reserves of oil and gas in the world.[102] Yet Murray viewed the U.S. policy as shortsighted, dangerous, and immoral. While other countries' diplomats in Uzbekistan kept silent about this arrangement, Murray spoke out, putting his career and life in jeopardy.

Murray described Karimov as "one of the most vicious dictators in the world, a man who is responsible for the death of thousands of people." Uzbek authorities, he said, "raped children in front of their parents" to force confessions to fictitious crimes. Prisoners were routinely raped, even with broken bottles; their teeth were smashed with hammers, their limbs broken, their fingernails pulled out. Other common methods of torture included using electroshock on prisoners' genitals, boiling body parts, and asphyxiation with a gas mask.[103]

Through interviews with Uzbek citizens, Murray discovered that Karimov was using the war on terror to further silence political dissent. In a country that is 88 percent Muslim, Karimov was imprisoning and killing moderate Muslims under the guise of fighting religious extremism and terrorism.[104] Murray found little history of political or terrorist violence in Uzbekistan and no evidence that Muslims in Uzbekistan were advocating violence of any kind.[105]

After a fact-finding visit to Uzbekistan in late 2002, UN Special Rapporteur on Torture Theo van Boven described torture as "widespread and systematic."[106] In a list that included North Korea and Burma, Amnesty International, Human Rights Watch, and other international organizations ranked Uzbekistan as one of the five worst dictatorships on earth.[107] Criticizing the regime or working for democracy or human rights in Uzbekistan could get you arrested, killed or locked in a mental asylum.[108]

Informed citizens in the rest of the world were appalled by the hypocrisy of the U.S.'s support of Karimov while justifying the war in Iraq by the need to spread freedom and democracy. It reinforced suspicions that the war on terror was really a war on Islam, and that the U.S.'s only real interest was assuring access to Uzbekistan's strategically located airbase and valuable resources.[109] Through his writings and advocacy, Craig Murray drew wide attention to these contradictory policies in the war on terror, embarrassing both London and Washington.[110]

In October 2002, just three months after arriving in Uzbekistan, Murray shocked a gathering of diplomats and top Uzbek officials by becoming the first western official in years to state publicly that "Uzbekistan is not a functioning democracy, nor does it appear to be moving in the direction of democracy."[111] He condemned the brutality of Karimov's system and mentioned the two men who had been boiled to death, saying, "All of us know that this is not an isolated incident."[112] His speech infuriated the American ambassador and President Karimov.[113] It was not the information that shocked everyone in the room; it was the fact that Murray was saying it publicly.

In the British Foreign Office, "there was total confusion. The speech had been authorised but clearly no one had realised that it would cause such offence."[114] Murray's speech garnered extra international attention because UN Secretary General Kofi Annan was scheduled to meet with President Karimov the next day. During that meeting, Annan expressed his concern about Uzbekistan's human rights violations. When Annan mentioned Murray's speech, Karimov became furious. While the Foreign Office officially supported Murray, saying that he "'accurately reflects our concerns,' there was a sudden awareness that London had a problem."[115]

In addition to speaking out publicly, Murray sent a number of classified memos to the Foreign Office. On September 16, 2002, in one of his first reports, Murray wrote that "Karimov is a dictator who is committed to neither political nor economic reform." Murray also criticized the U.S. and UK support of Uzbekistan, warning his superiors that it would backfire. Using Karimov as an ally in the war on terror might provide some short-term benefits, but in the end, Murray warned, this policy would create the very thing it was trying to destroy—more extremism and more terrorism.[116]

In another classified memo, Murray described Uzbekistan as "a one-party state without freedom of speech, without freedom of media, without freedom of movement, without freedom of assembly, without freedom of religion."[117] All opposition parties were banned. When two prominent dissidents demonstrated for human rights, Karimov had them committed to an insane asylum and kept them drugged to the point that they were effectively given chemical lobotomies.[118]

Murray informed the Foreign Office that most people in Uzbekistan were living in abject poverty, in large part due to government policies. Uzbekistan is the second-largest exporter of cotton in the world. The crop provides a huge source of income for the regime while Uzbeks are forced to work on cotton farms for seven cents a day.[119]

Soon after arriving in Uzbekistan, Murray received photos of a body that had been tortured. The man's coffin had been nailed shut and delivered to his mother's house for burial the next day. A soldier stood guard to ensure that the mother did not open the coffin. But the soldier fell asleep, and the old woman pried open the coffin and secretly photographed her son's deformed body. She sent the photos to Murray, who already had a reputation as a champion of human rights, and Murray sent the photos to a pathology department in the UK to be examined. The verdict came back that the man had been severely beaten, then boiled alive.[120] Uzbek authorities said that the man's burns were from a fight with a fellow prisoner over a teakettle.[121]

Murray also attended the trial of a man accused of being a Muslim terrorist. The man's uncle, who was old and frail, was brought into the court to testify that his nephew supported Osama bin Laden. In the middle of his rehearsed statement, the old man stopped and said to the judge, "They tortured my grandchildren in front of me until I signed this statement." He told the judge that he was just a poor farmer and his family had not even heard of bin Laden before this. The judge, infuriated, had the old man removed from court to face punishment himself.[122]

Murray later traveled to the city of Samarkand to talk with a literature professor who had written to President Bush and Prime Minister Blair, telling them about the torture that dissidents in Uzbekistan experience on a daily basis. Hours after the professor met with Murray, the mutilated corpse of his grandson was thrown onto his doorstep. The Uzbek secret police had kidnapped the professor's grandson, then tortured and killed him to discourage dissidents from speaking out. Despite the fact that the grandson's body had smashed elbows and knees, an arm that had been boiled until the skin peeled off, and a crushed skull, Uzbek authorities said that the young man died of a drug overdose.[123]

Murray read classified British intelligence reports about Uzbekistan and found much of the information in them to be preposterous. One report mentioned Islamic extremists who had set up training camps in the hills above Samarkand. Murray knew that there were no training camps there.[124] Another report identified an Uzbek dissident as a member of al Qaeda. Murray knew that the man was a Jehovah's Witness, and noted sarcastically, "There are very few Jehovah's Witnesses in al Qaeda." The constant theme in these reports was "that any dissident in Uzbekistan, any opposition figure," was an Islamic militant. And most of the time, the intelligence identified the dissidents as al Qaeda members who had traveled to Afghanistan to meet with bin Laden. Murray doubted this, because Uzbek citizens could not get visas to leave their country. Even if they *had* found a way to leave Uzbekistan, it did not make sense that so many ordinary Uzbek citizens could have met with bin Laden when no one in the West could find him.[125]

Murray realized much of this information had been obtained through torture by the Uzbek security forces and was then passed on to MI6 from the CIA. He sent his deputy to talk with the CIA chief in Tashkent, who confirmed that "torture was deployed in obtaining intelligence" in Uzbekistan," but "we don't see that as a problem" in the context of a war on terror.[126] Murray sent a classified memo to the Foreign Office warning them that the intelligence in the MI6 report was "nonsense and probably obtained by torture"[127] and received no reply. He sent another in February 2003, with additional evidence. This time the Foreign Office called him back to London and reprimanded him.[128] Sir Michael Wood, the Foreign Office's chief legal adviser, told Murray it was legal for Britain "to obtain this information that was got under torture," as long as the UK did not request that a particular person be tortured. Wood told Murray to stop complaining, because the British Secretary of State and the head of MI6 had decided it was important for the UK to keep obtaining the intelligence information, all of it CIA-sourced, and that some of the information had "a direct bearing on the war on terror."[129]

Ten days after Murray was reprimanded in London, he was back in Tashkent, watching on television as President Bush addressed the U.S.

on March 17, 2003. Bush had just given Saddam Hussein forty-eight hours to leave Iraq or be attacked. Speaking directly to the Iraqi people, he instructed them that the U.S.-led coalition would "tear down the apparatus of terror and...help you to build a new Iraq that is prosperous and free. In a free Iraq, there will be...no more executions of dissidents, no more torture chambers and rape rooms."[130] Murray was appalled by Bush's double standard. He immediately sent a classified memo to the Foreign Office pointing out the hypocrisy of the Bush administration's support of Karimov's regime, where "systematic torture and rape appear to be treated as peccadilloes, not to affect the relationship and to be downplayed" internationally, and stating that "Washington was financing Uzbekistan, rather than invading it."[131] Murray was especially disturbed that his own government was helping the U.S. cover up Karimov's gross human rights abuses. He had recently learned that at the UN Commission for Human Rights in Geneva, "the U.S. had pressured the European Union to withdraw a motion on Human Rights in Uzbekistan."[132]

The Bush administration was infuriated by Murray's criticism and pushed the UK to get rid of him. A senior source within the Blair administration later revealed that Murray was pressured "to stop his repeated criticisms of the brutal Karimov regime." Tony Blair found Murray's "outspokenness about the compromises Washington was prepared to make in its 'war on terror' increasingly embarrassing in the lead-up to the Iraq War."[133]

In August 2003, Murray was again summoned to London to be reprimanded. His superiors told him he should resign his post in Uzbekistan so that he could be reassigned as an ambassador somewhere more peaceful, such as Copenhagen."[134] When Murray refused, he was handed a list of eighteen accusations, including trading British visas for sex, being drunk at work, stealing, and unpatriotic behavior. The Foreign Office told Murray he had one week to resign and that he was not allowed to discuss the charges with anyone or he would face prosecution, even jail, under the Official Secrets Act.[135] Murray wondered why the Foreign Office would fabricate such serious charges, and he realized that, as much as they wanted to get rid of him, they couldn't legally fire him. Murray again refused to resign, and the allegations were leaked to the media.[136] His superiors openly questioned his sanity, and his personal life was "publicly shredded."[137] Sources close to the case believe that it was either the Foreign Office or MI6 behind this smear campaign, since Murray "was jeopardizing a strategic military outpost."[138] Following what one Foreign Office source described as "a campaign of systematic undermining,"[139] Murray suffered a nervous breakdown and spent weeks in a London psychiatric hospital.

After five months, the Foreign Office officially exonerated Murray, yet warned him not to talk to anyone about the charges.[140] Murray returned to Uzbekistan against the wishes of the Foreign Office. Although he officially remained ambassador, he was banned from entering the British embassy in Tashkent. Then, just two days after returning to Tashkent, Murray nearly died from blood clots in both of his lungs.[141] He was rushed back to London, but doctors could find no obvious cause for his near-fatal illness. Despite the extreme pressure, Murray stayed in his post in Uzbekistan for another year. In an attempt to keep him quiet, the Foreign Office gave him the "strictest instruction not to speak to the media in Tashkent."[142]

In July 2004, Murray wrote yet another strongly worded classified memo to his superiors, stating, "We receive intelligence obtained under torture from the Uzbek intelligence services via the U.S. We should stop. It is bad information anyway. Tortured dupes are forced to sign up to confessions showing what the Uzbek government wants the U.S. and UK to believe, that they and we are fighting the same war against terror." Murray argued that using torture-tainted intelligence "is morally, legally and practically wrong."[143] He decided to highlight the contradiction in the UK's diplomatic policy because, while he was being silenced, British Foreign Secretary Jack Straw was speaking publicly in response to the Abu Ghraib scandal, "saying how terrible torture was."[144]

Once again, his bosses in the Foreign Office were furious. They told him "that the intelligence gleaned in Uzbekistan could still be used by British officials, even if it was elicited by torture, as long as the mistreatment was not at the hands of British interrogators." Murray later said in an interview, "It was as if the goalposts had moved. Their perspective had changed" since the September 11th attacks.[145]

Murray was fired in October 2004, after his July 2004 confidential memo was leaked to the *Financial Times*.[146] Murray insists that he did not leak the memo and suspects the leak came from his superiors, who then could claim cause to fire him.[147] According to the Foreign Office, Murray was dismissed because "he no longer had the confidence of ministers and colleagues."[148] They insist that Murray was let go for operational reasons rather than for his outspokenness. Uzbek citizens called Murray a hero and protested his firing outside the British Embassy, no small act of courage in a country with no freedom of speech, assembly, or press.[149]

Murray had broken the unspoken rules of diplomacy and spoken the truth in public, believing that his government's actions were illegal and immoral and would also backfire. Traditionally, the role of the diplomat is to implement the policies of his government. If Murray felt unable to carry out those policies, many in the Foreign Office felt he should have asked to be transferred or resigned. Instead, Craig Murray rocked the boat.

Some journalists and politicians focused on the fact that Murray had broken civil service rules by speaking out. Others took a broader view and considered what kind of legal and moral compromises the West should be willing to make. The *Guardian* described Murray's actions as a "valuable public service," because what he revealed was part of "a broader and worrying pattern that is visible both at home and abroad."[150] By following his conscience, Murray held a spotlight to a dangerous and unethical policy.[151] The *Financial Times* noted that Murray may have been too blunt, "but his political masters cannot escape from its truth."[152]

Craig Murray continues to speak out about the hypocrisy of the U.S. and British war on terror. He has appeared on *60 Minutes, World News Tonight,* and *Democracy Now!* to discuss what happens when a country sacrifices its principles in an attempt to safeguard its security.

In January 2006, Murray posted on his website classified memos that he had written and received while ambassador to Uzbekistan, supplying concrete evidence that the British government was obtaining intelligence by torture and hiding its policy from its citizens. Murray viewed Sir Michael Wood's March 2003 memo as particularly damning, because Wood officially stated that it was not illegal for the UK "to receive or possess information under torture." The British government demanded that Murray remove the memos immediately, stating that he had violated the Official Secrets Act. Murray refused and, instead, encouraged others to post the memos on their websites, so the British government could not censor them all.

The British media chastised him for doing this. A *Guardian* editor wrote, "Some members of Britain's governing classes don't seem to see any longer what is to be gained by keeping their mouths shut."[153] A BBC correspondent warned, "An ambassador has to weigh up whether his or her personal views outweigh the necessities of government."[154] Were these simply Murray's personal views, or was he right in exposing the British government's illegal complicity in torture and other gross human rights violations?

The silence in the West over the atrocities in Uzbekistan began to wane in mid-2005, but not for the noble reasons expressed. Although the American government and media portrayed the U.S. departure from Uzbekistan as a response to Karimov's brutality, the facts reveal a different story. In May 2005, when the Uzbek government massacred hundreds of unarmed people demonstrating for democracy in the town of Andijan, the U.S. continued to protect Karimov. Weeks after the massacre, the U.S. government opposed a NATO proposal demanding an international investigation into the killings.[155]

While the Bush administration would like to have people believe the U.S. voluntarily left Uzbekistan in response to gross human rights violations in places like Andijan, Murray says that this claim is completely untrue.[156] The U.S. government did not speak out about Karimov's brutality until the Uzbek regime served notice to the United States, in mid-2005, to leave the country, which meant the U.S. had to abandon its prized military base in Uzbekistan.[157] Six months earlier, Karimov had signed an exclusive oil and gas development deal with the Russian monopoly Gazprom, one of the world's largest gas companies. Russian President Vladimir Putin insisted that this deal hinged upon the removal of the U.S. from Uzbekistan.[158]

In the end, the American policy of overlooking human rights abuses and giving huge amounts of money for access to the strategically impor-tant military base did not pay off. Murray lamented that, in exchange for "all that loss of moral authority, all that waste of money and resources," the U.S. and the UK governments got nothing.[159] Even worse, Murray notes, is that prior to 9/11, "there was virtually nobody in Uzbekistan who was anti-American . . . After three years of solid American support for that dictatorship a huge number of people in Uzbekistan hate the United States."[160]

Two hundred fifty years ago, Irish philosopher Edmund Burke said, "All that is necessary for evil to triumph is that good men do nothing." Driven by "a deep personal commitment,"[161] Craig Murray still refuses to be silenced. "I think it's just what any decent person would do. I mean, when you come across people being boiled and their fingernails pulled out or having their children raped in front of them, you just can't go along with it and sleep at night."[162] Murray warns his fellow British citizens "to kick up a fuss about it . . . [otherwise] this won't be a coun-try . . . to be proud of."[163]

The Foreign Office threatened legal action to block his memoir, *Murder in Samarkand,* from publication, and the wrangling dragged on until June 2006, when the book was published in the UK.[164] His story is also being made into a film by acclaimed director Michael Winter-bottom.[165]

✎ Frank Grevil

Denmark was among the first countries to join the Coalition of the Willing, providing 500 troops, a submarine, and a corvette (military ship) to the war effort.[166] In August 2002, the Danish government asked its military intelligence service to produce intelligence estimates on Iraq's weapons of mass destruction.

Major Frank Grevil, a Danish military intelligence officer, helped write these classified WMD intelligence reports for Prime Minister Anders Fogh Rasmussen. The reports, from August 2002 until March 2003, clearly and consistently stated that there was no evidence that Iraq had any weapons of mass destruction.[167]

The day before the invasion of Iraq, Prime Minister Rasmussen told the Danish Parliament, "Iraq has weapons of mass destruction. This is not something we just believe. We know."[168] Grevil was stunned. To convince Parliament to vote to go to war, Rasmussen completely ignored the intelligence reports.

In fact, in July 2002, Secretary of State Powell had told the Danish Minister of Foreign Affairs, Per Stig Moeller, that the U.S. had decided to remove Saddam Hussein from power by any means necessary. Much evidence reveals that Danish leaders knew the U.S. decision to go to war in Iraq was not based on WMD but was focused on regime change. And yet, during the five months before the war began, the Prime Minister and Minister of Foreign Affairs told Parliament more than 100 times that "the conflict was about disarming Iraq."[169]

Frank Grevil was deeply disturbed that his Prime Minister was distorting the intelligence on WMD to make the case for war. He believed that Parliament hadn't received the information it needed to make an informed decision whether to go to war.[170] But for almost a year, he kept his frustrations to himself. When no WMD were found in Iraq, the Parliament began hotly debating the prewar intelligence. In January 2004, Grevil approached two Danish journalists and told them the Prime Minister had misled Parliament and the country in making the case for war. The journalists told him they needed hard evidence, and after a few days, Grevil decided to leak the intelligence reports he had helped write. "I couldn't as a democratic citizen live with the fact that the government was withholding crucial documents,"[171] he told Amy Goodman eight months later. "It was my conscience that led me to provide these documents."[172]

In February 2004, the headline story "that there had in fact been no credible evidence that Iraq had possessed" WMD ran in *Berlingske Tidende*, one of Denmark's three major newspapers, and the Prime Minister denied the story. By March, Danish police identified Grevil as the source of the leak[173] and arrested him for revealing state secrets. Grevil confessed and was "dismissed" from his job,[174] tried, and sentenced to six months in prison, later reduced to four months.

Grevil became the focus of a government smear campaign. One former military officer denounced his actions, arguing that "Grevil should have attempted to get his boss to declassify the Iraq assessments, or else he should have kept his mouth shut."[175] At the same time, one member of Parliament criticized the government's prosecution of Grevil, arguing that it was more about protecting the Prime Minister's credibility than protecting state security.[176] Although widely denounced, Grevil also received international support from pro-democracy groups. In September 2004, eleven former and current U.S. and UK government employees issued an open letter supporting Grevil, noting that leaking classified documents without authorization is often the only way a person who believes strongly in a democratic system can expose wrongdoing.[177]

According to a 2004 Danish poll, 57 percent of Danes wanted a Parliamentary investigation into the government's decision to support the U.S.-led war in Iraq.[178] The poll also found that the majority of Danes found Frank Grevil more credible than Prime Minister Rasmussen.[179]

In April 2006, the Danish government charged the two *Berlingske Tidende* journalists with leaking state secrets and "undermining state security" for printing the classified reports.[180] In November, both journalists and their editor stood trial and faced up to two years in prison. All three were acquitted on December 4, 2006.[181]

✍ Andrew Wilkie

Andrew Wilkie served in the Australian Defence Force from 1980 to 2000, attaining the rank of Lieutenant Colonel. After retiring from the military, he became a senior civilian analyst in the Office of National Assessments, Australia's premier intelligence agency. In 2002, he was assigned to assess the threat that Iraq posed to the international community. The intelligence that Wilkie gathered indicated that WMD and Saddam's supposed link to al Qaeda were not the primary reasons the U.S. was going to war. Yet Australian Prime Minister John Howard repeatedly told his country that Iraq had WMD and posed a serious threat to the world.[182]

During the build-up to war, three out of every four Australians opposed the invasion of Iraq. Prime Minister Howard, on the other hand, had a close alliance with President Bush in fighting the war on terror and did all he could to drum up support for war. Wilkie knew that the intelligence did not support Howard's claims and felt increasingly alarmed as he witnessed his government politicizing the intelligence.[183] Just as in the U.S., UK, and Denmark, leaders of the Australian government were deceiving their citizens to convince them to support waging war on Iraq.

In March 2003, as soon as it became clear that his government was going to be part of the coalition invading Iraq, Andrew Wilkie resigned from the Office of National Assessments in protest. He explained, "There are all sorts of things that public servants disagree with, but to my mind, I was looking at government misconduct on an extraordinary scale. So much so that I felt I couldn't support the government any longer and, also, that I had an obligation to speak out publicly." Wilkie told the media that "intelligence on Iraq's WMD programs did not justify going to war." He did not harbor illusions that he could stop the war by resigning, but he did hope he might be able to "energize the public discussion of it."[184]

The day he resigned, the Australian government told the media that Wilkie had not worked on assessing Iraq's threat. Top officials suggested that Wilkie was mentally unstable, and journalists, in turn, downplayed the important role Wilkie had played in the intelligence assessments.[185]

Ray McGovern, former CIA analyst and cofounder of Veteran Intelligence Professionals for Sanity, wrote, "Those who dismiss such efforts [as Andrew Wilkie's public resignation and disclosures] as an exercise in futility should know that, on October 7, [2003,] the Australian Senate, in a rare move, censured Howard for misleading the public in justifying sending Australian troops off to war... One senator accused Howard of 'unprecedented deceit.' This important story received little attention in the U.S. media. We call it to your attention as a reminder of what one honest person can do."[186]

When the Australian Parliament conducted the Flood Inquiry into Australia's intelligence failures on Iraq in 2004,[187] Wilkie testified that the Australian government had distorted the intelligence so much that it was "pure dishonesty." He later felt that the Flood Inquiry vindicated his judgment.[188]

Wilkie points out that the investigations into intelligence failures in the U.S., UK, and Australia focused their inquiries too narrowly. They examined failures within the intelligence agencies and kept the "governments' misuse of intelligence material" beyond the scope of investigations. In this way, the inquiries protected the top decision makers from scrutiny.[189] Wilkie insists that these leaders must be held accountable for their deadly deceptions.[190]

Andrew Wilkie remains convinced that the Bush administration decided first to go to war in Iraq and then "went to the intelligence community and demanded that they present valid reasons to base a declaration of war on." His analysis led him to believe that the U.S., the UK, and Australian governments "very deliberately" distorted the intelligence in order to make uncertainties about the threat that Iraq posed seem certain.[191] He expands on this thesis in his book, *Axis of Deceit: The Story of the Intelligence Officer Who Risked All to Tell the Truth About WMD and Iraq.*

While Andrew Wilkie was being vilified by his government for speaking out and was even receiving death threats from fellow citizens, he was named 2004 Whistleblower of the Year by the United Nations Association of Australia[192] and stood for office as a Green Party candidate. He continues to speak out against the war.[193]

4

U.S. Whistleblowers

We must not confuse dissent with disloyalty.
When the loyal opposition dies, I think the soul
of America dies with it.
    −Edward R. Murrow, pioneer TV journalist

An informed public is essential to democracy. At a time of government secrecy, the suppression of dissent, and a dearth of mainstream investigative journalism, we rely on government insiders and courageous media outlets to reveal the truth. When a President uses executive privilege to withhold information from the legislature, the judiciary, and the public, how can we learn the truth if not from those with inside knowledge? Much of what we know about the run-up to the war in Iraq has come from whistleblowers.

"It is through whistleblowers that America has learned of the torture memos, the Abu Ghraib prison abuse scandal, secret CIA 'black site' detention facilities abroad," and warrantless wiretapping.[1] What is dangerous for our country is that the Bush administration has routinely retaliated "against government employees who uncover weaknesses in our ability to prevent terrorist attacks or protect the public's safety."[2]

In 1971, the *New York Times,* the *Washington Post,* and seventeen other newspapers published selections from the Pentagon Papers,[3] despite efforts by the Nixon White House to stop them.[4] In 2005, when the Downing Street Memos were first leaked in the London *Times,* they made major news in Europe but were barely mentioned in the U.S. In an era of media consolidation and government intimidation, the large corporations that own the media seem, at times, to prefer upholding administration fabrications to investigating the truth. Talk-show host Phil Donohue told Bill Moyers that MSNBC, where he worked, had a biased policy for guest selection during the run-up to the Iraq

War: "You could have the supporters of the President [on the air] alone, and they would say why this war is important. You couldn't have a dissenter alone. Our producers were instructed to feature two conservatives for every liberal."[5]

In December 2001, Attorney General John Ashcroft made it clear that the executive branch regarded any questioning of the powers they sought through the Patriot Act as bordering on treason. Referring to Americans alarmed by restrictions of their fundamental liberties, Ashcroft said, "To those who scare peace-loving people with phantoms of lost liberty, my message is this: Your tactics only aid terrorists, for they erode our national unity and diminish our resolve. They give ammunition to America's enemies and pause to America's friends."[6] This is a sharply different message from that of Theodore Roosevelt, who stated, "To announce that there must be no criticism of the President or that we are to stand by the President right or wrong is not only unpatriotic and servile, but is morally treasonable to the American public."[7] President Bush says his actions since 9/11 have been motivated by concern for national security—to protect the American people—and we have been advised to stay silent for the good of our country. But classified documents reveal that his actions—illegally eavesdropping on the United Nations Security Council members, Democrats, antiwar activists, and ordinary citizens—have been taken first and foremost to protect his administration's power.[8]

Bill Moyers observes, "Never has there been an administration so disciplined in secrecy, so precisely in lockstep in keeping information from the people at large and—in defiance of the Constitution—from their representatives in Congress."[9] Because of this secrecy, it has taken us years to understand the details about the build-up to war in Iraq—a deeply disturbing pattern of deception to foster support for an illegal and unnecessary war that has consumed military and financial resources, fueled Islamic fundamentalism, and destabilized the Middle East and America's role in the world. In June 2007, columnist Paul Krugman reminded an audience of booksellers and publishers, "It's really hard to remember how frightening it was to be critical [of the administration] just a few years ago."[10] It was a time of superpatriotism, when dissent was dangerous.[11]

It takes courage to speak out. Sometimes dissenters—including Joseph Wilson, Richard Clarke, Clare Short, Craig Murray, and Kofi Annan—become the targets of smear campaigns. Soon after Secretary General Annan declared the war in Iraq to be illegal under the UN Charter,[12] Republicans accused him of being part of the Oil-for-Food scandal, even as most countries in the world, including the UK, dismissed the charges.

Since 9/11, the number of government employees who have filed whistleblower disclosures has increased nearly 50 percent. Rather than being embraced, they are being retaliated against for coming forward. Many were star employees who had served for decades before revealing information they felt needed to be disclosed. One Federal Bureau of Investigation (FBI) agent told his superiors that their investigation into meetings between terrorist suspects had been jeopardized because other agents had violated wiretapping rules. Instead of being applauded, "his accusations were ignored, his reputation ruined, and his career obliterated."[13]

William Weaver, senior adviser to the National Security Whistleblowers Coalition, says that he used to encourage whistleblowers but now warns them against speaking out. "Most of the time they go ahead and do it anyway," he says, "and end up with their lives destroyed."[14] Current and former employees of the National Security Agency (NSA) claim that the agency "frequently retaliates against whistleblowers by falsely labeling them 'delusional,' 'paranoid,' or 'psychotic.'"[15]

What should a government insider do when she witnesses her country's leaders purposefully making inaccurate statements, withholding vital information, or committing a crime? Sometimes exposing your government's actions is in itself illegal. But what is legal and what is right are not always identical. Dr. Martin Luther King, Jr., warned, "We should never forget that everything Adolph Hitler did in Germany was 'legal' and everything the Hungarian freedom fighters did in Hungary was 'illegal.'"[16]

Daniel Ellsberg, who leaked the Pentagon Papers, exposing decades of deception behind U.S. involvement in Vietnam and contributing to that war's end, writes, "Revealing lies, cover-ups, and abuses is not disloyal. It is an expression of overarching loyalty to the Constitution, the

rule of law, and the sovereign public, transcending party and administration. It is a courageous and patriotic act."[17]

Whistleblowers are those who "commit the truth," often to their
detriment but almost always for the benefit of society.[18] They are ordinary people who, when faced with an untenable inner and outer conflict, stand up and speak truth to power. According to C. Fred Alford,
author of *Whistleblowers: Broken Lives and Organizational Power,* "A real
cynic isn't going to blow the whistle. A real conformist isn't going to
blow the whistle. And a real radical probably won't be in a position to
do it. It takes someone who believes in the system far more than the
system even believes in itself."[19]

It isn't always easy to tell the truth. Ellsberg tells the story of a U.S.
senator who, when asked in 1971 to help reveal the Pentagon Papers,
said he couldn't afford to look ridiculous.[20] Those who stand up sometimes look foolish, are ostracized, or even receive threats to their freedom and well-being. Whistleblowers lose their jobs, careers, houses,
and relationships. Some have been committed to psychiatric hospitals to silence them and ruin their reputations.[21] When asked why they
risked everything to tell the truth, whistleblowers give a variation on
the following statements: I had to. I had no other choice. I couldn't live
with myself if I hadn't. I have to look at myself in the mirror.[22] Louis
Clark, executive director of the Government Accountability Project,
notes that "despite intense personal anguish and frequent despair, most
would do it again."[23]

The Whistleblower Protection Act (WPA), passed by Congress
in 1989, guarantees "investigations into disclosures made by federal
employees and protects whistle-blowers from retaliation."[24] "The WPA
protects disclosure of information that a government employee reasonably believes evidences illegality, gross waste, flagrant mismanagement,
abuse of authority, or a substantial and specific danger to public health
or safety. The disclosure can be made to Congress, an interest group,"
or the press.[25]

Employees of intelligence-gathering agencies—the Central Intelligence Agency (CIA), Defense Intelligence Agency (DIA), National
Security Agency (NSA), and "certain other intelligence agencies excluded

by the President"[26]—are not covered by the Whistleblower Protection Act because they have access to classified information, which needs to be handled more carefully. The Intelligence Community Whistleblower Protection Act (ICWPA) of 1998 gives intelligence-community whistleblowers "access to Congress through the intelligence committees or through the Inspector General of their respective agencies."[27] However, "a series of court rulings, legal changes, and new security and secrecy policies" have made it easier than at any time since the Nixon era to punish whistleblowers.[28]

Throughout history, whistleblowers have provided a critical window into the improper and illegal workings of government: it is important for Congress to protect whistleblowers. Daniel Ellsberg implores today's government insiders to expose administration lies and machinations in order to save lives and renew America's reputation around the world, especially with regard to impending plans to attack Iran. Ellsberg's only regret, he says, is that he didn't leak the Pentagon Papers eight years earlier, before the Vietnam War escalated and more than 58,000 Americans and hundreds of thousands of Vietnamese were killed.[29]

Following are the stories of seven whistleblowers in the U.S. government. All have suffered in some manner for their acts of courage in shining light on abuse and incompetence.

✎ Bunnatine Greenhouse
Senior Contracting Officer, Army Corps of Engineers

In October 2004, Bunnatine Greenhouse publicly charged the U.S. Army Corps of Engineers (USACE) with violating Army regulations by giving no-bid contracts in Iraq to Vice President Cheney's former company, Halliburton, and its subsidiary, Kellogg, Brown and Root (KBR).[30] As the USACE's top civilian contracting officer—a position she had held since 1997—Greenhouse was responsible for ensuring "that any work contracted out by the Army Corps to private industry ... was granted in a fair and aboveboard way."[31] Her signature was required on all Army Corps of Engineers' contracts over $10 million.[32]

In February 2003, a month before the invasion of Iraq, U.S. leaders were concerned Saddam Hussein would ignite Iraqi oil fields. They met at the Pentagon to discuss issuing a contract—named Restore Iraqi Oil (RIO)—to a private company to extinguish fires on the oil fields as soon as the invasion began. Greenhouse was shocked to see several KBR executives in the room, because it was completely against protocol. Greenhouse, who holds master's degrees in business management, engineering management, and national resources strategy, viewed this as a conflict of interest.

In fact, since KBR employees had helped to prepare the RIO contract,[33] their company should have been excluded from consideration. "It was strict protocol in the procurement business that the contractor who drew up the contingency plan for a job should not be allowed to bid on the job itself."[34] Greenhouse insisted that the KBR executives leave the meeting. The general who complied with her request to remove the KBR representatives seemed adamant that the award needed to go to KBR based on "compelling emergency."[35]

The next day, Greenhouse received, for her approval, the final RIO contract awarded to KBR, a no-bid contract worth up to $7 billion over five years.[36] Although she had numerous reservations, Greenhouse signed the contract but not before adding a handwritten note below her signature: "I caution that extending this sole source effort beyond a one-year period could convey an invalid perception that there is not strong intent for a limited competition."[37]

After repeatedly questioning Halliburton's and its subsidiary KBR's contracts, Greenhouse stopped being included in major contracting decisions. Army officials referred her accusations to the Pentagon's investigations bureau and promised to protect her position.[38] But in late 2003, when Pentagon auditors found that Halliburton may have overcharged the government $61 million for fuel, the Army Corps of Engineers waived the concern and determined that the price was "reasonable."[39] Greenhouse complained that Corps officials had excluded her from this decision and had one of her subordinates sign off on the waiver.[40] This secretly granted waiver meant "the Pentagon investigation into KBR's fuel surcharges ground to a halt."[41]

A year later, on October 6, 2004, the commander of the Army Corps of Engineers, Lieutenant General Carl Strock, told Greenhouse that "because her last two performance ratings had been 'less than fully successful,' she must be removed from her post as chief of all contracting and demoted from the Senior Executive Service." He probably reminded her that she was eligible for retirement.[42] The Corps had tried to demote her a year earlier, but was foiled when Lieutenant General Joe Ballard, the former commander of the agency and the person who had hired her in 1997, wrote in a sworn affidavit that senior officials of the Corps who "were associated with favorite companies" resisted Greenhouse's "strict and ethical application" of rules intended to encourage fairness and competition."[43] He added, "I did not believe that females and minorities are always treated fairly at the Corps, because of long-standing 'good ole boy' mentality by a number of the members of the Command."[44]

For two years, Greenhouse had tried "to make KBR accountable from the inside, by doing her job and questioning contracts."[45] After being threatened with demotion, Greenhouse "hired a lawyer" and went public.[46] On October 21, 2004, Greenhouse's lawyer sent a letter on her behalf to the acting Secretary of the Army, demanding an investigation of alleged violations by the Corps. Once again, her demotion was delayed.

Greenhouse alleged that the Corps had engaged in "a pattern of favoritism toward Halliburton that imperils the integrity of the federal contracting program . . . without following rules designed to ensure competition and fair prices to the government."[47] When the terms of the RIO contract became public, Congressional and media outrage led to the contract being shortened to one year and replaced by a competitive process, as Greenhouse had recommended."[48]

In June 2005, Greenhouse testified before Congress that the RIO contract awarded to KBR was "the most blatant and improper contract abuse" she had witnessed "in twenty years of government service."[49] Weeks after this testimony, she was officially demoted and relieved of overseeing major contracts.[50] In his dismissal letter, Lt. Gen. Strock said that Greenhouse's removal was "based on her performance and not in retaliation for any disclosures of alleged improprieties she may have made." She was moved to a lesser post in the Corps' civil works division.[51]

While there is no concrete proof that Vice President Cheney or anyone in his office influenced the awarding of the RIO contract to KBR, there were indications to that effect. *Time* reported that an internal Pentagon email from an Army Corps of Engineers official said that action on RIO had already been "coordinated ... with the Vice President's office" before the contract was awarded.[52] The *Wall Street Journal* reported that "Halliburton executives then met directly with Cheney's staff."[53] KBR continues to maintain that the Vice President had nothing to do with any of its Iraq contracts.[54]

The National Whistleblower Center has established a defense fund for Bunnatine Greenhouse. See www.whistleblowers.org.

✎ Jesselyn Radack
Attorney, Department of Justice

Yale Law School graduate Jesselyn Radack entered the Department of Justice (DOJ) in 1995 through the prestigious Attorney General's Honor Program and began work in the Professional Responsibility Advisory Office (PRAO), the DOJ's ethics division.[55]

On December 7, 2001, a DOJ counterterrorism prosecutor contacted her to ask if an FBI agent in Afghanistan could ethically interview "American Taliban" John Walker Lindh without the lawyer his parents had retained being present. After consulting with PRAO's senior legal adviser, Radack recommended by email that the FBI refrain from interrogating Lindh, as it "would be a pre-indictment, custodial event interview which is not authorized by law."[56] Several days later, the same prosecutor informed her that the FBI agent had already interrogated Lindh without his attorney present. Radack advised him that the information gained from the interrogation could be used for intelligence purposes, but not for criminal prosecution.[57] Radack immediately told her supervisor, Claudia Flynn, that PRAO's advice had been ignored. Flynn responded by saying, "PRAO's involvement in the matter [is] over."[58]

Lindh's confession that he was fighting for the Taliban was crucial to the FBI's case. The question was, was the confession legal? When, on January 15, 2002, Attorney General John Ashcroft announced criminal charges against Lindh, he stressed that Lindh's rights had been "carefully, scrupulously honored,"[59] adding that Lindh had waived his right to an attorney, which Radack knew was not true.[60]

In March 2002, the lead prosecutor in the Lindh case notified Radack that the judge had ordered all DOJ correspondence on the Lindh case turned over to the court. He said he had two emails between Radack and the terrorism unit and asked if there were others. Radack remembered at least a dozen emails, but when she pulled Lindh's file, she found only three.[61] She asked Flynn about the others, and Flynn told her, "I sent [the judge] everything that was in the file."[62] Radack was surprised to learn that neither of the two emails the DOJ gave the judge "included her comments that the [Lindh] interrogation had been improper."[63]

With the help of a DOJ technician, Radack was able to recover fourteen emails about the case from her computer.[64] She printed them for Claudia Flynn and offered to fax them to the prosecutor. Flynn said she would take care of it.[65]

Instead, in April 2002, Jesselyn Radack received a blistering, out-of-cycle performance evaluation and was forced out of her DOJ job.[66] She began working for a private Washington, DC, law firm. In June 2002, Radack was listening to National Public Radio (NPR) and heard a story about John Walker Lindh, in which "the DOJ claimed it 'never' took the position that Lindh was entitled to counsel while in custody in Afghanistan."[67] Stunned to hear something so blatantly untrue, she realized that Claudia Flynn had never turned the emails over to the judge. Radack then gave the missing December 2001 emails to *Newsweek*,[68] "because my complaints through internal channels had fallen on deaf ears."[69] Michael Isikoff used the emails in a June 24, 2002, *Newsweek* story and posted thirteen of them on *Newsweek*'s website.[70]

The Department of Justice immediately began an investigation, not of departmental wrongdoing, but of the leak of the emails. It also informed Radack's law firm that "they had just hired a criminal,"[71] and pressured the firm to fire her,[72] which it did in November 2002.[73]

In January 2003, the DOJ inspector general told Radack that she had been referred for criminal prosecution, but he refused to identify the charges. Nine months later, the government dropped its investigation into the criminal case against her.[74] The DOJ then gave the Maryland and District of Columbia Bar Associations copies of a confidential report to which Radack never had access and recommended that she be disbarred. After a year, the Maryland Bar dismissed the charges.[75] As of July 2007, four years after receiving the confidential report, the DC Bar was still considering the charges. Radack was, nonetheless, elected to serve on the DC Bar Association's legal ethics committee. Following her departure from the Department of Justice, she was unable to find work in any Washington law firm until early 2007.[76]

Radack has written numerous articles on the rights of whistleblowers, torture, and enemy combatants. In early 2006, she became an adjunct professor at the American University School of Law, where she taught professional responsibility. She also works with the American Bar Association's Task Force on Treatment of Enemy Combatants.[78]

With the Lindh case, Radack believes something bigger than the case itself is at stake: "The consequences of playing fast and loose with the ethics rules would not only delegitimize the integrity of any conviction, but debase the entire legal system."[79] In 2006, she wrote and self-published *The Canary in the Coalmine: Blowing the Whistle in the Case of "American Taliban" John Walker Lindh.*

Jesselyn Radack says one of the lessons she learned from her experience with the Bush administration Justice Department is, "Those who speak out for reasons of conscience get punished."[80]

For information on her Coalition for Civil Rights and Democratic Liberties, visit www.cradl.info.

✎ Mary Ryan
Assistant Secretary of State for Consular Affairs

On October 12, 2001, Ambassador Mary Ryan testified to a Senate panel that American Embassy consular officers might have been able to stop some of the 9/11 terrorists from entering the country if the

CIA, FBI, and other agencies had shared information about the suspected terrorists with the State Department.[81] From May 1993 until July 2002, Ryan was the head of the State Department's Bureau of Consular Affairs and had received the Presidential Distinguished Service Award twice.

Although consular officers at U.S. Embassies worldwide are responsible for issuing visas to those who want to enter the United States, these officers must rely on the FBI, CIA, and other law enforcement and intelligence agencies to provide appropriate data that alerts consular officers to potential terrorists whom they may block from entering the country by refusing them visas.[82] The Immigration and Customs Enforcement Service (ICE), formed in March 2003, processes visas at U.S. border entry points and decides whether someone with a visa can enter the United States. ICE also tracks those who overstay their visas.

In her testimony to the Senate, Ryan said there had been a "colossal intelligence failure, or there was information that wasn't shared with us," and blamed the hijackers' entry into the U.S. on this lack of information.[83] The Immigration and Customs Enforcement Service subsequently acknowledged that thirteen of the nineteen suspected hijackers had been issued legal visas.[84] Consular officers were distraught to learn they had allowed entry to the 9/11 hijackers, Ambassador Ryan told the committee. Mohamed Atta, the suspected leader of the hijackers, had received his visa in May 2000, even though intelligence agencies possibly knew before then, that he had met with operatives associated with Osama bin Laden as early as January 2000.[85]

Ryan said that "the FBI has refused for a decade to provide the State Department with access to its National Crime Information Center (NCIC) databases, including a database on gang and terrorist group members. The FBI's reason: The State Department is not a law enforcement agency."[86] In 2003, the FBI did grant ICE, "a fellow Justice Department agency, access to the NCIC databases, but then only at two entry points into the United States... Similarly, the ICE and the FBI developed separate fingerprint identification databases beginning in 1989."[87] This lack of integration may have contributed to the ability of several of the September 11th terrorists to enter the country undetected. Ryan stressed the need for information sharing to protect this country from attacks.[88] It would take "an act of Congress to require the FBI to share data," Ryan said, after dealing with the FBI's reluctance to provide data to the State Department.[89]

In July 2002, Secretary of State Powell asked Mary Ryan, the U.S.'s longest-serving career diplomat at the time and the State Department's third-ranking career officer, to retire amid revelations that more than seventy visas had been issued illegally by the U.S. Embassy in Qatar, several to men with ties to the 9/11 hijackers. Powell said that his request was unrelated to Ryan's testimony or to the Visa Express scandal, where certain Saudi travel agents had been authorized to expedite U.S. visas for Saudi citizens. Many felt that Mary Ryan was the administration's scapegoat for the 9/11 terrorists' entering the United States.[90] Ironically, Powell asked her to step down after she was criticized by Congress for the very charge she had brought to Congress' attention, that security changes were needed in the wake of September 11.[91]

On January 26, 2004, Mary Ryan testified at a hearing of the National Commission on Terrorist Attacks upon the United States: "I wish that there had been a perfect way of detecting terrorists as they applied for visas, but the only tools at our disposal were the ones I have mentioned. They combined careful data collection and sharing with powerful information technology that put the data at the fingertips of the consular in the field in real time. They were reinforced by a system of multiple checks at our ports of entry and within the United States. They obviously were not infallible, but . . . were the best we had at the time, and I believe that they will get better every day as we learn more about the threats we face. I think that Consular Affairs and consular officers in the field did all we could, using the information and the tools we had available prior to September 11, 2001. However, as we know now, we lacked critical information . . . If there is a single point that I want to leave with the Commission, it is that, by any name, a check system is and will be as good as the information that is in it. One lesson of 9/11 is that Consular Affairs had no information on any of the nineteen terrorists."[92]

Mary Ryan died in Washington, DC, in April 2006, at the age of 65.

✎ Sibel Edmonds

Translator, Federal Bureau of Investigation

> *We fear that the designation of information as*
> *classified in some cases serves to protect the executive*
> *branch against embarrassing revelations and full*
> *accountability.*
>
> > –Senators Leahy and Grassley,
> >   in a letter to Attorney General Ashcroft
> >   about Sibel Edmonds

Sibel Edmonds was born in Iran in 1970, the daughter of an Azerbaijani doctor.[93] One of her first memories is of SAVAK, the Shah's brutal secret police, searching her family home in Tehran for left-leaning books. After the revolution led by the Ayatollah Khomeini, soldiers from the Revolutionary Guard threatened 11-year-old Sibel with jail because her head covering was not modest enough. Soon after, Edmonds and her family fled to Turkey.[94]

Six years later, in 1988, Edmonds came to the U.S. to attend George Washington University, where she received bachelor's degrees in both psychology and criminal justice. In 1992, she married Matthew Edmonds, an American, and became a naturalized U.S. citizen.[95]

Because Edmonds is fluent in Turkish, Farsi, and Azeri—"three languages crucial to intelligence-gathering in the Middle East"[96]—she was hired by the FBI soon after September 11, 2001, and given top secret security clearance to translate conversations and documents the FBI had obtained from wiretaps and from suspected terrorists detained in the U.S. and abroad.[97] At the same time, she was also earning her master's degree in public policy and international commerce from George Mason University.

It wasn't long before Edmonds found herself disturbed by the work environment of the FBI's language division. It was, she told CBS's Ed Bradley, "riddled with incompetence and corruption."[98] From her first day on the job, she "was told repeatedly by one of her supervisors that there was no urgency" in translating the documents. She was advised to take longer so that the department would appear overworked and understaffed and thus secure a bigger budget to hire more translators the following year. In an effort to slow her down, her supervisor would even erase completed translations from her computer after she'd left work for the day. When she arrived the next day, she would have to retranslate the same documents. Her supervisor told her, "Consider it a lesson and don't talk about it to anybody else."[99]

Edmonds also became troubled by a coworker at the FBI's language division, a Turkish woman named Jan Dickerson. According to Edmonds, Dickerson tried to recruit Sibel into the American-Turkish Council (ATC), a legitimate organization but one that Sibel knew "was a target of top secret surveillance" by the FBI.[100] As part of her job, Edmonds had listened to wiretaps that "suggested to her that the Washington office of the ATC was being used as a front for criminal activity."[101]

Dickerson also insisted that she (Dickerson) be the only one to translate the wiretaps of certain Turkish suspects who were the targets of counterintelligence investigations.[102] When Edmonds didn't agree, Dickerson threatened her: "Why would you want to place your life and your family's life in danger by translating these tapes?"[103]

Edmonds secretly reviewed Dickerson's translations and discovered that Dickerson had left out information crucial to the FBI's ongoing investigation of the ATC—information Edmonds said would have revealed that the Turkish suspects "had spies working for [them] inside the U.S. State Department and at the Pentagon."[104] Edmonds said she found at least eighteen translations and "communications that were extremely important for the ongoing investigations of these individuals," but Dickerson had marked them as "not important to be translated." Edmonds told CBS that these documents revealed "activities to obtain United States military and intelligence secrets."[105]

Edmonds told her FBI bosses about this repeatedly, but "nobody wanted to hear about it." The agent in charge said that her allegations implied that FBI security officers were not doing their jobs and warned that if she insisted on an investigation, he would make sure it would become an investigation about her.[106]

Frustrated, she wrote a letter to her immediate superiors and to a top official at the FBI. After several months with no response, she contacted the Justice Department's inspector general and Senator Charles Grassley of the Judiciary Committee, which oversees the FBI, to alert them of security breaches and corruption. Senator Grassley found Edmonds to be "very credible…because people within the FBI have corroborated a lot of her story."[107]

In March 2002, the FBI fired Sibel Edmonds, saying only that her contract had been terminated for the government's convenience. "Three months later, the FBI conceded that on at least two occasions, Dickerson had, in fact, left out significant information from her translations," but attributed it to lack of experience rather than a malicious act.[108]

After being fired, Edmonds told her story to congressional investigators, the Justice Department, and the commission investigating the 9/11 attacks.[109] Senator Grassley expressed concern about internal security at the FBI: "You shouldn't have somebody (Dickerson) in your organization that's compromising our national security by not doing the job right, whether it's lack of skills or whether it's intentional."[110]

Edmonds filed a lawsuit in July 2002 "to challenge the FBI's retaliatory actions."[111] She "alleged that her rights under the Privacy Act and her First and Fifth Amendment rights had been violated by the government," because they "leaked confidential information about her to several publications." Edmonds sought "monetary damages and reinstatement to a contract job."[112]

In 2004, "the FBI took the highly unusual step of retroactively classifying information" it had given to Congress two years earlier concerning the Sibel Edmonds' case.[113] Congressional letters investigating the case—one from Senators Grassley and Leahy to the Justice Department "asking specific questions about Edmonds' allegations" and revealing that the FBI had already confirmed many of her allegations in unclassified briefings, and another from Senator Leahy to Attorney General Ashcroft "asking for a speedy and thorough investigation of Edmonds' case"—were also retroactively reclassified.[114]

In court, the FBI and Justice Department argued that Edmonds' "lawsuit should be dismissed because much of the information needed to be considered for it was protected by the 'state secrets privilege,' which is meant to protect classified national security information from being disclosed."[115]

"In defending the invocation of the state secrets privilege, Attorney General Ashcroft wrote to the court, 'Based on my personal consideration of the matter, I have concluded that further disclosure of the information underlying in this case, including the nature of the duties of the plaintiff or the other contract translators at issue in this case, reasonably could be expected to cause serious damage to the national security interests of the United States.'"[116]

In July 2004, a federal judge dismissed Edmonds' lawsuit, because the information she needed to prove her case had recently been "classified and protected by the 'state secrets privilege.'"[117] Edmonds' lawyers argued that the decision represented an example of the Executive Branch abusing secrecy as a weapon against whistleblowers.[118]

Two weeks after Edmonds' case was dismissed, the Justice Department Inspector General completed his classified investigation and "concluded that Edmonds' allegations 'were at least a contributing factor in why the FBI terminated her services.'"[119] John Roberts, former chief of the FBI's Internal Affairs Department, confirmed that Edmonds' case was part of a larger pattern at the FBI of hiding internal misconduct while punishing the whistleblower.[120]

During subsequent investigations, the FBI revealed that "critical shortages of experienced Middle Eastern language translators have plagued the FBI and the rest of the U.S. intelligence community for years," acknowledging that some individuals in their language department did not even speak English or the language they were supposed to be translating adequately.[121]

Edmonds' case raised controversy on several fronts. Information she provided to the Senate Judiciary Committee several years earlier was deemed classified in 2004 under the state secrets privilege.[122] Attorneys who fled a lawsuit stemming from the 9/11 terrorist attacks wanted to depose her, but their request was denied for the same reason. "Edmonds has testified in closed session to the 9/11 Commission and has made claims that the FBI possessed some information prior to the attacks on the World Trade Center and the Pentagon that could have proved helpful in preventing the terrorist strikes."[123]

In August 2004, Edmonds founded the National Security Whistleblowers Coalition to lobby Congress to provide protections for whistleblowers from the national security communities, including the FBI, CIA, NSA, Justice Department, State Department, and Department of Defense.[124] Currently there are no federal protections for national security whistleblowers.[125]

In 2005, the Justice Department Inspector General revealed that many of Edmonds' charges "were substantiated by witnesses and documents and that her allegations, in fact, were the most significant factor in the FBI's decision to terminate her services."[126]

Edmonds was awarded the 2006 PEN/Newman's Own First Amendment Award, for fighting "courageously, despite adversity, to safeguard the First Amendment right to freedom of expression as it applies to the written word."[127] In announcing the award, the the PEN American Center maintained that "Sibel Edmonds' Kafkaesque ordeal underscores how easily government powers, especially powers wielded in the name of national security, can be abused to keep the public in the dark about official failings."[128]

What gives Edmonds the courage to persevere? One day when she was young, the Iranian police came to arrest her for the immodesty of her head covering. Her father told her, "Sibel, you only live your life once. How do you choose to live? According to your principles or in fear?" She has never forgotten those words.[129]

Sibel Edmonds' website is www.JustACitizen.org. The website for the National Security Whistleblowers Coalition is www.nswbc.org.

✑ Russell Tice
*Intelligence Specialist, Defense Intelligence Agency
and National Security Agency*

On December 16, 2005, the *New York Times* revealed that the U.S. National Security Agency (NSA) had been conducting a clandestine domestic spying program since 2002, at the direction of the President, using wiretaps to eavesdrop on American citizens without the legally required warrants from the Foreign Intelligence Surveillance Act (FISA) court.[130] The *Times* article cited national security officials who questioned "whether the surveillance has stretched, if not crossed, constitutional limits on legal searches."[131] The Bush administration argued it was operating within the law, "based on classified legal opinions that assert that the president has broad powers to order such searches," in part because Congress authorized the President after 9/11 to use force against "al Qaeda and other terrorist groups."[132]

The *Times* learned about this program in 2004, before the presidential elections, but refrained from printing the story for more than a year.[133] When they finally did decide to publish this story, President Bush personally summoned *Times* publisher Arthur Sulzberger and executive editor Bill Keller to the Oval Office to try to dissuade them.[134] In late December 2005, the Justice Department launched a criminal investigation into the leak of the eavesdropping program's existence.[135]

Russell Tice, an eighteen-year intelligence veteran who had worked for both the NSA and the Defense Intelligence Agency (DIA), admitted being one of the *Times'* sources for the story.[136] Tice said the NSA's warrantless wiretapping program was illegal, because it violated both the Constitution as well as FISA, which was enacted in 1978 in response to flagrant CIA and FBI eavesdropping abuses.[137] The act "created a special court to issue wiretap warrants for cases in which the government says national security is involved."[138] Violating FISA is a felony.[139]

Tice said he'd been taught early in his NSA career, "You will not spy on Americans. It is drilled into our heads over and over and over again in security briefings, at least twice a year, where you ultimately have to sign a paper that says you have gotten the briefing. Everyone at NSA who is a Signals Intelligence (SIGINT) officer knows that you do not do this. Ultimately, so do the leaders of NSA, and apparently the leaders of NSA have decided that they were just going to go against the tenets of something that's a gospel to a SIGINT officer."[140] Equally troubling was the revelation that the NSA was sharing the information from this secret spying program with other intelligence agencies including the FBI and the DIA, which is another violation of FISA.[141]

Because employees of intelligence agencies have access to classified materials, they are not protected by the Whistleblower Protection Act (WPA).[142] Instead, these employees are covered under the Intelligence Community Whistleblower Protection Act (ICWPA), which offers "a legal means to contact Congress" to inform them about something improper or illegal occurring in the intelligence community.[143] On December 18, 2005, Tice wrote to the House and Senate intelligence committees offering to testify about the secret spying program and requesting whistleblower protection under the ICWPA.[144]

In his letter, Tice explained, "It is with my oath as a U.S. intelligence officer weighing heavy on my mind that I wish to report to Congress acts that I believe are unlawful and unconstitutional. The freedom of the American people cannot be protected when our constitutional liberties are ignored and our nation has decayed into a police state."[145]

Tice said he spoke out because he was concerned that the actions of senior government officials who condone warrantless wiretapping have harmed NSA and the security of the United States. Tice said, "I think the American people need to be concerned about allegations that the intelligence community is spying on Americans. One of my fears is that this would cause . . . the good work that's being done at NSA to be ineffective. The NSA is very important to this country's security. I certainly hope that some bad apples, even if these bad apples were at the top of NSA, don't ultimately destroy the capabilities of NSA to protect the American people."[146] Tice's revelations sparked a national debate on the warrantless wiretapping program and laid the groundwork for the Senate Judiciary Committee to hold hearings on illegal government actions.[147]

On January 1, 2006, two weeks after exposing the existence of the secret domestic spying program, the *Times* reported that in March 2004, the Justice Department had refused to reauthorize the program "amid concerns about its legality and oversight."[148] At the time, Attorney General John Ashcroft had been hospitalized. His deputy, James Comey, who was acting Attorney General, objected to parts of the surveillance program and refused to approve its continued use. The White House sent two top Bush aides, Andrew Card and Alberto Gonzales, to visit Ashcroft in intensive care to seek his approval for the program.[149] Ashcroft refused.[150] The next day, "the White House approved the executive order without any signature from the Justice Department certifying its legality."[151] In mid-2007, Comey testified to the Senate Judiciary Committee that the program continued for several weeks until Ashcroft,

Comey, FBI Director Robert Mueller, and several others threatened to resign. At that point, President Bush suspended parts of the program and the Justice Department finally approved it.

Russell Tice's disclosures were instrumental in getting a short-lived pause in the administration's illegal spying on American citizens. On August 17, 2006, U.S. District Judge Anna Diggs Taylor ruled that the NSA's warrantless surveillance program violated the Constitution and FISA, because it authorizes illegal searches.[152] She dismissed the Bush administration argument that the congressional resolution known as the Authorization for Use of Military Force (AUMF) passed after 9/11 had given the President the authority to create the program. That resolution, "says nothing whatsoever of intelligence or surveillance," Diggs concluded. "We must first note that the Office of the Chief Executive has itself been created, with its powers, by the Constitution. There are no hereditary Kings in America and no powers not created by the Constitution. So all 'inherent powers' must derive from that Constitution. . . . The public interest is clear, in this matter. It is the upholding of our Constitution."[153] The Bush administration quickly filed notice of appeal.[154]

In January 2007, before the appeal was heard in court, President Bush announced he would allow the FISA court to oversee the NSA program.[155] Six months later, on July 6, 2007, a federal appeals court reversed Judge Taylor's order that the NSA warrantless wiretapping program must be shut down.[156] The next month, Congress buckled to pressure from the Bush administration that played on Democrats' fear of being seen as weak on terrorism, and agreed to amend the Foreign Intelligence Surveillance Act of 1978.[157] On August 4, 2007, Congress passed the Protect America Act that broadly expanded the administration's "authority to eavesdrop" on American citizens' international calls and emails without warrants or oversight.[158]

⤳ Coleen Rowley

Chief Counsel, Federal Bureau of Investigation
Minneapolis Field Office

Coleen Rowley, chief counsel for the FBI's Minneapolis Field Office, had been an FBI Special Agent for twenty-two years when, on May 21, 2002, she sent a thirteen-page memorandum to Director Robert Mueller, accusing FBI headquarters "of deliberately obstructing measures that could have helped disrupt the September 11th attacks."[159] She charged that FBI supervisors in Washington "systematically dismissed and undermined requests" from Minneapolis FBI agents for a special "warrant to wiretap and search the computer"[160] and possessions of "Zacarias Moussaoui, who had been learning to fly a 747 jumbo jet at an Eagan, Minnesota, flight school."[161]

Rowley revealed that the FBI's lack of information sharing prevented connecting Moussaoui's flight lessons with "an earlier report from a Phoenix field agent raising suspicions about Middle Eastern men attending flight schools."[162] In her memo she wrote, "It's at least possible we could have gotten lucky and uncovered one or two more of the terrorists in flight training prior to September 11. There is at least some chance that we may have limited the September 11th attacks and resulting loss of life."[163] Moussaoui, the only person brought to trial in the U.S. in connection with the 9/11 attacks, was sentenced to life imprisonment in 2006 for his role in the attacks.[164]

Rowley wrote that Mueller and senior aides "omitted, downplayed, glossed over and or/mischaracterized" the investigation of Moussaoui by her Minneapolis office.[165] Because Mueller and other senior FBI officials had consistently denied the FBI had any information "that Islamic terrorists might be planning an attack involving hijacked airplanes," Rowley wrote in her letter, "I have deep concerns that a delicate shading/skewing of facts by you and others at the highest levels of FBI management has occurred and is occurring." She closed her letter by acknowledging "the frankness with which I have expressed myself" and asked for federal whistle-blower protection.[166] She was just two years away from retirement and feared reprisals.

For her courage in speaking out, Rowley was one of three women named Persons of the Year by *Time* magazine in 2002. The others were Sherron Watkins, who had warned Enron's Kenneth Lay "that the company's methods of accounting were improper," and Cynthia Cooper, who informed the WorldCom Board of Directors "that the company had covered up $3.8 billion in losses through...phony bookkeeping."[167] In choosing these three women, *Time* maintained, "Democratic capitalism requires that people trust in the integrity of public and private institutions alike. As whistleblowers, these three became fail-safe systems that did not fail." They risked their jobs, health, privacy, and sanity. "They were people who did right just by doing their jobs rightly."[168]

In early 2003, Rowley made public a letter she wrote urging Mueller to oppose the imminent U.S. invasion of Iraq because of its domestic impact. She argued that a war in Iraq could result in "a flood of terrorism" on a scale the bureau was not prepared to handle.[169]

The FBI Agents Association called her comments about an area in which, they alleged, she lacked expertise, "demoralizing to the many FBI employees who have been achieving significant successes in this area."[170] Although Mueller "had promised there would be no reprisals for her earlier criticisms," Rowley was reassigned "from her job as the chief division counsel in the Minneapolis office, accepting a lower-level job and a pay cut."[171]

During 2003 and 2004, "with FBI clearances to talk about ethics and civil liberties," she traveled throughout the United States, speaking to organizations such as the American Civil Liberties Union, "National Aeronautics and Space administration, nuclear power plant security officials, accountants, health care compliance officers, church groups, and college students."[172]

Rowley ended her twenty-four-year FBI career in January 2005, "just eleven days after turning 50," when she was eligible for a full pension.[173] Since her retirement, she has continued to travel around the country speaking about ethics, integrity, and civil liberties. Rowley asked "to be considered for appointment to the new federal Privacy and Civil Liberties Oversight Board," which "would give her a chance to use her background as a constitutional law adviser at the bureau." "The new law overhauling the nation's intelligence apparatus directs the Department of Homeland Security to create the board to ensure that counterterrorism investigations and arrests do not infringe on people's rights."[174] Although Rowley was nominated for the board by a majority of Minnesota senators and congresspersons, the Bush administration chose not appoint her.[175] Rowley has written numerous articles about "the importance of preserving civil liberties in the nation's anti-terrorism climate."[176]

Putting her experience in government to use, Rowley ran for the U.S. House of Representatives from Minnesota's second district but lost the election in November 2006.[177]

Coleen Rowley's letter to FBI Director Robert Mueller spelling out her concerns about the FBI's handling of investigations of potential terrorists prior to September 11, 2001, is remarkable for its frankness and courage. She put her career on the line to make public her views on the FBI's failures that stifled field initiatives that might have unraveled the 9/11 plot before the tragic events of that day.

☙

Coleen Rowley's Letter to FBI Director Robert Mueller[178]

May 21, 2002
FBI Director Robert Mueller
FBI Headquarters
Washington, DC

Dear Director Mueller:

I feel at this point that I have to put my concerns in writing concerning the important topic of the FBI's response to evidence of terrorist activity in the United States prior to September 11th. The issues are fundamentally ones of INTEGRITY and go to the heart of the FBI's law enforcement mission and mandate. Moreover, at this critical juncture in fashioning future policy to promote the most effective handling of ongoing and future threats to United States citizens' security, it is of absolute importance that an unbiased, completely accurate picture emerges of the FBI's current investigative and management strengths and failures.

To get to the point, I have deep concerns that a delicate and subtle shading/skewing of facts by you and others at the highest levels of

FBI management has occurred and is occurring. The term "cover up" would be too strong a characterization, which is why I am attempting to carefully (and perhaps over laboriously) choose my words here. I base my concerns on my relatively small, peripheral but unique role in the Moussaoui investigation in the Minneapolis Division prior to, during and after September 11th and my analysis of the comments I have heard both inside the FBI (originating, I believe, from you and other high levels of management) as well as your congressional testimony and public comments.

I feel that certain facts, including the following, have, up to now, been omitted, downplayed, glossed over and/or mischaracterized in an effort to avoid or minimize personal and/or institutional embarrassment on the part of the FBI and/or perhaps even for improper political reasons:

1. The Minneapolis agents who responded to the call about Moussaoui's flight training identified him as a terrorist threat from a very early point. The decision to take him into custody on August 15, 2001, on the INS "overstay" charge was a deliberate one to counter that threat and was based on the agents' reasonable suspicions. While it can be said that Moussaoui's overstay status was fortuitous, because it allowed for him to be taken into immediate custody and prevented him receiving any more flight training, it was certainly not something the INS coincidentally undertook of their own volition. I base this on the conversation I had when the agents called me at home late on the evening Moussaoui was taken into custody to confer and ask for legal advice about their next course of action. The INS agent was assigned to the FBI's Joint Terrorism Task Force and was therefore working in tandem with FBI agents.

2. As the Minneapolis agents' reasonable suspicions quickly ripened into probable cause, which, at the latest, occurred within days of Moussaoui's arrest when the French Intelligence Service confirmed his affiliations with radical fundamentalist Islamic groups and activities connected to Osama bin Laden, they became desperate to search the computer laptop that had been taken from Moussaoui as well as conduct a more thorough search of his personal effects. The agents

in particular believed that Moussaoui signaled he had something to hide in the way he refused to allow them to search his computer.

3. The Minneapolis agents' initial thought was to obtain a criminal search warrant, but in order to do so, they needed to get FBI Headquarters' (FBIHQ's) approval in order to ask for DOJ OIPR's approval to contact the United States Attorney's Office in Minnesota. Prior to and even after receipt of information provided by the French, FBIHQ personnel disputed with the Minneapolis agents the existence of probable cause to believe that a criminal violation had occurred/was occurring. As such, FBIHQ personnel refused to contact OIPR to attempt to get the authority.

While reasonable minds may differ as to whether probable cause existed prior to receipt of the French intelligence information, it was certainly established after that point and became even greater with successive, more detailed information from the French and other intelligence sources. The two possible criminal violations initially identified by Minneapolis agents were violations of Title 18 United States Code Section 2332b (Acts of terrorism transcending national boundaries, which, notably, includes "creating a substantial risk of serious bodily injury to any other person by destroying or damaging any structure, conveyance, or other real or personal property within the United States or by attempting or conspiring to destroy or damage any structure, conveyance, or other real or personal property within the United States") and Section 32 (Destruction of aircraft or aircraft facilities).

It is important to note that the actual search warrant obtained on September 11th was based on probable cause of a violation of Section 32.[179] Notably also, the actual search warrant obtained on September 11th did not include the French intelligence information. Therefore, the only main difference between the information being submitted to FBIHQ from an early date which HQ personnel continued to deem insufficient and the actual criminal search warrant which a federal district judge signed and approved on September 11th, was the fact that, by the time the actual warrant was obtained, suspected terrorists were known to have hijacked planes which they then deliberately crashed into the World Trade Center and the Pentagon.

To say then, as has been iterated numerous times, that probable cause did not exist until after the disastrous event occurred, is really to acknowledge that the missing piece of probable cause was only the FBI's (FBIHQ's) failure to appreciate that such an event could occur. The probable cause did not otherwise improve or change. When we went to the United States Attorney's Office that morning of September 11th, in the first hour after the attack, we used a disk containing the same information that had already been provided to FBIHQ; then we quickly added Paragraph 19, which was the little we knew from news reports of the actual attacks that morning.

The problem with chalking this all up to the "20–20 hindsight is perfect" problem (which I, like all attorneys who have been involved in deadly force training or the defense of various lawsuits, am fully appreciative of), is that this is not a case of everyone in the FBI failing to appreciate the potential consequences. It is obvious, from my firsthand knowledge of the events and the detailed documentation that exists, that the agents in Minneapolis who were closest to the action and in the best position to gauge the situation locally, did fully appreciate the terrorist risk/danger posed by Moussaoui and his possible co-conspirators even prior to September 11th.

Even without knowledge of the Phoenix communication (and any number of other additional intelligence communications that FBIHQ personnel were privy to in their central coordination roles), the Minneapolis agents appreciated the risk. So I think it's very hard for the FBI to offer the "20–20 hindsight" justification for its failure to act! Also intertwined with my reluctance in this case to accept the "20–20 hindsight" rationale is firsthand knowledge that I have of statements made on September 11th, after the first attacks on the World Trade Center had already occurred, made telephonically by the FBI Supervisory Special Agent (SSA) who was the one most involved in the Moussaoui matter and who, up to that point, seemed to have been consistently, almost deliberately thwarting the Minneapolis FBI agents' efforts (see number 5).

Even after the attacks had begun, the SSA in question was still attempting to block the search of Moussaoui's computer, characterizing the World Trade Center attacks as a mere coincidence with Minneapolis' prior suspicions about Moussaoui.[180]

4. In one of my peripheral roles on the Moussaoui matter, I answered an email message on August 22, 2001, from an attorney at the National Security Law Unit (NSLU). Of course, with (ever important!) 20–20 hindsight, I now wish I had taken more time and care to compose my response. When asked by NSLU for my "assessment of (our) chances of getting a criminal warrant to search Moussaoui's computer," I answered, "Although I think there's a decent chance of being able to get a judge to sign a criminal search warrant, our USAO seems to have an even higher standard much of the time, so rather than risk it, I advised that they should try the other route."

Leaked news accounts which said the Minneapolis Legal Counsel (referring to me) concurred with the FBIHQ that probable cause was lacking to search Moussaoui's computer are in error (or possibly the leak was deliberately skewed in this fashion?). What I meant by this pithy email response was that although I thought probable cause existed ("probable cause" meaning that the proposition has to be more likely than not, or if quantified, a 51 percent likelihood), I thought our United States Attorney's Office (for a lot of reasons including just to play it safe), in regularly requiring much more than probable cause before approving affidavits (maybe, if quantified, 75–80 percent probability and sometimes even higher), and depending on the actual AUSA who would be assigned, might turn us down.

As a tactical choice, I therefore thought it would be better to pursue the "other route" (the FISA search warrant) first, the reason being that there is a common perception, which for lack of a better term I'll call the "smell test," which has arisen that if the FBI can't do something through straight-up criminal methods, it will then resort to using less-demanding intelligence methods. Of course this isn't true, but I think the perception still exists. So, by this line of reasoning, I was afraid that if we first attempted to go criminal and failed to convince an AUSA, we wouldn't pass the "smell test" in subsequently seeking a FISA. I thought our best chances therefore lay in first seeking the FISA.

Both of the factors that influenced my thinking are areas arguably in need of improvement: requiring an excessively high standard of probable cause in terrorism cases and getting rid of the "smell test" perception. It could even be argued that FBI agents, especially in terrorism cases where time is of the essence, should be allowed to go directly to federal judges to have their probable cause reviewed for arrests or searches without having to gain the USAO's approval.[181]

5. The fact is that key FBIHQ personnel whose job it was to assist and coordinate with field division agents on terrorism investigations and the obtaining and use of FISA searches (and who theoretically were privy to many more sources of intelligence information than field division agents) continued to, almost inexplicably,[182] throw up roadblocks and undermine Minneapolis' by-now-desperate efforts to obtain a FISA search warrant, long after the French intelligence service provided its information and probable cause became clear.

HQ personnel brought up almost ridiculous questions in their apparent efforts to undermine the probable cause.[183] In all of their conversations and correspondence, HQ personnel never disclosed to the Minneapolis agents that the Phoenix Division had, only approximately three weeks earlier, warned of al Qaeda operatives in flight schools seeking flight training for terrorist purposes!

Nor did FBIHQ personnel do much to disseminate the information about Moussaoui to other appropriate intelligence/law enforcement authorities. When, in a desperate eleventh-hour measure to bypass the FBIHQ roadblock, the Minneapolis Division undertook to directly notify the CIA's Counter Terrorist Center (CTC), FBIHQ personnel actually chastised the Minneapolis agents for making the direct notification without their approval!

6. Eventually on August 28, 2001, after a series of emails between Minneapolis and FBIHQ, which suggest that the FBIHQ SSA deliberately further undercut the FISA effort by not adding the further intelligence information which he had promised to add that supported Moussaoui's foreign power connection and by making

several changes in the wording of the information that had been provided by the Minneapolis agent, the Minneapolis agents were notified that the NSLU Unit Chief did not think there was sufficient evidence of Moussaoui's connection to a foreign power.

Minneapolis personnel are, to this date, unaware of the specifics of the verbal presentations by the FBIHQ SSA to NSLU or whether anyone in NSLU ever was afforded the opportunity to actually read for him/herself all of the information on Moussaoui that had been gathered by the Minneapolis Division and the French intelligence service. Obviously verbal presentations are far more susceptible to mischaracterization and error. The email communications between Minneapolis and FBIHQ, however, speak for themselves, and there are far better witnesses than me who can provide their firsthand knowledge of these events, characterized in one Minneapolis agent's email as FBIHQ is "setting this up for failure."

My only comment is that the process of allowing the FBI supervisors to make changes in affidavits is itself fundamentally wrong, just as, in the follow-up to FBI Laboratory Whistleblower Frederic Whitehurst's allegations, this process was revealed to be wrong in the context of writing up laboratory results. With the Whitehurst allegations, this process of allowing supervisors to rewrite portions of laboratory reports was found to provide opportunities for overzealous supervisors to skew the results in favor of the prosecution. In the Moussaoui case, it was the opposite—the process allowed the Headquarters Supervisor to downplay the significance of the information thus far collected in order to get out of the work of having to see the FISA application through or possibly to avoid taking what he may have perceived as an unnecessary career risk.[184]

I understand that the failures of the FBIHQ personnel involved in the Moussaoui matter are also being officially excused because they were too busy with other investigations, the Cole bombing and other important terrorism matters, but the Supervisor's taking of the time to read each word of the information submitted by Minneapolis and then substitute his own choice of wording belies to some extent the notion that he was too busy. As an FBI division legal adviser for twelve years (and an FBI agent for over 21 years),

I can state that an affidavit is better and will tend to be more accurate when the agent has firsthand information of all the information he/she must attest to. Of necessity, agents must continually rely upon information from confidential sources, third parties and other law enforcement officers in drafting affidavits, but the repeating of information from others greatly adds to the opportunities for factual discrepancies and errors to arise.

To the extent that we can minimize the opportunity for this type of error to arise by simply not allowing unnecessary rewrites by supervisory staff, it ought to be done. (I'm not talking, of course, about mere grammatical corrections, but changes of some substance as apparently occurred with the Moussaoui information which had to be, for lack of a better term, "filtered" through FBIHQ before any action, whether to seek a criminal or a FISA warrant, could be taken.) Even after September 11th, the fear was great on the part of Minneapolis Division personnel that the same FBIHQ personnel would continue their "filtering" with respect to the Moussaoui investigation, and now with the added incentive of preventing their prior mistakes from coming to light.

For this reason, for weeks, Minneapolis prefaced all outgoing communications (ECs) in the PENTTBOM investigation with a summary of the information about Moussaoui. We just wanted to make sure the information got to the proper prosecutive authorities and was not further suppressed! This fear was probably irrational but was nonetheless understandable in light of the Minneapolis agents' prior experiences and frustrations involving FBIHQ. (The redundant preface information regarding Moussaoui on otherwise unrelated PENTTBOM communications has ended up adding to criminal discovery issues, but this is the reason it was done.)

7. Although the last thing the FBI or the country needs now is a witch hunt, I do find it odd that (to my knowledge) no inquiry whatsoever was launched of the relevant FBIHQ personnel's actions a long time ago. Despite FBI leaders' full knowledge of all the items mentioned herein (and probably more that I'm unaware of), the SSA, his unit chief, and other involved HQ personnel were allowed to

stay in their positions and, what's worse, occupy critical positions in the FBI's SIOC Command Center post September 11th. (The SSA in question actually received a promotion some months afterward!)

It's true we all make mistakes and I'm not suggesting that HQ personnel in question ought to be burned at the stake, but we all need to be held accountable for serious mistakes. I'm relatively certain that if it appeared that a lowly field office agent had committed such errors of judgment, the FBI's OPR would have been notified to investigate and the agent would have been, at the least, quickly reassigned. I'm afraid the FBI's failure to submit this matter to OPR (and to the IOB) gives further impetus to the notion (raised previously by many in the FBI) of a double standard which results in those of lower rank being investigated more aggressively and dealt with more harshly for misconduct while the misconduct of those at the top is often overlooked or results in minor disciplinary action. From all appearances, this double standard may also apply between those at FBIHQ and those in the field.

8. The last official "fact" that I take issue with is not really a fact, but an opinion, and a completely unsupported opinion at that. In the day or two following September 11th, you, Director Mueller, made the statement to the effect that if the FBI had only had any advance warning of the attacks, we (meaning the FBI), may have been able to take some action to prevent the tragedy. Fearing that this statement could easily come back to haunt the FBI upon revelation of the information that had been developed pre–September 11th about Moussaoui, I and others in the Minneapolis Office immediately sought to reach your office through an assortment of higher level FBIHQ contacts, in order to quickly make you aware of the background of the Moussaoui investigation and forewarn you so that your public statements could be accordingly modified.

When such statements from you and other FBI officials continued, we thought that somehow you had not received the message and we made further efforts. Finally, when similar comments were made weeks later, in Assistant Director Caruso's congressional testimony in response to the first public leaks about Moussaoui we faced the sad realization that the remarks indicated someone, possibly with your approval, had decided to circle the wagons at FBIHQ in an apparent effort to protect the FBI from embarrassment and the relevant FBI officials from scrutiny. Everything I have seen and heard about the FBI's official stance and the FBI's internal preparations in anticipation of further congressional inquiry had, unfortunately, confirmed my worst suspicions in this regard.

After the details began to emerge concerning the pre–September 11th investigation of Moussaoui, and subsequently with the recent release of the information about the Phoenix EC, your statement has changed. The official statement is now to the effect that even if the FBI had followed up on the Phoenix lead to conduct checks of flight schools and the Minneapolis request to search Moussaoui's personal effects and laptop, nothing would have changed and such actions certainly could not have prevented the terrorist attacks and resulting loss of life.

With all due respect, this statement is as bad as the first! It is also quite at odds with the earlier statement (which I'm surprised has not already been pointed out by those in the media!). I don't know how you or anyone at FBI Headquarters, no matter how much genius or prescience you may possess, could so blithely make this affirmation without anything to back the opinion up other than your stature as FBI Director. The truth is, as with most predictions into the future, no one will ever know what impact, if any, the FBI's following up on those requests would have had.

Although I agree that it's very doubtful that the full scope of the tragedy could have been prevented, it's at least possible we could have gotten lucky and uncovered one or two more of the terrorists in flight training prior to September 11th, just as Moussaoui was discovered after we made contact with his flight instructors. It is certainly not beyond the realm of imagination to hypothesize that Moussaoui's fortuitous arrest alone, even if he merely was the 20th hijacker, allowed the hero passengers of Flight 93 to overcome their terrorist hijackers and thus spare more lives on the ground. And even greater casualties, possibly of our nation's highest government officials, may have been prevented if al Qaeda intended for Moussaoui to pilot an entirely different aircraft.

There is, therefore at least some chance that discovery of other terrorist pilots prior to September 11th may have limited the September 11th attacks and resulting loss of life. Although it must be very reassuring for some in the FBI to hear your conclusion repeated so often (as if saying it's so may make it so), I think your statements demonstrate a rush to judgment to protect the FBI at all costs. I think the only fair response to this type of question would be that no one can pretend to know one way or another.

Mr. Director, I hope my observations can be taken in a constructive vein. They are from the heart and intended to be completely apolitical. Hopefully, with our nation's security on the line, you and our nation's other elected and appointed officials can rise above the petty politics that often plague other discussions and do the right thing.

You do have some good ideas for change in the FBI, but I think you have also not been completely honest about some of the true reasons for the FBI's pre–September 11th failures. Until we come clean and deal with the root causes, the Department of Justice will continue to experience problems fighting terrorism and fighting crime in general.

I have used the term "we" repeatedly herein to include facts about others in the Minneapolis Office at critical times, but none of the opinions expressed herein can be attributed to anyone but myself.

I know that those who know me would probably describe me as, by nature, overly opinionated and sometimes not as discreet as I should be. Certainly some of the above remarks may be interpreted as falling into that category, but I really do not intend anything as a personal criticism of you or anyone else in the FBI, to include the FBIHQ personnel who I believe were remiss and mishandled their duties with regard to the Moussaoui investigation.

Truly my only purpose is to try to provide the facts within my purview so that an accurate assessment can be obtained and we can learn from our mistakes. I have pointed out a few of the things that

I think should be looked at, but there are many, many more.[185] An honest acknowledgment of the FBI's mistakes in this and other cases should not lead to increasing the Headquarters bureaucracy and approval levels of investigative actions as the answer.

Most often, field office agents and field office management on the scene will be better suited to the timely and effective solution of crimes and, in some lucky instances, to the effective prevention of crimes, including terrorism incidents. The relatively quick solving of the recent mailbox pipe-bombing incidents, which resulted in no serious injuries to anyone, are a good example of effective field office work (actually several field offices working together), and there are hundreds of other examples.

Although FBIHQ personnel have, no doubt, been of immeasurable assistance to the field over the years, I'm hard-pressed to think of any case which has been solved by FBIHQ personnel and I can name several that have been screwed up! Decision-making is inherently more effective and timely when decentralized instead of concentrated.

Your plans for an FBI Headquarters "Super Squad" simply fly in the face of an honest appraisal of the FBI's pre–September 11th failures. The Phoenix, Minneapolis, and Paris Legal Attaché Offices reacted remarkably, exhibiting keen perception and prioritization skills regarding the terrorist threats they uncovered or were made aware of pre–September 11th. The same cannot be said for the FBI Headquarters' bureaucracy, and yet you want to expand that?!

Should we put the counterterrorism unit chief and SSA who previously handled the Moussaoui matter in charge of the new "Super Squad"?! You are also apparently disregarding the fact the Joint Terrorism Task Forces (JTTFs), operating out of field divisions for years (the first and chief one being New York City's JTTF), have successfully handled numerous terrorism investigations and, in some instances, successfully prevented acts of terrorism.

There's no denying the need for more and better intelligence and intelligence management, but you should think carefully about how much gatekeeping power should be entrusted with any HQ entity. If we are indeed in a "war," shouldn't the generals be on the battlefield instead of sitting in a spot removed from the action while still attempting to call the shots?

I have been an FBI agent for over 21 years and, for what it's worth, have never received any form of disciplinary action throughout my career. From the 5th grade, when I first wrote to the FBI and received the "100 Facts about the FBI" pamphlet, this job has been my dream. I feel that my career in the FBI has been somewhat exemplary, having entered on duty at a time when there was only a small percentage of female Special Agents. I have also been lucky to have had four children during my time in the FBI, and I am the sole breadwinner of a family of six.

Due to the frankness with which I have expressed myself and my deep feelings on these issues (which is only because I feel I have a somewhat unique, inside perspective of the Moussaoui matter, the gravity of the events of September 11th, and the current seriousness of the FBI's and United States' ongoing efforts in the "war against terrorism"), I hope my continued employment with the FBI is not somehow placed in jeopardy.

I have never written to an FBI Director in my life before, on any topic. Although I would hope it is not necessary, I therefore wish to take advantage of the federal "Whistleblower Protection" provisions by so characterizing my remarks.

∽ Joseph Wilson
Retired U.S. Ambassador on Special Assignment

On July 6, 2003, retired Ambassador Joseph Wilson, realizing that the Bush administration was being dishonest about the allegation that Saddam Hussein had tried to obtain yellowcake uranium from Niger, wrote an Op-Ed piece in *The New York Times* titled "What I Didn't Find in Africa."

Prior to the war, Wilson argued that "a strict containment regime backed by the threat of force was preferable to an invasion.... The act of war is the last option of a democracy, taken when there is a grave threat to our national security." He continued in the Op-Ed, "I was convinced before the war that the threat of weapons of mass destruction in the hands of Saddam Hussein required a vigorous and sustained international response to disarm him. Iraq possessed and had used chemical weapons; it had an active biological weapons program and quite possibly a nuclear research program—all of which were in violation of United Nations resolutions. Having encountered Mr. Hussein and his thugs in the run-up to the Persian Gulf War of 1991, I was only too aware of the dangers he posed."[186]

Wilson had been the acting U.S. Ambassador in Iraq before the first Gulf War. Because of his knowledge of Saddam's regime and his contacts in Niger from previous official visits while he was the State Department political adviser to the U.S. military's European Command, the CIA sent Wilson to Niger in February 2002 to investigate rumors about Saddam trying to purchase yellowcake uranium to use for WMD. The following month, still a year before the U.S.-led invasion of Iraq, he reported to the CIA that there was no evidence of a deal between Iraq and Niger. By this time, "the Niger reports had been discredited more than half a dozen times"—by the CIA, FBI, State Department, some Pentagon analysts, the U.S. Ambassador to Niger, and French intelligence.[187] But Vice President Dick Cheney had made clear to the CIA that he wanted evidence that Iraq had tried to buy uranium from Niger.[188] Ten months later, in his January 2003 State of the Union address, President Bush warned Americans: "The British Government has learned that Saddam Hussein recently sought significant quantities of uranium from Africa." Wilson was stunned, and assumed the President must have been referring to a different African country.[189] When he learned that Bush was referring to the debunked claims about Niger, he published his concerns in the *Times,* alleging the Bush administration had twisted the intelligence on Iraq's nuclear program "to exaggerate the Iraqi threat."[190] The following day, the Bush administration admitted publicly that the allegations connecting Iraq and Niger were unproven and should not have appeared in the State of the Union address.[191]

The Bush administration then embarked on a campaign to discredit and intimidate Wilson, disclosing that his wife, Valerie Plame, was a covert CIA agent. In March 2007, Vice President Cheney's chief of staff, Lewis "Scooter" Libby, was convicted in federal court of obstruction of justice, giving false statements to the FBI, and perjuring himself. He was sentenced to two and a half years in prison and a $250,000 fine. On July 2, 2007, hours after a federal appeals panel ruled that Libby could not delay his prison term, President George Bush commuted Libby's jail time.[192]

On July 19, 2007, U.S. District Judge John D. Bates dismissed on jurisdictional grounds Plame and Wilson's lawsuit alleging that Vice President Cheney, Cheney's Chief of Staff Scooter Libby, Presidential senior adviser Karl Rove, and Deputy Secretary of State Richard Armitage violated the couple's privacy and constitutional rights by participating in discussions that led to Plame's identity being publicly revealed. The Wilsons alleged that the leaks to reporters were an illegal effort to retaliate against Wilson for his criticism of the Iraq War, had ruined Plame's chance for career advancement, and were meant to harass them.

The judge wrote, "The alleged means by which defendants chose to rebut Mr. Wilson's comments and attack his credibility may have been highly unsavory, but there can be no serious dispute that the act of rebutting public criticism, such as that levied by Mr. Wilson against the Bush administration's handling of prewar foreign intelligence, by speaking with members of the press, is within the scope of defendants' duties as high-level Executive Branch officials."[193]

Judge Bates is a 2001 Bush appointee to the bench, who previously worked with Independent Counsel Ken Starr on the prosecution of President Clinton's Whitewater real estate investments and the 1997 release of thousands of pages of White House documents related to Hillary Clinton's conversations about Whitewater. Since 2001, Judge Bates has strongly supported the White House's assertion of executive privilege on a wide range of legal challenges. In December 2002, he dismissed a lawsuit filed by the Government Accountability Office against Vice President Cheney that sought access to the Vice President's energy task force documents.[194]

5

Opposition Within the Military

The commitment of our forces to this fight was done with a casualness and swagger that are the special province of those who have never had to execute these missions—or bury the results.

    –Marine Lieutenant General (Ret.) Greg Newbold

OFFICERS

I n the United States military, officers and enlisted personnel are subordinate to the civilian elected government. They provide advice to the civilian decision makers, but once a decision is made, unless it is unlawful, it is the military's responsibility to follow the civilian leadership's orders. If someone in the military believes that an order or policy is illegal, challenging it can be risky for that person's career, reputation, and, possibly, freedom.

Once President Bush declared a war on terror following the events of September 11, 2001, important advice given by senior military commanders to the civilian leadership was ignored, questions regarding the legality of certain U.S. actions were quashed, and those who attempted to sound an alarm were silenced. General Eric Shinseki, who challenged the civilian leadership, was publicly excoriated, setting an example to others. As the drumbeat for war on Iraq intensified, few active-duty military leaders spoke out.

However, several retired generals did voice opposition to beginning a war on Iraq. These included Lieutenant General Brent Scowcroft, National Security Adviser to President Ford and the first President Bush; General Anthony Zinni, former U.S. Central Command Chief; and Lieutenant General William Odom, head of the NSA during the Reagan administration. Later, general officers who were on active duty during the invasion and occupation of Iraq, spoke out publicly about their concerns—after their retirements.

In addition, a large number of general officers, in recent years, have been so concerned about the Bush administration's decisions on the treatment of detainees and the Geneva Conventions that they wrote public letters to the President and the Senate Armed Services Committee. One group wrote that they were worried that the Military Commissions Act, by downgrading the standards of treatment of detainees, could pose a grave threat to American servicemembers and, in their opinion, violated the core principles of the Geneva Conventions. Despite their concerns, Congress passed the Military Commissions Act in October 2006.

Another group of general officers asked President Bush to ensure "that the United States has a single standard of conduct specified in law that governs all interrogations, regardless of the legal status or the location of the detainee being interrogated."

A third group urged the Senate Judiciary Committee to explore in detail with Attorney General–nominee Alberto R. Gonzales "whether he intends to . . . [maintain] a military that operates within the rule of law," adding U.S. detention and interrogation operations in Afghanistan, Iraq, and Guantánamo "have fostered greater animosity toward the United States, undermined our intelligence-gathering efforts, and added to the risks facing our troops serving around the world."

This outpouring of concern by general officers about the impact of an administration's policies on the professionalism, ethical, and moral foundation of the military is unprecedented.

✆ General Eric Shinseki

Army Chief of Staff General Eric Shinseki challenged Secretary of Defense Donald Rumsfeld on the number of troops needed in post-invasion Iraq. In February 2003, he told a congressional committee that several hundred thousand troops would be needed. Deputy Secretary of Defense Paul Wolfowitz called this "wildly off the mark," and he and Rumsfeld "castigated [Shinseki] in public, nominated his replacement a year before his retirement, and marginalized him in his remaining months in his post."[1]

ꙮ Lieutenant General (Ret.) Brent Scowcroft

In an Op-Ed piece in the *Wall Street Journal* seven months before the invasion, retired General Brent Scowcroft—military assistant to President Richard Nixon, and National Security Adviser to Presidents Gerald Ford and George H. W. Bush—cautioned that a war on Iraq would divert attention from the war on terrorism: "The central point is that any campaign against Iraq, whatever the strategy, cost, and risks, is certain to divert us for some indefinite period from our war on terrorism. Worse, there is a virtual consensus in the world against an attack on Iraq at this time. So long as that sentiment persists, it would require the U.S. to pursue a virtual go-it-alone strategy against Iraq, making any military operations correspondingly more difficult and expensive. The most serious cost, however, would be to the war on terrorism. Ignoring that clear sentiment would result in a serious degradation in international cooperation with us against terrorism. And make no mistake, we simply cannot win that war without enthusiastic international cooperation, especially on intelligence."[2]

Scowcroft warned there would be outrage in the region: "Possibly the most dire consequences would be the effect in the region. The shared view in the region is that Iraq is principally an obsession of the U.S. The obsession of the region, however, is the Israeli–Palestinian conflict. If we were seen to be turning our backs on that bitter conflict—which the region, rightly or wrongly, perceives to be clearly within our power to resolve—in order to go after Iraq, there would be an explosion of outrage against us. We would be seen as ignoring a key interest of the Muslim world in order to satisfy what is seen to be a narrow American interest."[3]

He also worried that an attack on Iraq would play into hands of those who wanted to upset the balance of power in the Middle East: "Even without Israeli involvement, the results could well destabilize Arab regimes in the region, ironically facilitating one of Saddam's strategic objectives. At a minimum, it would stifle any cooperation on terrorism, and could even swell the ranks of the terrorists. Conversely, the more progress we make in the war on terrorism, and the more we are seen to be committed to resolving the Israeli–Palestinian issue, the greater will be the international support for going after Saddam."[4]

"If we are truly serious about the war on terrorism," he wrote, "it must remain our top priority. However, should Saddam Hussein be found to be clearly implicated in the events of September 11, that could make him a key counterterrorist target, rather than a competing priority, and significantly shift world opinion toward support for regime change."[5]

The advice of one of the country's most experienced military and security officials was ignored by the Bush administration, and Scowcroft himself was ridiculed by members of the President's staff.

✍ General (Ret.) Anthony Zinni

In the months leading up to the war, while he was still President Bush's Middle East envoy, retired four-star Marine General Anthony Zinni told Congress, "This is, in my view, the worst time to take this on. And I don't feel it needs to be done now." He said Iraq was "the wrong war at the wrong time—with the wrong strategy," that it was "a war the generals didn't want—but it was a war the civilians wanted." Later he added, "I can't speak for all generals, certainly. But I know we felt that this situation was contained. Saddam was effectively contained. The no-fly, no-drive zones. The sanctions that were imposed on him." He said most generals believed we should have dealt with one problem at a time, first complete the actions against al Qaeda in Afghanistan.[6]

In his book *Battle Ready,* Zinni wrote: "In the lead-up to the Iraq War and its later conduct, I saw at a minimum, true dereliction, negligence and irresponsibility, at worst, lying, incompetence and corruption ... I think there was dereliction in insufficient forces being put on the ground and fully understanding the military dimensions of the plan. I think there was dereliction in lack of planning ... The president is owed the finest strategic thinking. He is owed the finest operational planning. He is owed the finest tactical execution on the ground ... He got the latter. He didn't get the first two."[7]

✎ Lieutenant General (Ret.) William Odom

Lieutenant General William Odom, former chief of Army intelligence and the Director of the National Security Agency during the Reagan administration, says the Iraq War is "the worst strategic mistake in the history of the United States," and concludes that U.S. strategy in Iraq, as in Vietnam, has served almost exclusively the interests of our enemies. Odom, now a senior fellow at the Hudson Institute, recalls that U.S. objectives in Vietnam passed through three phases leading to defeat: (1) 1961–65, "containing" China; (2) 1965–68, obsession with U.S. tactics, leading to "Americanization" of the war; and (3) 1968–75, phony diplomacy and self-deluding "Vietnamization." Odom states that U.S. involvement in Iraq has now completed two similar phases and is entering the third, phony diplomacy and self-deluding "Iraqization."[8]

✎ Lieutenant General (Ret.) Gregory Newbold

Marine Lieutenant General Gregory Newbold was Director of Operations for the Joint Staff. He says that he felt the invasion force of 125,000 troops was too small and regrets not confronting Secretary of Defense Rumsfeld. "I should have had the gumption to confront him. The right thing to do was to confront, and I didn't. It's something I'll have to live with for a long time."[9]

After his retirement, in April 2006, Newbold wrote an article for *Time* saying that he held civilian leadership accountable and that Rumsfeld had to be replaced. "My sincere view is that the commitment of our forces to this fight was done with a casualness and swagger that are the special province of those who have never had to execute these missions—or bury the results."[10]

Newbold also criticized his military colleagues: "Flaws in our civilians are one thing; the failure of the Pentagon's military leaders is quite another. Those are men who know the consequences of war but, with few exceptions, acted timidly when their voices urgently needed to be heard. When they knew the plan was flawed, saw intelligence distorted to justify a rationale for war, or witnessed arrogant micromanagement that at times crippled the military's effectiveness, many leaders who wore the uniform chose inaction. A few of the most senior officers actually supported the logic for war. Others were simply intimidated, while still others must have believed that the principle of obedience does not allow for respectful dissent. The consequence of the military's quiescence was that a fundamentally flawed plan was executed for an invented war, while pursuing the real enemy, al Qaeda, became a secondary effort."[11]

"Inside the military family, I made no secret of my view that the zealots' rationale for war made no sense. And I think I was outspoken enough to make those senior to me uncomfortable. But I now regret that I did not more openly challenge those who were determined to invade a country whose actions were peripheral to the real threat—al Qaeda."[12]

Newbold now calls on senior military leaders to end their silence for the protection of the enlisted personnel who have no voice: "It is time for senior military leaders to discard caution in expressing their views and ensure that the President hears them clearly."[13]

"Every military officer must have a limit to what he's willing to subordinate to pure obedience, and I can't think of a limit that is more important than the sacrifice of the young patriots to what the national leadership called them to do. And if you see it so flagrantly abused, then I think I personally set a limit, and that limit was crossed. To the man who has no limit I have only sympathy."[14]

✍ Major General (Ret.) Paul Eaton

During 2003 and 2004, Army Major General Paul Eaton was responsible for overseeing the creation of the new Iraqi Army. In a *New York Times* Op-Ed piece on March 19, 2006, he called for Secretary of Defense Donald Rumsfeld's resignation: "Defense Secretary Donald Rumsfeld is not competent to lead our armed forces. First, his failure to build coalitions with our allies from what he dismissively called 'old Europe' has imposed far greater demands and risks on our soldiers in Iraq than necessary. Second, he alienated his allies in our own military, ignoring the advice of seasoned officers and denying subordinates any chance for input. In sum, he has shown himself incompetent strategically, operationally, and tactically, and is far more than anyone else responsible for what has happened to our important mission in Iraq … Mr. Rumsfeld must step down."[15] "In the five years Mr. Rumsfeld has presided over the Pentagon, I have seen a climate of groupthink become dominant and a growing reluctance by experienced military men and civilians to challenge the notions of the senior leadership."[16]

✍ Major General (Ret.) John Batiste

Major General John Batiste, served as assistant to Deputy Secretary of Defense Paul Wolfowitz from March 2001 to June 2002, and as commander of the 1st Infantry Division in Iraq in 2004 and 2005. He retired in November 2005. He says he told Wolfowitz about troop shortages causing a "shell game" with soldiers, "moving them from one hot spot to another," allowing insurgents to come back. Even though he was "fuming" over the decision to disband the Iraqi Army and about Rumsfeld's "shitty war plan," Batiste said he kept quiet. He had the opportunity to tell Rumsfeld in front of reporters that his units needed many things, but he didn't. "We don't air our differences in public." Then he adds, "I didn't trust Rumsfeld a bit. I had seen the way he treated other officers and discounted their advice." Five months after retiring, Major General Batiste began speaking publicly about Rumsfeld. Among other things, he said that "Rumsfeld's plan allowed the insurgency to take root and metastasize to where it is today." He also said, "Secretary Rumsfeld's dismal strategic decisions resulted in the unnecessary deaths of American servicemen and women, our allies, and the good people of Iraq."[17]

Why don't more senior officers speak out? "Everyone's working for defense contractors. Their bread is buttered by the Department of Defense." Batiste says the Army is managed by technocrats and bureaucrats rather than by experienced warriors.[18]

Another retired major general stated privately, "For our generation, Iraq will be Vietnam with the volume turned way up. Three decades ago, the retired generals who are now speaking out against the Iraq War were junior officers in Vietnam. The seniors who trained and mentored us, and who became generals but who kept silent, did not speak out after retirement against Vietnam."[19]

‿

Letters of Concern to the President and the Congress from Retired U.S. Military Leaders

On the Geneva Conventions

September 12, 2006
The Honorable John Warner, Chairman
The Honorable Carl Levin, Ranking Member
Senate Armed Services Committee
United States Senate
Washington, DC 20510

Dear Chairman Warner and Senator Levin:

As retired military leaders of the U.S. Armed Forces and former officials of the Department of Defense, we write to express our profound concern about a key provision of S. 3861, the Military Commissions Act of 2006, introduced last week at the behest of the President. We believe that the language that would redefine Common Article 3 of the Geneva Conventions as equivalent to the standards contained in the Detainee Treatment Act violates the core principles of the Geneva Conventions and poses a grave threat to American service-members, now and in future wars.

We supported your efforts last year to clarify that all detainees in U.S. custody must be treated humanely. That was particularly important, because the Administration determined that it was not bound by the basic humane treatment standards contained in Geneva Common Article 3. Now that the Supreme Court has made clear that treatment of al Qaeda prisoners is governed by the Geneva Convention standards, the Administration is seeking to redefine Common Article 3, so as to downgrade those standards. We urge you to reject this effort.

Common Article 3 of the Geneva Conventions provides the minimum standards for humane treatment and fair justice that apply to anyone captured in armed conflict. These standards were specifically designed to ensure that those who fall outside the other, more extensive, protections of the Conventions are treated in accordance with the values of civilized nations. The framers of the Conventions, including the American representatives, in particular wanted to ensure that Common Article 3 would apply in situations where a state party to the treaty, like the United States, fights an adversary that is not a party, including irregular forces like al Qaeda. The United States military has abided by the basic requirements of Common Article 3 in every conflict since the Conventions were adopted. In each case, we applied the Geneva Conventions—including, at a minimum, Common Article 3—even to enemies that systematically violated the Conventions themselves.

We have abided by this standard in our own conduct for a simple reason: the same standard serves to protect American servicemen and women when they engage in conflicts covered by Common Article 3. Preserving the integrity of this standard has become increasingly important in recent years when our adversaries often are not nation-states. Congress acted in 1997 to further this goal by criminalizing violations of Common Article 3 in the War Crimes Act, enabling us to hold accountable those who abuse our captured personnel, no matter the nature of the armed conflict.

If any agency of the U.S. government is excused from compliance with these standards, or if we seek to redefine what Common Article 3 requires, we should not imagine that our enemies will take notice of the technical distinctions when they hold U.S. prisoners captive. If degradation, humiliation, physical and mental brutalization of prisoners is decriminalized or considered permissible under a restrictive interpretation of Common Article 3, we will forfeit all credible objections should such barbaric practices be inflicted upon American prisoners.

This is not just a theoretical concern. We have people deployed right now in theaters where Common Article 3 is the only source of legal protection should they be captured. If we allow that standard to be eroded, we put their safety at greater risk.

Last week, the Department of Defense issued a Directive reaffirming that the military will uphold the requirements of Common Article 3 with respect to all prisoners in its custody. We welcome this new policy. Our servicemen and women have operated for too long with unclear and unlawful guidance on detainee treatment, and some have been left to take the blame when things went wrong. The guidance is now clear.

But that clarity will be short-lived if the approach taken by the Administration's bill prevails. In contrast to the Pentagon's new rules on detainee treatment, the bill would limit our definition of Common Article 3's terms by introducing a flexible, sliding scale that might allow certain coercive interrogation techniques under some circumstances, while forbidding them under others. This would replace an absolute standard—Common Article 3—with a relative one. To do so will only create further confusion.

Moreover, were we to take this step, we would be viewed by the rest of the world as having formally renounced the clear strictures of the Geneva Conventions. Our enemies would be encouraged to interpret the Conventions in their own way as well, placing our troops in jeopardy in future conflicts. And American moral authority in the war would be further damaged.

All of this is unnecessary. As the senior serving Judge Advocates General recently testified, our armed forces have trained to Common Article 3 and can live within its requirements while waging the war on terror effectively.

As the United States has greater exposure militarily than any other nation, we have long emphasized the reciprocal nature of the Geneva Conventions. That is why we believe—and the United States has always asserted—that a broad interpretation of Common Article 3 is vital to the safety of U.S. personnel. But the Administration's bill would put us on the opposite side of that argument. We urge you to consider the impact that redefining Common Article 3 would have on Americans who put their lives at risk in defense of our Nation. We believe their interests, and their safety and protection should they become prisoners, should be your highest priority as you address this issue.

With respect,
General John Shalikashvili, USA (Ret.), General Joseph Hoar, USMC (Ret.), Admiral Gregory G. Johnson, USN (Ret.), Admiral Jay L. Johnson, USN (Ret.), General Paul J. Kern, USA (Ret.), Admiral Charles R. Larson, USN (Ret.), General David M. Maddox, USA (Ret.), General Merrill A. McPeak, USAF (Ret.), Admiral Stansfield Turner, USN (Ret.), General William G. T. Tuttle Jr., USA (Ret.), General Anthony Zinni, USMC (Ret.), Lieutenant General Daniel W. Christman, USA (Ret.), Lieutenant General Paul E. Funk, USA (Ret.), Lieutenant General Robert G. Gard Jr., USA (Ret.), Lieutenant General Jay M. Garner, USA (Ret.), Vice Admiral Lee F. Gunn, USN (Ret.), Lieutenant General Arlen D. Jameson, USAF (Ret.), Lieutenant General Claudia J. Kennedy, USA (Ret.), Lieutenant General Donald L. Kerrick, USA (Ret.), Vice Admiral Albert H. Konetzni Jr., USN (Ret.), Lieutenant General Charles Otstott, USA (Ret.),Vice Admiral Jack Shanahan, USN (Ret.), Lieutenant General Harry E. Soyster, USA (Ret.), Lieutenant General Paul K. Van Riper, USMC (Ret.), Major General John Batiste, USA (Ret.), Major General Eugene Fox, USA (Ret.), Major General John L. Fugh, USA (Ret.), Rear Admiral Don Guter, USN (Ret.), Major General Fred E. Haynes, USMC (Ret.), Rear Admiral John D. Hutson, USN (Ret.), Major General Melvyn Montano, ANG (Ret.), Major General Gerald T. Sajer, USA (Ret.), Major General Michael J. Scotti Jr., USA (Ret.), Brigadier General David M. Brahms, USMC (Ret.), Brigadier General James P. Cullen, USA (Ret.), Brigadier General Evelyn P. Foote, USA (Ret.), Brigadier General David R. Irvine, USA (Ret.), Brigadier General John H. Johns, USA (Ret.), Brigadier General Richard O'Meara, USA (Ret.), Brigadier General Murray G. Sagsveen, USA (Ret.), Brigadier General John K. Schmitt, USA (Ret.), Brigadier General Anthony Verrengia, USAF (Ret.), Brigadier General Stephen N. Xenakis, USA (Ret.), Ambassador Pete Peterson, USAF (Ret.), Colonel Lawrence B. Wilkerson, USA (Ret.), Honorable Richard Danzig, Honorable Walter B. Slocombe, Honorable William H. Taft IV, Frank Kendall III, Esq.

On the Treatment of Detainees

January 18, 2006
The Honorable George W. Bush
President of the United States
The White House
1600 Pennsylvania Avenue NW
Washington, DC 20500

Dear President Bush:

We write to thank you for publicly endorsing Senator McCain's amendment on the treatment of detainees in U.S. custody, and for signing it into law. The new law, implemented and enforced in accordance with Congressional intent, will ensure that the United States has a single standard for interrogating enemy prisoners that is effective, lawful, and humane. The primary reason we strongly supported Senator McCain's effort is that we believe this law, if effectively and forcefully implemented, will help protect our troops in Iraq and elsewhere, now and in the future.

Past abuses have damaged military discipline, put American military personnel at greater risk, undermined U.S. intelligence gathering efforts, and greatly harmed America's image around the world. It is incumbent on you as President and Commander-in-Chief to ensure that all senior members of your administration speak with a consistent voice to make clear that the United States now has a single standard of conduct specified in law that governs all interrogations, regardless of the legal status or the location of the detainee being interrogated. Accountability and deterrence have never been more important to end all torture and abuse in America's name, and thereby restore America's reputation in the world. This long overdue corrective action will require strong leadership from you and others in positions of authority.

Mr. President, we welcome your attention to this issue and stand ready to assist in any way we can to ensure the effective implementation of this new law. Clear and unambiguous implementation will help ensure that our brave men and women in uniform will never again feel that to prevail against the enemy they must risk their honor or the values they fight to protect.

Sincerely,
General Joseph Hoar, USMC (Ret.), Lieutenant General Robert G. Gard Jr., USA (Ret.), Lieutenant General Claudia J. Kennedy, USA (Ret.), Vice Admiral Albert H. Konetzni Jr., USN (Ret.), Lieutenant General Charles Otstott, USA (Ret.), Vice Admiral Jack Shanahan, USN (Ret.), Major General Eugene Fox, USA (Ret.), Major General John L. Fugh, USA (Ret.), Rear Admiral Don Guter, USN (Ret.), Major General Fred E. Haynes, USMC (Ret.), Rear Admiral John D. Hutson, USN (Ret.), Major General Melvyn Montano, ANG (Ret.), Major General Gerald T. Sajer, USA (Ret.), Major General Robert H. Scales, USA (Ret.), Major General Michael J. Scotti Jr., USA (Ret.), Brigadier General David M. Brahms, USMC (Ret.), Brigadier General James P. Cullen, USA (Ret.), Brigadier General Evelyn P. Foote, USA (Ret.), Brigadier General David R. Irvine, USA (Ret.), Brigadier General Richard O'Meara, USA (Ret.), Brigadier General John K. Schmitt, USA (Ret.), Brigadier General Stephen N. Xenakis, USA (Ret.)

On the Nomination of Alberto Gonzales for Attorney General

The Honorable Members
United States Senate Committee on the Judiciary
224 Dirksen Senate Office Building
Washington, DC 20510

Dear Senator
    We, the undersigned, are retired professional military leaders of the U.S. Armed Forces. We write to express our deep concern about the nomination of Alberto R. Gonzales to be Attorney General, and to urge you to explore in detail his views concerning the role of the Geneva Conventions in U.S. detention and interrogation policy and practice.
    During his tenure as White House Counsel, Mr. Gonzales appears to have played a significant role in shaping U.S. detention and interrogation operations in Afghanistan, Iraq, Guantánamo Bay, and elsewhere.

Today, it is clear that these operations have fostered greater animosity toward the United States, undermined our intelligence gathering efforts, and added to the risks facing our troops serving around the world. Before Mr. Gonzales assumes the position of Attorney General, it is critical to understand whether he intends to adhere to the positions he adopted as White House Counsel, or chart a revised course more consistent with fulfilling our nation's complex security interests, and maintaining a military that operates within the rule of law.

Among his past actions that concern us most, Mr. Gonzales wrote to the President on January 25, 2002, advising him that the Geneva Conventions did not apply to the conflict then underway in Afghanistan. More broadly, he wrote that the "war on terrorism" presents a "new paradigm [that] renders obsolete Geneva's" protections.

The reasoning Mr. Gonzales advanced in this memo was rejected by many military leaders at the time, including Secretary of State Colin Powell who argued that abandoning the Geneva Conventions would put our soldiers at greater risk, would "reverse over a century of U.S. policy and practice in supporting the Geneva Conventions," and would "undermine the protections of the rule of law for our troops, both in this specific conflict [Afghanistan] and in general." State Department adviser William H. Taft IV agreed that this decision "deprives our troops [in Afghanistan] of any claim to the protection of the Conventions in the event they are captured and weakens the protections afforded by the Conventions to our troops in future conflicts." Mr. Gonzales' recommendation also ran counter to the wisdom of former U.S. prisoners of war. As Senator John McCain has observed: "I am certain we all would have been a lot worse off if there had not been the Geneva Conventions around which an international consensus formed about some very basic standards of decency that should apply even amid the cruel excesses of war."

Mr. Gonzales' reasoning was also on the wrong side of history. Repeatedly in our past, the United States has confronted foes that, at the time they emerged, posed threats of a scope or nature unlike any we had previously faced. But we have been far more steadfast in the past in keeping faith with our national commitment to the rule of law.

During the Second World War, General Dwight D. Eisenhower explained that the allies adhered to the law of war in their treatment of prisoners because "the Germans had some thousands of American and British prisoners and I did not want to give Hitler the excuse or justification for treating our prisoners more harshly than he already was doing." In Vietnam, U.S. policy required that the Geneva Conventions be observed for *all* enemy prisoners of war—both North Vietnamese regulars and Viet Cong—even though the Viet Cong denied our own prisoners of war the same protections. And in the 1991 Persian Gulf War, the United States afforded Geneva Convention protections to more than 86,000 Iraqi prisoners of war held in U.S. custody. The threats we face today—while grave and complex—no more warrant abandoning these basic principles than did the threats of enemies past.

Perhaps most troubling of all, the White House decision to depart from the Geneva Conventions in Afghanistan went hand in hand with the decision to relax the definition of torture and to alter interrogation doctrine accordingly. Mr. Gonzales' January 2002 memo itself warned that the decision not to apply Geneva Convention standards "could undermine U.S. military culture which emphasizes maintaining the highest standards of conduct in combat, and could introduce an element of uncertainty in the status of adversaries." Yet Mr. Gonzales then made that very recommendation with reference to Afghanistan, a policy later extended piece by piece to Iraq. Sadly, the uncertainty Mr. Gonzales warned about came to fruition. As James R. Schlesinger's panel reviewing Defense Department detention operations concluded earlier this year, these changes in doctrine have led to uncertainty and confusion in the field, contributing to the abuses of detainees at Abu Ghraib and elsewhere, and undermining the mission and morale of our troops.

The full extent of Mr. Gonzales' role in endorsing or implementing the interrogation practices the world has now seen remains unclear. A series of memos that were prepared at his direction in 2002 recommended official authorization of harsh interrogation methods, including waterboarding, feigned suffocation, and sleep deprivation. As with the recommendations on the Geneva Conventions, these memos ignored established U.S. military policy, including doctrine prohibiting "threats, insults, or exposure to inhumane treatment as a means of or aid to interrogation." Indeed, the August 1, 2002, Justice Department memo analyzing the law on interrogation references health care administration law more than five times, but never once cites the U.S. Army Field Manual on interrogation. The Army Field Manual was the product of decades of experience—experience that had shown, among other things that such interrogation methods produce unreliable results and often impede further intelligence collection. Discounting the Manual's wisdom on this central point shows a disturbing disregard for the decades of hard-won knowledge of the professional American military.

The United States' commitment to the Geneva Conventions—the laws of war—flows not only from field experience, but also from the moral principles on which this country was founded, and by which we all continue to be guided. We have learned first hand the value of adhering to the Geneva Conventions and practicing what we preach on the international stage. With this in mind, we urge you to ask of Mr. Gonzales the following:

1. Do you believe the Geneva Conventions apply to all those captured by U.S. authorities in Afghanistan and Iraq?
2. Do you support affording the International Committee of the Red Cross access to all detainees in U.S. custody?
3. What rights under U.S. or international law do suspected members of Al Qaeda, the Taliban, or members of similar organizations have when brought into the care or custody of U.S. military, law enforcement, or intelligence forces?
4. Do you believe that torture or other forms of cruel, inhuman and degrading treatment—such as dietary manipulation, forced nudity, prolonged solitary confinement, or threats of harm—may lawfully be used by U.S. authorities so long as the detainee is an "unlawful combatant" as you have defined it?
5. Do you believe that CIA and other government intelligence agencies are bound by the same laws and restrictions that constrain the

operations of the U.S. Armed Forces engaged in detention and interrogation operations abroad?

Signed,

Brigadier General David M. Brahms, USMC (Ret.), Brigadier General James Cullen, USA (Ret.), Brigadier General Evelyn P. Foote, USA (Ret.), Lieutenant General Robert Gard, USA (Ret.), Vice Admiral Lee F. Gunn, USN (Ret.), Admiral Don Guter, USN (Ret.), General Joseph Hoar, USMC (Ret.), Rear Admiral John D. Hutson, USN (Ret.), Lieutenant General Claudia Kennedy, USA (Ret.), General Merrill McPeak, USAF (Ret.), Major General Melvyn Montano, ANG (Ret.), General John Shalikashvili, USA (Ret.)

⤙

The Generals Who Signed These Letters

General John Shalikashvili, USA (Ret.), was Chairman of the Joint Chiefs of Staff and NATO's Supreme Allied Commander for Europe.

General Joseph Hoar, USMC (Ret.), served as Commander in Chief, U.S. Central Command.

Admiral Gregory G. Johnson, USN (Ret.), was Senior Military Assistant to the Secretary of Defense and Commander of the U.S. Sixth Fleet.

Admiral Jay L. Johnson, USN (Ret.), was Chief of Naval Operations.

General Paul J. Kern, USA (Ret.), was Commanding General, Army Materiel Command, and led the military's internal investigation into the abuses at Abu Ghraib prison.

Admiral Charles R. Larson, USN (Ret.), served as Commander in Chief of United States military forces in the Pacific and Superintendent of the U.S. Naval Academy.

General David M. Maddox, USA (Ret.), was Commander in Chief, U.S. Army, in Europe.

General Merrill A. McPeak, USAF (Ret.), served as the Chief of Staff of the U.S. Air Force and Commander in Chief of the U.S. Pacific Air Forces.

Admiral Stansfield Turner, USN (Ret.), was Director of Central Intelligence and Commander in Chief of NATO's Southern Flank.

General William G. T. Tuttle Jr., USA (Ret.), was commander of the U.S. Army Materiel Command.

General Anthony Zinni, USMC (Ret.), was Commander of U.S. forces in the Middle East and was President Bush's Presidential Envoy to the Middle East.

General Daniel W. Christman, USA (Ret.), served as Superintendent of the U.S. Military Academy at West Point and as assistant to the Chairman of the Joint Chiefs of Staff.

Lieutenant General Paul E. Funk, USA (Ret.), served as Commander of the 3rd Armored Division in Saudi Arabia, Iraq, and Kuwait in the Persian Gulf War.

Lieutenant General Robert G. Gard Jr., USA (Ret.), is president emeritus of the Monterey Institute for International Studies.

Lieutenant General Jay M. Garner, USA (Ret.), served as Vice Chief of Staff, U.S. Army and as Director of Reconstruction and Humanitarian Assistance for Iraq.

Vice Admiral Lee F. Gunn, USN (Ret.), was Inspector General of the Department of the Navy.

Lieutenant General Arlen D. Jameson, USAF (Ret.), was chief of staff, U.S. Strategic Command.

Lieutenant General Claudia J. Kennedy, USA (Ret.), served as Deputy Chief of Staff for Army Intelligence and Commander of the U.S. Army Recruiting Command. She is the only woman to achieve the rank of three-star general in the U.S. Army.

Lieutenant General Donald L. Kerrick, USA (Ret.), was Deputy National Security Adviser to the President of the United States, Assistant to the Chairman of the Joint Chiefs of Staff, and Director of Operations of the Defense Intelligence Agency.

Vice Admiral Albert H. Konetzni Jr., USN (Ret.), served as Chief of Staff of the U.S. Atlantic Fleet and Commander, Submarine Force, of the U.S. Pacific Fleet.

Lieutenant General Charles Otstott, USA (Ret.), was Deputy Chairman, NATO Military Committee.

Vice Admiral Jack Shanahan, USN (Ret.), was Commander of the North Atlantic fleet.

Lieutenant General Harry E. Soyster, USA (Ret.), was Director of the Defense Intelligence Agency and Director of Operations, Joint Chiefs of Staff.

Lieutenant General Paul K. Van Riper, USMC (Ret.), was Commanding General, Marine Corps Combat Development Command, President of the Marine Corps University, and Director of Intelligence.

Major General John Batiste, USA (Ret.), commanded the First Infantry Division in Kosovo and Iraq and was Senior Military Assistant to Deputy Secretary of Defense Paul Wolfowitz.

Major General Eugene Fox, USA (Ret.), was Deputy Director of the Strategic Defense Initiative Office.

Major General John Fugh, USA (Ret.), was Judge Advocate General of the U.S. Army and first Chinese-American to attain General officer status in the U.S. Army.

Rear Admiral Don Guter, USN (Ret.), was the Navy's Judge Advocate General.

Major General Fred E. Haynes, USMC (Ret.), was a Captain in the regiment that seized Mt. Suribachi, Iwo Jima, in World War II and raised the American flag there.

Rear Admiral John D. Hutson, JAGC, USN (Ret.), was the Navy's Judge Advocate General.

Major General Melvyn Montano, ANG (Ret.), was the Adjutant General of the New Mexico National Guard and the first Hispanic Air National Guard officer appointed adjutant general in the U.S.

Major General Gerald T. Sajer, USA (Ret.), was Adjutant General of the Pennsylvania National Guard.

Major General Michael J. Scotti Jr., USA (Ret.), commanded all Army medical forces in Europe.

Brigadier General David M. Brahms, USMC (Ret.), served as the Marine Corps' senior legal adviser.

Brigadier General James P. Cullen, USA (Ret.), served as the Chief Judge of the U.S. Army Court of Criminal Appeals.

Brigadier General Evelyn P. Foote, USA (Ret.), was Commanding General of Fort Belvoir and served as Vice Chair of the Army's Senior Review Panel on Sexual Harassment.

Brigadier General David R. Irvine, USA (Ret.), was Deputy Commander for the 96th Regional Readiness Command. He served four terms in the Utah House of Representatives.

Brigadier General John H. Johns, USA (Ret.), Ph.D., helped developed the Army's counterinsurgency doctrine and served as a Deputy Assistant Secretary of Defense.

Brigadier General Richard O'Meara, USA (Ret.), fought in Vietnam before joining the Army's Judge Advocate General Corps.

Brigadier General Murray G. Sagsveen, USA (Ret.), was the senior judge advocate in the Army National Guard.

Brigadier General John K. Schmitt, USA (Ret.), was Assistant Chief of Staff for Operations, Kosovo Forces (KFOR).

Brigadier General Anthony Verrengia, USAF (Ret.), served as commander of an Air Force Command and on the Air Staff.

Brigadier General Stephen N. Xenakis, USA (Ret.), was Commanding General of the Southeast Regional Army Medical Command.

Ambassador Pete Peterson, USAF (Ret.), a POW in Vietnam for more than six years, was U.S. ambassador to the Socialist Republic of Vietnam and a three-term congressman from Florida.

Colonel Lawrence B. Wilkerson, USA (Ret.), was Special Assistant to General Colin Powell when Powell was Chairman of the U.S. Joint Chiefs of Staff and Secretary of State.

Honorable Richard Danzig was Secretary of the Navy.

Honorable Walter B. Slocombe was Under Secretary of Defense for Policy, Senior Adviser for National Security and Defense in the

Coalition Provisional Authority for Iraq, and a member of the Commission on Intelligence Capabilities Regarding WMD.

Honorable William H. Taft IV was Legal Adviser to the Department of State, U.S. Permanent Representative to NATO, and Deputy Secretary of Defense.

Frank Kendall III, Esq. was Vice Chairman of the Defense Intelligence Agency Advisory Board and Assistant Deputy Under Secretary of Defense for Strategic Defense Systems.

MILITARY LAWYERS

Many military lawyers steadfastly opposed the Bush administration's views on significant aspects of the war on terror. In December 2001 and January 2002, the four Judge Advocates General, the top military lawyer of each of the armed services, argued for providing traditional Geneva Convention protections for combatants in Afghanistan. They said that U.S. troops would be in jeopardy if the United States failed to uphold international law.[20] The same military lawyers argued against expanding interrogation techniques to allow for what amounts to torture. Additionally, military lawyers have won cases in the Supreme Court against the Bush administration's decisions to deny rights to prisoners held at the Guantánamo Bay prison camp.

In early 2006, two Seton Hall University Law professors completed a study of the backgrounds of 517 detainees at Guantánamo. They based their study on the review by military lawyers of the status, or classification, of each detainee, (i.e.) whether he was still an unlawful enemy combatant, a lawful enemy combatant, or an innocent civilian. The Seton Hall study determined that only 8 percent of those being held at Guantánamo were classified as al Qaeda, 40 percent have no connection with al Qaeda, and 18 percent have no connection with either al Qaeda or the Taliban. The study also shows that U.S. forces "purchased" 95 percent of those in Guantánamo from Afghan warlords and others who turned in alleged al Qaeda and Taliban for a bounty. U.S. forces captured only 5 percent of those detained in Guantánamo. Fifty-five

percent of those detained have been determined to have *not* committed any hostile acts against the United States or Coalition allies.[21] In
October 2004, then-deputy commander of Guantánamo, Brigadier
General Martin Lucenti, had told the London *Times*, "Most of these
guys at Guantánamo weren't [captured] fighting. They were running.[22]

✑ Lieutenant Commander Charles Swift

In 2006, Navy Lieutenant Commander Charles Swift argued and won
the case *Hamdan v. Rumsfeld*. The U.S. Supreme Court ruled that President Bush overstepped his authority in setting up military tribunals to
try Guantánamo prisoners, including Swift's client, alleged al Qaeda
operative Salim Ahmed Hamdan. Just days earlier, Swift had been
named by the *National Law Journal* one of the hundred most influential lawyers in America. After the embarrassing setback for the Bush
administration, Swift was passed over for promotion, and in October
2006, the Navy announced plans to dismiss him under its "up or out"
policy. This policy requires an officer to retire when he reaches twenty
years of service if he has not been promoted. Lt. Commander Swift
retired when he reached twenty years of service in the spring of 2007.

The statement of Commander Swift when he received the American Civil Liberties Union (ACLU) Courageous Advocate award on
December 11, 2006, explains the challenge military lawyers face in
providing legal advice to prisoners in Guantánamo. He called the military commission more of an inquisition than a commission: "In December 2003, I was given the assignment of representing a 34-year-old
Yemeni with a fourth-grade education named Salim Ahmed Hamdan
for unspecified charges before a military commission. The rules for trial
permitted Salim to be tried and convicted on evidence that he was not
permitted to see, much less confront, and for that evidence to be the
product of interrogations that used sleep deprivation, agonizing stress
positions, physical and mental humiliation, and even water-boarding
to induce the sense of drowning. The commission, in short, bore a closer
resemblance to an inquisition than it did to the military justice system
that I was so very proud to be a part of."

Swift said that his access to his client was based on his client pleading guilty; the operation of the commission was not a part of America he had sworn to defend: "The prosecution's letter requesting counsel for Salim made clear that my access to him was conditioned on the negotiation of a guilty plea. That's right: Unless Salim agreed to plead guilty, he would not be able to continue to have access to a lawyer, much less a day in court. This was not the America I had sworn to defend. I discussed Salim's situation with Professor Neal Katyal, and we decided that I could offer Salim another option. I could promise Salim that if he did not want to plead guilty I would take a writ of *habeas corpus* on his behalf to the federal courts seeking a regular trial affording all of the guarantees necessary to ensure justice."

As a military lawyer, Swift saw the extreme conditions his client lived under and the extraordinary psychological stress to which he was subjected: "When I met Salim, he had been sitting in solitary confinement for almost two months and because he exercised only at night had not seen the sun for almost two months. I told Salim what the government wanted from him and . . . and my plan to file suit on his behalf if he so desired. When I finished, Salim said simply, 'The guards say there is no law here.' I replied, 'I do not believe that. I think that there is law everywhere but we are going to have to fight for it. We are going to have to go to the Supreme Court of the United States and win.' Salim then asked, 'Will this make me famous?' and I replied that it might. He responded, 'I do not want to be famous. I want to go home.' I said it is the only way. Ultimately he agreed, and so we began a journey."[23]

☙ Lieutenant Commander Matthew Diaz

In 2004 the U.S. Supreme Court ruled that the Center for Constitutional Rights (CCR), based in New York, could represent the prisoners at Guantánamo, but Secretary of Defense Donald Rumsfeld gave orders not to release to CCR the names of the 550 prisoners CCR was to defend. Lieutenant Commander Matthew Diaz, a Navy lawyer of nineteen years, assigned to the prison at Guantánamo, felt it was wrong to withhold the names after the Supreme Court had ruled to provide them. Diaz said, "My oath as a commissioned officer is to the Constitution of the United States. I'm not a criminal. I had observed the stonewalling, the obstacles we continued to place in the way of the attorneys. I knew my time was limited. I had to do something. I felt [providing the names] was the right decision, the moral decision, the decision that was required by international law. No matter how the conflict was identified, we were to treat [the prisoners] in accordance with Geneva, and it just wasn't being done."

The Navy didn't agree. Diaz was court-martialed and, on May 18, 2007, sentenced to six months in a Navy brig and given a Dishonorable discharge for releasing the names of the Guantánamo prisoners.[24]

MILITARY WHISTLEBLOWERS

Whistle-blowing in the military can result in other soldiers receiving disciplinary action, including jail time. Due to the camaraderie and loyalty toward fellow servicemembers instilled as part of military training, these acts of conscience are generally met with anger, retribution, and even physical harm. It takes courage to reveal wrongdoing in the military. If it hadn't been for whistleblowers, we would not have known about the criminal acts committed by military personnel against prisoners at Abu Ghraib.

✍ Specialist Joe Darby

Army Specialist Joe Darby was a military policeman at Abu Ghraib prison. In January 2004, a fellow guard handed him a compact disc containing photos of a pyramid of naked prisoners, prisoners with women's underwear on their heads, two soldiers posing over the dead body of a prisoner, dogs being used to scare prisoners, and many other photos depicting humiliating treatment by the U.S. guards. Darby gave a copy of the CD to the Criminal Investigative Division (CID) of his command, and an investigation into prisoner abuse at Abu Ghraib began.

On April 29, 2004, CBS's *60 Minutes* broadcast some of the photos, forcing Secretary of Defense Rumsfeld to address the abuses. He responded by naming Darby on national TV as the person who had provided the CD. Darby was eating dinner in a mess hall when he heard Rumsfeld on TV say his name, and he felt his life was in danger.[25]

Darby called home that day and learned that his wife was being treated badly by people in their small town in Maryland who had heard that Darby had blown the whistle on military personnel, even though those military personnel had abused Iraqi prisoners. He was flown out of Iraq the next day and his family met him at Dover Air Force Base. Because of the threats against him Specialist Darby never returned home:

> People there don't look at the fact that I knew right from wrong. They look at the fact that I put an Iraqi before an American. But I don't regret any of it. I made my peace with my decision before I turned the pictures in. I knew that if people found out it was me, I wouldn't be liked. That's why I wanted to be anonymous. I knew what the mentality is up there. But the only time I ever regretted it was when I was in Iraq and my family was going through a lot. Other than that, I never doubted that it was the right thing. It forced a big change in my life, but the change has been good and bad.[26]

The Army provided six bodyguards for Joe Darby at the military base where he was transferred. After his discharge from the military he went into federal protective custody to begin life in a new place.[27] Joe Darby received a Profile in Courage Award from the John F. Kennedy Library Foundation in Boston in May 2005.[28]

∾ Captain Ian Fishback

U.S. Army Captain Ian Fishback, a West Point graduate, served two combat tours with the 82nd Airborne Division, one in Afghanistan and one in Iraq. On September 16, 2005, he sent a letter to Senator John McCain stating his concern about the abuse of prisoners. He was called to testify before Congress the following month, and he stated that soldiers frequently beat and abused Iraqi prisoners during the period

September 2003 to April 2004 at Camp Mercury, near Fallujah. Based in part on Fishback's testimony, Senator McCain, along with Senators John Warner and Lindsey Graham, wrote an amendment to a Senate bill to make previous Bush administration claims for the use of extreme methods of abuse illegal. On May 8, 2006, Captain Fishback was chosen by *Time* magazine as one of the 100 most influential people in the world for taking a stand against torture.[29]

∾ Sergeant Samuel Provance

From September 2003 to February 2004, U.S. Army Sergeant Samuel Provance was assigned to work at Abu Ghraib Prison. He reported to Army investigators the abuse that he'd witnessed, but they did not pursue the leads he gave them. Taking his frustration to the media, in May 2004, he was interviewed on ABC's *World News Tonight with Peter Jennings*. Military retaliation came immediately. He was reprimanded, although his immediate commander wanted a more severe punishment through court-martial. His top secret security clearance was suspended, and he was reduced in rank. He was given an Honorable discharge from the Army in October 2005. In February 2006, Samuel Provance testified before the House Committee on Government Reform during a briefing on "Protecting National Security Whistleblowers in the Post-9/11 Era."[30]

U.S. MILITARY RESISTERS

Anyone who joins the military knows he or she may be ordered to war by the country's civilian leadership. The military depends on the obedience of its servicemembers. However, when given an order to perform an illegal action, servicemen and women are duty bound to refuse. Commissioned officers take an oath to support and defend the Constitution of the United States against all enemies, foreign and domestic. They do not swear allegiance to a person or political party.

Many international attorneys and military personnel see the war in Iraq as an illegal act of aggression, which is a war crime. This belief is at the heart of the actions of most of the resisters whose stories follow. Since March 2003, tens of thousands of U.S. military personnel have gone absent without leave (AWOL), defined as unauthorized absence from one's unit for less than thirty days. Another 10,500 have deserted, defined as absence from one's unit for longer than thirty days. And the number choosing to go AWOL or to desert is rising each year. At the height of the Vietnam War, in 1971, 33,000 military personnel, or 3.4 percent of all forces, had deserted.

The military does not disclose the number of deserters who turn themselves in and are given administrative discharges. A service-member who returns from AWOL or deserter status and refrains from speaking out against the war usually receives a General or Less than Honorable discharge. But if a serviceman or woman speaks out pub-licly while AWOL or in deserter status, he or she is generally court-martialed, sentenced to prison, and given a Bad Conduct or Undesirable discharge. Not all who go AWOL or desert are protesting the war. Family situations, the inability to adapt to military life, and other issues can also cause soldiers to desert.

In June 2006, Army First Lieutenant Ehren Watada became the first U.S. military officer to refuse orders to deploy to Iraq. After exten-sive soul searching and research, Lt. Watada came to the conclusion that the war on Iraq is illegal. He stated clearly that he is not against war in general, but he believes that the President, Congress, and mil-itary leaders who support this war are a "threat to the Constitution,"[31] and the Constitution is what he took an oath to protect. Following a court-martial mistrial in February 2007, Lt. Watada was scheduled to be retried in October 2007.

On January 16, 2007, a group of active-duty U.S. soldiers traveled to Washington, DC, to deliver to Congress an Appeal for Redress of Grievances, calling for "the prompt withdrawal of all American mili-tary forces and bases from Iraq." The Appeal has been signed by more than 1,800 active-duty U.S. military troops, most of whom have spent at least one tour of duty in Iraq. These troops believe the war in Iraq is not working and a different solution must be found.[32]

Many people say that when you join the military, you take what comes. Resisters and deserters respond that they didn't volunteer to participate in a war of aggression, and they willingly risk imprisonment rather than fight in an illegal war. Whether you agree with them or not, the depth of their beliefs and the courage it takes to face the consequences of these actions merit respect.

As retired Major General Paul Eaton acknowledged in his Op-Ed in which he called for the resignation of Donald Rumsfeld, "Our most important, and sometimes most severe, judges are our subordinates."[33] Among the most severe critics of the war are the enlisted men and women who join the military trusting that the civilian and military leadership will put them in harm's way only for the most important of purposes, the defense of the country. Many of these servicemen and women have seen clearly, some early and some later, the failure of the checks and balances of our government and the falsehoods told by our leaders. Some of them decided to protect themselves and others by speaking the truth, no matter what the consequences, while others refuse to continue to participate in military service altogether and face the consequences of that decision, whether it be court-martial or living in another country away from family and friends.

In the following pages, we tell the stories of some of these servicemen and women who made the difficult decision to be court-martialed or go to Canada rather than serve in a war they feel is illegal. Almost all of these men and women had already served in Iraq when they chose to resist further deployment. There are many more resisters whose stories are every bit as compelling, but, unfortunately, we do not have room to include them all.

✎ Camilo Mejía

In 1994, at the age of 18, Camilo Mejía, a Nicaraguan citizen, moved to Florida with his mother. The following year, he enlisted in the U.S. Army for three years and rose to the rank of Staff Sergeant. After completing his active duty service, he joined the Florida National Guard to qualify for tuition assistance so he could attend the University of

Florida. In April 2003, as Mejía was entering his final semester of college, his National Guard unit was ordered to active duty in Iraq. By this time, he had spent more than seven years in the military, including three years of active duty.

Camilo Mejía was deeply affected by what he saw in Iraq—firefights, ambushes, excessive use of force, soldiers who were poorly trained and equipped, commanders who put glory over good strategy. He watched Iraqi citizens turn from welcoming the American forces to becoming hostile in response to the roadblocks, raids on their homes, and the senseless killing of civilians. He also witnessed the abuse of Iraqi prisoners. Months before the Abu Ghraib prison photos were made public, Mejía notified his superiors about conditions at a makeshift detention camp near Baghdad's airport, "where Iraqis were arbitrarily arrested and detained and where he and his men were directed by three unidentified interrogators to 'soften up' prisoners for questioning." Mejía says he was taught to stage mock executions, clicking a pistol trigger near the ears of hooded prisoners, and to bang on metal walls with sledgehammers to keep prisoners awake for up to forty-eight hours.[34]

After six months in Iraq, Camilo Mejía returned home on leave. He applied for conscientious objector (CO) status and refused to return to his unit in Iraq, citing moral reasons, the legality of the war, and the conduct of U.S. troops toward Iraqi civilians and prisoners." He became the first combatant in the Iraq War to publicly refuse to return.

After five months of being AWOL from his unit, on March 15, 2004, Staff Sergeant Mejía spoke at a rally and held a press conference at the Peace Abbey, near Boston, and then turned himself in to military police. On May 21, 2004, he was court-martialed for desertion. During his trial at Fort Stewart, Georgia, his commanding officers and men in his squad described Mejía as "exemplary and popular."[35] The military court found him guilty and sentenced him to the maximum one-year imprisonment, reduction in rank to E-1, forfeiture of two-thirds of his pay for one year, and a Bad Conduct discharge. Amnesty International declared him a prisoner of conscience. On February 15, 2005, after serving nine months of his sentence, Camilo Mejía was released from prison. He continues to speak publicly against the war.

Mejía has written about his experiences in *Road from Ar Ramadi: The Private Rebellion of Staff Sergeant Mejía.*

∾

Camilo Mejía's Statement
Written while in prison at Fort Sill, Oklahoma

I was deployed to Iraq in April 2003 and returned home for a two-week leave in October. Going home gave me the opportunity to put my thoughts in order and to listen to what my conscience had to say. People would ask me about my war experiences, and answering them took me back to all the horrors—the firefights, the ambushes, the time I saw a young Iraqi dragged by his shoulders through a pool of his own blood, or an innocent man decapitated by our machine gun fire. The time I saw a soldier broken down inside because he killed a child, or an old man on his knees, crying, with his arms raised to the sky, perhaps asking God why we had taken the life of his son.

I thought of the suffering of a people whose country was in ruins and who were further humiliated by the raids, patrols, and curfews of an occupying army.

And I realized that none of the reasons we were told about why we were in Iraq turned out to be true. There were no weapons of mass destruction. There was no link between Saddam Hussein and al Qaeda. We weren't helping the Iraqi people, and the Iraqi people didn't want the U.S. there. We weren't preventing terrorism or making Americans safer. I couldn't find a single good reason for having been there, for having shot at people and been shot at.

Coming home gave me the clarity to see the line between military duty and moral obligation. I realized that I was part of a war that I believed was immoral and criminal, a war of aggression, a war of imperial domination. I realized that acting upon my principles became incompatible with my role in the military, and I decided that I could not return to Iraq.

By putting my weapon down, I chose to reassert myself as a human being. I have not deserted the military or been disloyal to the men and women of the military. I have not been disloyal to a country. I have only been loyal to my principles.

When I turned myself in, with all my fears and doubts, I did it not only for myself. I did it for the people of Iraq, even for those who fired upon me—they were simply on the other side of a battleground where war itself was the only enemy. I did it for the Iraqi children, who are victims of mines and depleted uranium. I did it for the thousands of unknown civilians killed in war. My time in prison is a small price to pay compared to the price Iraqis and Americans have paid with their lives. Mine is a small price compared to the price humanity has paid for war.

Many have called me a coward; others have called me a hero. I believe I can be found somewhere in the middle. To those who have called me a hero, I say that I don't believe in heroes, but I believe that ordinary people can do extraordinary things.

To those who have called me a coward, I say that they are wrong. They are wrong when they think that I left the war for fear of being killed. I admit that fear was there, but also the fear of killing innocent people, the fear of putting myself in a position where to survive means to kill. There was the fear of losing my soul in the process of saving my body, the fear of being lost to my daughter, to the people who love me, to the man I used to be, the man I wanted to be. I was afraid of waking up one morning to realize my humanity had abandoned me.

I say without any pride that I did my job as a soldier. I commanded an infantry squad in combat and we never failed to accomplish our mission. But those who called me a coward are also right without knowing it. I was a coward not for leaving the war, but for having been a part of it in the first place. Refusing and resisting this war was my moral duty, a moral duty that called me to take a principled action. I failed to fulfill my moral duty as a human being, and, instead, I chose to fulfill my duty as a soldier. All because I was afraid. I was terrified, I did not want to stand up to the government and the Army, I was afraid of punishment and humiliation. I went to war because at that moment I was a coward. I apologize to my soldiers for not being the type of leader I should have been.

I also apologize to the Iraqi people. To them, I say I am sorry for the curfews, for the raids, for the killings. May they find it in their hearts to forgive me.

One reason I did not refuse the war from the beginning was that I was afraid of losing my freedom. Today, as I sit behind bars, I realize that there are many types of freedom, and that in spite of my confinement I remain free in many important ways. What good is freedom if we are afraid to follow our conscience? What good is freedom if we are not able to live with our own actions? I am confined to a prison but I feel, today more than ever, connected to all humanity. Behind these bars I sit a free man because I listened to a higher power, the voice of my conscience.

While I was confined in total segregation, I came across a poem written by a man who refused and resisted the government of Nazi Germany. For doing so he was executed. His name is Albrecht Hanshofer, and he wrote this poem as he awaited execution.

Guilt

The burden of my guilt before the law
weighs light upon my shoulders; to plot
and to conspire was my duty to the people;
I would have been a criminal had I not.
I am guilty, though not the way you think,
I should have done my duty sooner, I was wrong,
I should have called evil more clearly by its name
I hesitated to condemn it for far too long.
I now accuse myself within my heart:
I have betrayed my conscience far too long
I have deceived myself and fellow man.
I knew the course of evil from the start
My warning was not loud nor clear enough!
Today I know what I was guilty of...

To those who are still quiet, to those who continue to betray their conscience, to those who do not call evil more clearly by its name, to those of us who are still not doing enough to refuse and resist, I say, "Come forward." I say, "Free your minds." Let us, collectively, free our minds, soften our hearts, comfort the wounded, put down our weapons, and reassert ourselves as human beings by putting an end to war.[36]

⤷ Pablo Paredes

On December 5, 2004, Navy Petty Officer Pablo Paredes, a weapons-control technician, refused to board the *USS Bonhomme Richard* in San Diego as it was preparing to sail to the Persian Gulf. Paredes previously had been stationed in Japan and hadn't had a direct role in the war on Iraq, which he'd opposed from the start. He did not want to be "part of a ship that's taking 3,000 Marines over there, knowing a hundred or more of them won't come back. I can't sleep at night knowing that's what I do for a living." Paredes said he was young and naive when he joined the Navy in 2000 and "never imagined, in a million years, we would go to war with somebody who had done nothing to us." He had twenty months left on his six-year enlistment.[37] In mid-December, Paredes turned himself in to military authorities and applied for conscientious objector status. The Navy denied his application.

At his May 11, 2005, court-martial, Paredes' attorney called international law professor Marjorie Cohn to the stand as an expert witness, and she testified that in her professional legal opinion, the war on Iraq was an illegal war of aggression, a war crime. The military judge found Paredes guilty of refusing deployment to the Persian Gulf and sentenced him to three months of hard labor while confined to the Naval Base, but no time in the brig. He was also demoted from petty officer third class to seaman recruit, the lowest rank in the Navy. In discussing the light sentence, the military judge acknowledged, "Based on the evidence at the court-martial, any seaman recruit has reasonable cause to believe that the wars in Yugoslavia, Afghanistan, and Iraq were illegal."[38] Paredes' lawyers called it a victory for war resisters, as prosecutors had asked the judge to sentence Paredes to nine months of confinement and a Bad Conduct discharge.[39]

Pablo Paredes continues to actively oppose the war. Through the GI Rights Hotline, he counsels other men and women in the military who are facing crises of conscience.

On May 12, 2005, before his sentencing, Paredes read the following statement to the presiding judge at the military court-martial.

↷

Pablo Paredes' Statement

Your Honor, and to all present, I'd like to state first and foremost that it has never been my intent or motivation to create a mockery of the Navy or its judicial system. I do not consider military members adversaries. I consider myself in solidarity with all servicemembers. It is this feeling of solidarity that was at the root of my actions. I don't pretend to be in a position to lecture anyone on what I perceive as facts concerning our current political state of affairs. I accept that it is very possible that my political perspective on this war could be wrong. I don't think that rational people can even engage in debate if neither side is willing to accept the possibility that their assertions, no matter how well researched, can be tainted with inaccuracy and falsehoods. I do believe that accepting this in no way takes away from one's confidence in their own convictions.

I am convinced that the current war in Iraq is illegal. I am also convinced that the true causality for it lacked any high ground in the topography of morality. I believe, as a member of the Armed Forces, beyond having duty to my chain of command and my President, I have a higher duty to my conscience and to the supreme law of the land. Both of these higher duties dictate that I must not participate in any way, hands-on or indirectly, in the current aggression that has been unleashed on Iraq. In the past few months I have been continually asked if I regret my decision to refuse to board my ship and to do so publicly. I have spent hour upon hour reflecting on my decision, and I can tell you with every fiber of certitude that I possess that I feel in my heart I did the right thing.

This does not mean I have no regrets. I regret dearly exposing the families of Marines and sailors to my protest. While I do not feel my message was wrong, I know that those families were facing a difficult moment. This moment was made in some ways more difficult by my actions, and this pains me. That day on the pier, I restrained myself from answering the calls of "coward" and even some harsher variations of the same term. I did so because I knew this wasn't the time to engage these families in debate. I thought that I became in many ways a forum for venting their fears and sadness. And I didn't want to turn that into a combative situation in which the families were more distracted by our debate than simply empowered by their ability to chastise my actions. All that being said, I still feel my actions made some people very unhappy and made others feel that I was taking away from their child's or their husband's good-bye, and I regret this.

I also regret the pain and stress I have caused those near and dear to me. I know that my lawyers feel that it is ill-advised for me to say these things. My lawyers have had a very difficult time with me. They also thought that it was ill-advised for me to plead not guilty. It is this I truly want to explain, both to them and to the court. I acknowledge I did not board the *Bonhomme Richard* on December 6 and that I left after ship personnel and the Pier Master-at-Arms refused to arrest me. Given these confessions, one may find it hard to understand why anyone would admit to the action but not plead guilty to the crime. This question has also been a topic of much reflection for me.

I never deny my actions, nor do I run from their consequences. But pleading guilty is more than admission of action. It is also acceptance that that action was wrong and illegal. These two things I do not and cannot accept. I feel, even with all the regrets and difficulties that have come as a result of my actions, that they were in fact my duty as a human being and as a servicemember. I feel in my mind and heart that this war is illegal and immoral. The moral argument is one that courts have little room for, and it has been articulated in my conscientious objector (CO) application. It is an argument that encompasses all wars as intolerable in my system of morals. The legal argument is quite relevant, although motions filed and approved have discriminated against it to the point it was not allowed in this trial.

I have long now been an ardent reader of independent media, and, in my opinion, less corrupted forms of media, such as TruthOut.org, *Democracy Now!*, books from folks like Steven Zunes and Chalmers Johnson, articles from people like Noam Chomsky and Naomi Klein. These folks are very educated in matters of politics and are not on the payroll of any major corporate news broadcaster such as CNN or

Fox News Network. They all do what they do for reasons other than money, as they could earn much more if they joined the corporate-controlled ranks. I have come to trust their research and value their convictions in assisting me to form my own. They have unanimously condemned this war as illegal, as well as made resources available for me to draw my own conclusions—such as Kofi Annan's statements about how, under the UN Charter, the Iraq War is illegal, and Marjorie Cohn's articles providing numerous sources and reasons why the war is illegal under international as well as domestic law. I could speak extensively about the arguments as to the legality of the war on Iraq. But again, I don't presume to be in a position to lecture anyone here on law. I mean only to provide insight on my actions on December 6.

I understood very well before that date what the precedent was for servicemembers participating in illegal wars. I read the arguments and the outcomes to Nazi German soldiers and imperial Japanese soldiers in the Nuremberg and Tokyo Trials, respectively. In all I read, I came to the overwhelming conclusion, supported by numerous examples, that in the eyes of international law any servicemember who knowingly participates in an illegal war can find no haven in the fact that he was following orders.

Nazi aggression and imperialist Japan are very charged moments of history, and simply mentioning them evokes many emotions and memories of many atrocities. So I want to be very clear that I am in no way comparing our current government to any historical counterparts. I am not comparing the leaders nor their acts, not their militaries nor their acts. I am only citing the trials because they are the best example of judicial precedent for what a soldier or sailor is expected to do when faced with the decision whether or not to participate in what he perceives is an illegal war.

I think we would all agree that a servicemember must not participate in random, unprovoked, illegitimate violence simply because he is ordered to. What I submit to you and the court is that I am convinced that the current war is exactly that. So, if there's anything I could be guilty of, it is my beliefs. I am guilty of believing this war is illegal. I'm guilty of believing war in all forms is immoral and useless, and

I am guilty of believing that as a servicemember I have a duty to refuse to participate in this war, because it is illegal.

I do not expect the court to rule on the legality of this war, nor do I expect the court to agree with me. I only wish to express my reasons and convictions surrounding my actions. I acted on my conscience. Whether right or wrong in my convictions, I will be at peace knowing I followed my conscience.[40]

∽ Kevin Benderman

Sergeant Kevin Benderman was a ten-year Army veteran, a mechanic trained to fix Bradley armored vehicles. During six months in combat in Iraq in 2003, "he saw a young Iraqi girl with her arm horribly burned and blackened, standing helplessly on a roadside as [his] convoy rushed past. He saw dogs feasting on civilian corpses that had been dumped into pits." He saw his fellow American soldiers "treat war like a video game with few qualms about killing or the effects of the invasion on ordinary Iraqis." Badly shaken by his experiences in Iraq, on December 20, 2004, Kevin Benderman applied for conscientious objector status, and the Army turned down his application. With one tour in Iraq behind him, when his unit was ordered to return to Iraq, he refused to go with them. Serveant Benderman did not go AWOL or desert; he remained on his base.[41]

On July 28, 2005, Benderman was acquitted of desertion and found guilty of missing military movement. He was sentenced to fifteen months in prison and given a Dishonorable discharge. Benderman completed thirteen months of imprisonment at Fort Lewis, Washington, and was released on August 19, 2006, two months early, for good behavior. He has appealed his conviction and Dishonorable discharge, stating, "I did not do anything dishonorable, so I don't think I deserve that."[42]

Kevin Benderman's Statement

Having observed life from the standpoint of a soldier for ten years, I always felt there was no higher honor than to serve my country and defend the values that established this country. My family has a history of serving this country dating back to the American Revolution, and I felt that to continue on in that tradition was the honorable thing to do.

As I went through the process that led to my decision to refuse deployment to Iraq for the second time, I was torn between thoughts of abandoning the soldiers that I serve with or following my conscience, which tells me: war is the ultimate destruction and waste of humanity.

The idea that we could, and should, consider better ways to solve our differences with other people in the world has crossed my mind on numerous occasions. This was the driving force that made me refuse deployment to Iraq a second time. Some people may say I am doing so out of fear of combat; I am not going to tell you that the thought of going back to that place isn't scary, but that is not the reason for my decision not to return.

I want people to know that the longer I thought about just how stupid the concept of war really is, the stronger I felt about not participating in war. Why do we tell our children not to solve their differences with violence, then turn around and commit the ultimate in violence against people in another country who have nothing to do with the political attitudes of their leaders?

Having read numerous books on the subject of war and having heard the arguments for war, I have come to the conclusion that there are no valid arguments for the destructive force of war. People are destroyed, nations are destroyed, and yet we continue on with war. The young people that I went with to the combat zone looked at it like it was a video game they played back in their childhood.

When you contemplate the beauty of the world around us and the gifts we have been given, you have to ask yourself, Is this what humanity is meant to do, wage war against one another? Why can't we teach our children not to hate or not to be afraid of someone else just because they are different from us? Why must it be considered honorable to train young men and women to look through the sights of a high-powered rifle and to kill another human being from 300 meters away?

Consider, if you will, the positive things that could be accomplished without war in our lives: prescription medication that is affordable for seniors, college grants that are available for high school students. I could give a list of reasons not to waste our resources on war. The most important is to let the children of the world learn war no more.

I've received emails from people who said that I was a coward for not going to war, but I say to them that I have already been, so I do not have anything to prove to anyone anymore. What is there to prove any-way—that I can kill someone I do not even know and who has never done anything to me? What is in that concept that anyone could con-sider honorable?

I first realized that war was the wrong way to handle things in this or any other country when I went to the war zone and saw the dam-age that it causes. Why must we resort to violence when things do not go our way? Where is the logic of that? I have felt that there are bet-ter ways to handle our business than to bomb each other into oblivion. When you are on the water in a boat and you have a chance to see dolphins playing with each other as they go about their business, you realize that if they can live without war, then humanity should be able to as well.

Can't we teach our children to leave war behind, in history, where it belongs? We realized that slavery and human sacrifice were obsolete institutions, and we left them behind us. When are we going to have the same enlightened attitude about war?

I look at my stepchildren and realize that war has no place with me in giving them what they need to survive the trials and tribulations of early adulthood. And if you look at all the times soldiers miss in the course of fighting wars, such as birthdays and anniversaries, their children going to the senior prom and college graduations, and other memories that can never be replaced, then you have to come to the un-derstanding that war steals the sense of humanity from more than just soldiers. It also steals some of that humanity from their family.

I have learned from firsthand experience that war is the destroyer of everything that is good in the world; it turns our young into soulless killers, and we tell them that they are heroes when they master the "art" of killing. That is a very deranged mindset, in my opinion. It destroys the environment, life, and the resources that could be used to create more life by advancing our endeavors.

War should be left behind us; we should evolve to a higher mindset even if it means going against what most people tell us in this country, such as that we can never stop fighting with other people in the world. I have made the decision not to participate in war any longer, and some people in this country cannot comprehend that concept, but to me it is simple. I have chosen not to take part in war, and it was easy to come to that decision.

I cannot tell anyone else how to live his or her life, but I have determined how I want to live mine—by not participating in war any longer, as I feel that it is stupid and against everything that is good about our world.[43]

ᴄ Stephen Funk

Twenty-year-old Stephen Funk's Marine Reserve Corps unit was mobilized to deploy to Iraq in February 2003, and Funk went AWOL. Forty-seven days later, he turned himself in to military authorities and declared himself a conscientious objector.

He said he'd made a mistake enlisting and hoped his public resistance might prevent others from doing the same. Funk, who had excelled as a rifleman during boot camp, said, "I refuse to kill. I object to war, because I believe that it is impossible to achieve peace through violence. I am a conscientious objector, because there is no way for me to remain a Marine without sacrificing my entire sense of self-respect." Funk said he would rather face the military's punishment than act against his beliefs.[44]

"I was lacking direction, and I needed a sense of belonging, and I wanted some discipline," he said. "I thought the Marines would provide that. But as soon I set foot in Camp Pendleton in San Diego

County for basic training, I knew this wasn't the life for me." He couldn't bring himself to hit other soldiers during hand-to-hand combat drills, and when he was ordered to say, "Kill! Kill!" during training, Funk would say "Jill! Jill!" or "Phil! Phil!"[45]

On September 6, 2003, the Marine Corps court-martialed Funk, convicted him of unauthorized absence, and sentenced him to six months in prison and a Bad Conduct discharge. He was acquitted of desertion. Funk completed the six-month sentence in military prison at Camp Lejeune, North Carolina, and was released in March 2004.

↭

Stephen Funk's Statement

I refuse to kill. I object to war because I believe that it is impossible to achieve peace through violence. I am a conscientious objector, because there is no way for me to remain a Marine without sacrificing my entire sense of self-respect. When I enlisted in February 2002, I was living on my own for the first time and saw the Marine Reserves as a way to learn things such as teamwork and leadership—things you can learn in Boy Scouts. I saw it as a way to learn new things and meet new people. I caved in to pressure from a recruiter who capitalized on my vulnerability. The Marines don't advertise that they kill people. I didn't really realize the full implications of what I was doing. I would rather face the military's punishment than act against my beliefs.[46]

↭ Abdullah Webster

Sergeant First Class Abdullah Webster joined the U.S. Army in 1985 and served in the first Gulf War, Korea, and Bosnia. While in the military, Webster became a Muslim. In April 2003, while he was based in Bamberg, Germany, Webster's unit was notified that it would deploy to Iraq later in the year. In September 2003, he applied for conscientious objector status, stating that "his religion prohibited him from participating in any aggressive war, or in any oppression or injustice to Muslims or non-Muslims." When he learned that his application was going to be rejected, he withdrew it, instead requesting reassignment to noncombatant service. He was ordered to deploy to Iraq in February 2004, and he refused on religious grounds. He reapplied for conscientious objector status and was rejected because "his objection was not to war in general but to the Iraq War in particular."

Webster was charged with failing to obey commands from his superior and missing his brigade's movements. At his court-martial hearing on June 3, 2004, Webster was sentenced to fourteen months' imprisonment, a Bad Conduct discharge, suspension of his salary, and loss of pension and other benefits. He had been due to retire from the Army in 2005, after twenty years of service. He was released from prison on May 1, 2005.[47] Webster is the highest-ranking noncommissioned officer to be court-martialed for refusing to go to Iraq.

✍

Abdullah Webster's Statement

I want to thank everyone at Amnesty International for their prayers and support, which really helped me during my time in the prisons at Mannheim, Germany, and Fort Lewis, Washington. Thanks to Amnesty International, I received letters from all around the world. I am touched that you took the time to encourage me throughout the past eleven months.

Since being out, I have noticed various inaccurate accounts of why I refused to go to Iraq. What I informed my command is that we are taught to train soldiers to be mentally, physically, and spiritually prepared for war, but that the reason for this war was false. There have not been any weapons of mass destruction, and my faith forbids me to participate in an unjust war. I truly believe that I would have been held accountable before Allah (God) if I had gone, knowing the war to be unjust, and I would not have been able to function fully to the same capacity as I have the past nineteen years of my career as a soldier. It was therefore not an easy decision, nor one taken lightly, to refuse to go to Iraq.

During my time in Fort Lewis and Mannheim prisons, I met several soldiers who served in Iraq. I can recall a couple of stories that really cemented the fact that I had made the right decision. One soldier informed me that he was on a convoy when a group of local people blocked their path. He stopped his vehicle, but his commander told him to carry on. The group slowly broke up, with the exception of a child blocking their way. The soldier said that at night he could still see his vehicle hitting the little child and the vehicles behind him running over the child's body. He informed me that if he could do it all over again, he wouldn't have gone to Iraq. Another soldier told me that he regretted the fact that he didn't intervene or take any action when his fellow squad member was raping the wife and daughter of a man who refused to give them any information during their searches. How could I look my God and my family in the face had I gone and been present at incidents such as these?

My experience in confinement had its ups and downs. The lowest point during my time there was when I was not allowed to contact my family, but generally God enabled me to learn from my experience and draw strength from it. I was also able to try to help others while there. The good days were when I met several people who were willing to turn their lives around. Many people in confinement thought I was there unjustly, because of my faith. Several of the guys looked at how I dealt with my experience, given the way I had been treated and the good way I was coping with it, and it inspired them to cope better with their situations. Several of the soldiers—both inmates and guards— needed advice or a listening ear and would come to me. Even up to the day I left—they asked what they were going to do now that I was going. I said that they needed to rely on each other for their support.

I was surprised to find out that I had also been an inspiration to my wife while inside. I thought that she was a source of strength in keeping the family together and working so hard with organizations such as Amnesty International, letting people know what had happened to me as well as taking care of our 2-year-old daughter. Instead she told me that because I referred to each day as one day less inside, she began to view our circumstances in the same way. It truly was a blessing to be reunited with them again and to see how much my baby had grown.

If there is one thing I hope to come out of my experience, it is the fact that the Army needs to review its policy on how it treats conscientious objectors. The Army regulations pertaining to conscientious

objectors do not take account of a war being illegal or unjustly preventing a soldier from performing his duties in that particular war. It is too
cut-and-dry. Not all soldiers object to all wars—as in this case, the real
reasons for going to war seem somewhat obscure. Not all soldiers belong
to just one faith—there are many soldiers now from various religious
backgrounds, and the current conscientious objector regulations/guide-
lines do not take this into account. We can ascertain when a war is
wrong, and we may come across a situation such as this one where
the United Nations has recognized a war as illegal to the point that it
clashes with our religious belief. We should be given the option to resign
if no other options are available. Now soldiers have no other option but
to go AWOL, because they realize that the punishment for going
AWOL is less than going through their chain of command and object-
ing to a war which is unjust. This should not be the case, and we should
try to support those soldiers who are genuine in their conscientious
beliefs.

We all still wish to protect our families and our country, and it is my
hope that after my experience, soldiers in a similar situation will receive
the support they need in order to continue to carry out their duties.[48]

✎ Aidan Delgado

Aidan Delgado was attending college in Florida when he decided to
join the Army Reserve, on the morning of September 11, 2001. He
finished the paperwork and saw a TV broadcast of the burning World
Trade Center.

After joining the Army, Delgado began studying Buddhism and its
principles of nonviolence. By April 2003, when he began a yearlong
tour in Iraq, he was openly questioning whether he could, in good conscience, participate. Having grown up in Cairo and graduated from the
American-Cairo University, Delgado spoke Arabic and had a deep
appreciation of the cultures of the Middle East.[49]

Delgado was assigned to the 320th Military Police Company. He
spent six months in the southern Iraqi city of Nasiriyah and another
six months helping run the notorious Abu Ghraib prison, personally

witnessing abuses of prisoners by U.S. soldiers. Brutality, often racially motivated, he said, infected the entire prison system and military operation in Iraq.

A few months after arriving in Iraq, Delgado surrendered his rifle and told his officers he was a conscientious objector. He was punished by the officers and ostracized by his peers. One year later, after his unit returned to the U.S., he received conscientious objector status.[50]

≈

Aidan Delgado's Statement

My Buddhism developed parallel to being in the Army. I wasn't a Buddhist before I joined the military, but after I signed on, I had a couple of months before I went to basic training. That is when I started studying Buddhism intensely, doing research to cope with the stress of being in the Army. I went into advanced training the next summer and became really serious about Buddhism. I became a vegetarian. I started talking to my sergeants, saying, "I'm not sure the Army's right for me; I'm a Buddhist now."

Within a few months of arriving in Iraq, I told them that I wanted to be a conscientious objector and I wanted to leave the military because of my religious beliefs. It ended up taking over a year to get my status, so I served in the whole conflict as a conscientious objector. I finally got conscientious objector status after my unit returned to the U.S.

It was extremely difficult to get conscientious objector status. There is a huge burden of proof. You have to do an interview with an investigating officer who grills you on your beliefs to find out if you're just making it up or if you've really thought it out. You have to have some kind of documentation. I think one of my strongest points was that I had a lot of military paperwork showing that I had gradually identified myself as a Buddhist. I also had a lot of conversations with my superiors where I talked about being an objector and being a Buddhist, and they went on the record and said, Yes, he's talked about it progressively throughout the deployment. That really did a lot to establish my sincerity.

The command was extremely hostile to me, and there were all kinds of punitive measures. They wouldn't let me go on leave. They took my ballistic armor away—they told me that I didn't need the hard plate that goes inside your flak jacket, the part that actually protects you against bullets. They said that because I was an objector and I wasn't going to fight, I wouldn't need it. This proved not to be the case; when we got to Abu Ghraib, there was continuous mortar shelling. I did the whole year's deployment without that plate. I really feel that it was more maliciously motivated than anything else.

Also, I was socially ostracized. A lot of my fellow soldiers didn't want to eat with me or hang out with me or go on missions with me. They felt I was untrustworthy, because I was critical of the war and I was a Buddhist. My command "lost" my CO paperwork or misdirected it. They'd say, "We lost your copy. You'll have to do it again."

I eventually got my home leave back, because I threatened my commander that I was going to have them prosecuted for discriminating against me on religious grounds. My company commander, my company first sergeant, and my battalion commander had all decided they were not going to let me leave—they said I couldn't go home on a two-week leave, because I wouldn't come back. My stance was that they were just doing this because I'm a Buddhist and they didn't agree with my beliefs, and I was going to get the ACLU and the World Congress of Buddhists involved. Ultimately, they decided it wasn't worth the headache.[51]

❧ Katherine Jashinski

Army Texas National Guard Specialist Katherine Jashinski applied for conscientious objector status in 2004. A year and a half later, in October 2005, the Army denied her application. In November 2005, at Fort Benning, Georgia, she announced that with or without CO status, she would not go to Afghanistan, becoming the first woman in the military to publicly declare resistance to the wars in the Middle East. The same month, she was ordered to weapons training and deployment training at Fort Benning, and she had to choose between her legal obligation to the Army and her deep moral values. She believed that any person doing any job in the Army contributed in some way to the planning and preparation for war, and she refused to train with weapons. She would not compromise her beliefs for any reason, believing she had a moral obligation, not only to herself but to the world, that is more important than any contract.[52]

Early in March 2006, a federal judge denied her petition to force the Army to declare her a conscientious objector.[53] On May 23, 2006, Katherine Jashinski was court-martialed for refusing to train with weapons. She was convicted and received a Bad Conduct discharge and a sentence of 120 days' imprisonment. With credit for time served while awaiting court-martial, she had to serve an additional forty-seven days in prison. She was released from confinement in July 2006 and now works with the Austin, Texas, GI Rights Hotline.[54]

؈

Katherine Jashinski's Statement

My name is Katherine Jashinski. I am a specialist (SPC) in the Texas Army National Guard. I was born in Milwaukee, Wisconsin, and I am 22 years old. When I graduated from high school, I moved to Austin, Texas, to attend college. At age 19, I enlisted in the Guard as a cook, because I wanted to experience military life. When I enlisted, I believed that killing was immoral but also that war was an inevitable part of life and, therefore, an exception to the rule.

After enlisting, I began the slow transformation into adulthood. Like many teenagers who leave their homes for the first time, I went through a period of growth and soul searching. I encountered many new people and ideas that broadly expanded my narrow experiences. After reading essays by Bertrand Russell and traveling to the South Pacific and talking to people from all over the world, my beliefs about humanity and its relation to war changed. I began to see a bigger picture of the world, and I started to reevaluate everything that I had been taught about war as a child. I developed the belief that taking human life was wrong and war was no exception. I was then able to clarify who I am and what it is that I stand for.

The thing that I revere most in this world is life, and I will never take another person's life. Just as others have faith in God, I have faith in humanity. I have a deeply held belief that people must solve all conflicts through peaceful diplomacy and without the use of violence. Violence only begets more violence.

Because I believe so strongly in nonviolence, I cannot perform any role in the military. Any person doing any job in the Army contributes in some way to the planning, preparation, or implementation of war. For eighteen months, while my CO status was pending, I honored my commitment to the Army and did everything that they asked of me. However, I was ordered to Fort Benning last Sunday to complete weapons training in preparation to deploy for war.

Now I have come to the point where I am forced to choose between my legal obligation to the Army and my deepest moral values. I want to make it clear that I will not compromise my beliefs for any reason. I have a moral obligation not only to myself but to the world as a whole, and this is more important than any contract.

I have come to my beliefs through personal, intense reflection and study. These beliefs are everything that I am and all that I stand for. After much thought and contemplation about the effect my decision will have on my future, my family, the possibility of prison, and the inevitable scorn and ridicule that I will face, I am completely resolute.

I will exercise my every legal right not to pick up a weapon and not to participate in the war effort. I am determined to be discharged as a CO, and, while undergoing the appeals process, I will continue to follow orders that do not conflict with my conscience, until my status has been resolved. I am prepared to accept the consequences of adhering to my beliefs.

What characterizes conscientious objectors is our willingness to face adversity and uphold our values at any cost. We do this not because it is easy or popular, but because we are unable to do otherwise.[55]

✑ Melanie McPherson

Melanie McPherson joined a U.S. Army Reserve Public Affairs unit in Minnesota in 1999. In civilian life, she was an artist and the graphic designer for a newspaper. She was on inactive status from 2002 until April 2006, when she was activated. She believed that the invasion of Iraq was wrong, that it was about oil, but she was willing to serve in the job she had been trained for—public affairs and journalism.

During her predeployment training, McPherson learned that in Iraq journalists were being assigned to other jobs, such as military police and truck driving. Her commander wouldn't confirm that she would be working in public affairs.

Feeling she would be a danger to herself and others if she were sent to Iraq with virtually no training in military police duties, in July 2006, the day before her flight to Kuwait and on to Iraq, McPherson went AWOL. In September 2006, she turned herself in to military authorities. She rejected a summary court-martial that would have sentenced her to a month in prison and then deployment to Iraq. Instead she requested a special court-martial so she could have full legal representation.[56] In February 2007, McPherson pleaded guilty to being AWOL, was sentenced to three months' imprisonment, reduced in rank to private, and given a Bad Conduct discharge.[57]

&

Melanie McPherson's Statement

I love my country. I was hoping to use my God-given talent, not just be a bullet-catcher. I felt certain I was not going to be a public affairs journalist in Iraq. I believed that I was going to be given training in military police duties after I arrived in Iraq, with bullets flying around my head. I think it would be putting myself and others around me in grave danger. I need to get out. I don't fit the mold. I'm not as flexible as they want me to be.[58]

& Ehren Watada

First Lieutenant Ehren Watada joined the U.S. Army in 2003 and served one tour in Korea. In January 2006, Watada told his commanders at Fort Lewis, Washington, that he believed the war in Iraq was illegal, and therefore his orders to deploy there were unlawful and he did not have to obey them. However, he did not consider himself a conscientious objector, since he was willing to fight in wars that were justified, legal, and waged in defense of the nation. Watada's commanders told him that he could submit his resignation but that they would recommend disapproval. His resignation was rejected in May 2006. On June 7, 2006, Lieutenant Watada became the first commissioned officer to refuse deployment to Iraq.

He was charged with missing a deployment movement and multiple counts of "conduct unbecoming an officer and a gentleman" for his public opposition to the war on Iraq. Political charges of "contempt toward the President" were dropped. "The last known prosecution of this charge was in 1965, resulting from Lt. Henry Howe's opposition to U.S. foreign policy during the Vietnam War."[59]

Lt. Watada's February 2007 court-martial ended in a mistrial when the trial judge nullified the Stipulation of Facts that had been agreed to by the defense and prosecution a week before the trial began. The Army refiled charges, and a second court-martial was scheduled for October 2007. Ehren Watada faces up to six years' imprisonment for his act of conscience in refusing to be deployed to Iraq.

∽

Lieutenant Ehren Watada's Statement

Veterans for Peace Convention, Seattle, Washington, August 12, 2006

You are all true American patriots. Although long since out of uniform, you continue to fight for the very same principles you once swore to uphold and defend. No one knows the devastation and suffering of war more than veterans—which is why we should always be the first to prevent it.

Yes, I'm just a lieutenant. And yet, I feel as though we are all citizens of this great country and what I have to say is not a matter of authority—but from one citizen to another. We have all seen this war tear apart our country over the past three years. It seems as though nothing we've done, from vigils to protests to letters to Congress, have had any effect in persuading the powers that be. Tonight I will speak to you on my ideas for a change of strategy. My action is not the first and it certainly will not be the last. Yet, on behalf of those who follow, I require your help—your sacrifice—and that of countless other Americans. I may fail. We may fail. But nothing we have tried has worked so far. It is time for change and the change starts with all of us.

I stand before you today, not as an expert—not as one who pretends to have all the answers. I am simply an American and a servant of the American people. My humble opinions today are just that. I realize that you may not agree with everything I have to say. However, I did not choose to be a leader for popularity. I did it to serve and make better the soldiers of this country. And I swore to carry out this charge honorably under the rule of law.

Today, I speak with you about a radical idea. It is one born from the very concept of the American soldier (or service member). It became instrumental in ending the Vietnam War—but it has been long since forgotten. The idea is this: that to stop an illegal and unjust war, the soldiers can choose to stop fighting it.

Now it is not an easy task for the soldier. For he or she must be aware that they are being used for ill-gain. They must hold themselves responsible for individual action. They must remember duty to the Constitution and the people supersedes the ideologies of their leadership. The soldier must be willing to face ostracism by their peers, worry over the survival of their families, and of course the loss of personal freedom. They must know that resisting an authoritarian government at home is equally important to fighting a foreign aggressor on the battlefield. Finally, those wearing the uniform must know beyond any shadow of a doubt that by refusing immoral and illegal orders, they will be supported by the people not with mere words but by action.

The American soldier must rise above the socialization that tells them authority should always be obeyed without question. Rank should be respected but never blindly followed. Awareness of the history of atrocities and destruction committed in the name of America—either through direct military intervention or by proxy war—is crucial. They must realize that this is a war not out of self-defense but by choice, for profit and imperialistic domination. WMD, ties to al Qaeda, and ties to 9/11 never existed and never will. The soldier must know that our narrowly and questionably elected officials intentionally manipulated the evidence presented to Congress, the public, and the world to make the case for war. They must know that neither Congress nor this administration has the authority to violate the prohibition against preemptive war—an American law that still stands today. This same administration uses us for rampant violations of time-tested laws banning torture and degradation of prisoners of war. Though the American soldier wants to do right, the illegitimacy of the occupation itself, the policies of this administration, and rules of engagement of desperate field commanders will ultimately force them to be party to war crimes. They must know some of these facts, if not all, in order to act.

Mark Twain once remarked, "Each man must for himself alone decide what is right and what is wrong, which course is patriotic and which isn't. You cannot shirk this and be a man. To decide against your conviction is to be an unqualified and inexcusable traitor, both to yourself and to your country." By this, each and every American soldier, marine, airman, and sailor is responsible for their choices and their actions. The freedom to choose is only one that we can deny ourselves.

The oath we take swears allegiance not to one man but to a document of principles and laws designed to protect the people. Enlisting in the military does not relinquish one's right to seek the truth—neither does it excuse one from rational thought nor the ability to distinguish between right and wrong. "I was only following orders" is never an excuse.

The Nuremberg Trials showed America and the world that citizenry as well as soldiers have the unrelinquishable obligation to refuse complicity in war crimes perpetrated by their government. Widespread torture and inhumane treatment of detainees is a war crime. A war of aggression born through an unofficial policy of prevention is a crime against the peace. An occupation violating the very essence of international humanitarian law and sovereignty is a crime against humanity. These crimes are funded by our tax dollars. Should citizens choose to remain silent through self-imposed ignorance or choice, it makes them as culpable as the soldier in these crimes.

The Constitution is no mere document—neither is it old, outdated, or irrelevant. It is the embodiment of all that Americans hold dear: truth, justice, and equality for all. It is the formula for a government of the people and by the people. It is a government that is transparent and accountable to whom they serve. It dictates a system of checks and balances and separation of powers to prevent the evil that is tyranny.

As strong as the Constitution is, it is not foolproof. It does not fully take into account the frailty of human nature. Profit, greed, and hunger for power can corrupt individuals as much as they can corrupt institutions. The founders of the Constitution could not have imagined how money would infect our political system. Neither could they believe a standing army would be used for profit and manifest destiny. Like any common dictatorship, soldiers would be ordered to commit acts of such heinous nature as to be deemed most ungentlemanly and unbecoming that of a free country.

The American soldier is not a mercenary. He or she does not simply fight wars for payment. Indeed, the state of the American soldier is worse than that of a mercenary. For a soldier-for-hire can walk away if they are disgusted by their employer's actions. Instead, especially when it comes to war, American soldiers become indentured servants whether they volunteer out of patriotism or are drafted through economic desperation. Does it matter what the soldier believes is morally right? If this is a war of necessity, why force men and women to fight? When it comes to a war of ideology, the lines between right and wrong are blurred.

Soldier or officer, when we swear our oath it is first and foremost to the Constitution and its protectorate, the people. If soldiers realized this war is contrary to what the Constitution extols—if they stood up and threw their weapons down—no President could ever initiate a war of choice again. When we say, ". . . against all enemies foreign and domestic," what if elected leaders became the enemy? Whose orders do we follow? The answer is the conscience that lies in each soldier, each American, and each human being. Our duty to the Constitution is an obligation, not a choice.

The military, and especially the Army, is an institution of fraternity and close-knit camaraderie. Peer pressure exists to ensure cohesiveness, but it stamps out individualism and individual thought. The idea of brotherhood is difficult to pull away from if the alternative is loneliness and isolation. If we want soldiers to choose the right but difficult path—they must know beyond any shadow of a doubt that they will be supported by Americans. To support the troops who resist, you must make your voices heard. If they see thousands supporting me, they will know. I have heard your support, but many others have not. Increasingly, more soldiers are questioning what they are being asked to do. Yet, the majority lacks awareness of the truth that is buried beneath the headlines. Many more see no alternative but to obey. We must show open-minded soldiers a choice, and we must give them courage to act. Many soldiers don't refuse this war en masse because, like all of us, they value their families over their own lives and perhaps their conscience. Who would willingly spend years in prison for principle and morality while denying their family sustenance?

I tell this to you because you must know that to stop this war, for the soldiers to stop fighting it, they must have the unconditional support of the people. I have seen this support with my own eyes. Convince them that no matter how long they sit in prison, no matter how long this country takes to right itself, their families will have a roof over their heads, food in their stomachs, opportunities, and education. This is a daunting task. It requires the sacrifice of all of us. Why must Canadians feed and house our fellow Americans who have chosen to do the right thing? We should be the ones taking care of our own. Are we that powerless? Are we that unwilling to risk something for those who can truly end this war? How do you support the troops but not the war? By supporting those who can truly stop it. Let them know that resistance to participate in an illegal war is not futile and not without a future.

I have broken no law but the code of silence and unquestioning loyalty. If I am guilty of any crime, it is that I learned too much and cared too deeply for the meaningless loss of my fellow soldiers and my fellow human beings. If I am to be punished it should be for following the rule of law over the immoral orders of one man. If I am to be punished it should be for not acting sooner. Martin Luther King, Jr., once said, "History will have to record that the greatest tragedy of this period

... was not the strident clamor of the bad people, but the appalling silence of the good people."

Now, I'm not a hero. I am a leader of men who said enough is enough. Those who called for war prior to the invasion compared diplomacy with Saddam to the compromises made with Hitler. I say, we compromise now by allowing a government that uses war as the first option instead of the last to act with impunity. Many have said this about the World Trade Towers, "Never again." I agree. Never again will we allow those who threaten our way of life to reign free—be they terrorists or elected officials. The time to fight back is now—the time to stand up and be counted is today.

I'll end with one more Martin Luther King, Jr., quote: "One who breaks an unjust law that conscience tells him is unjust, and who willingly accepts the penalty of imprisonment in order to arouse the conscience of the community over its injustice, is in reality expressing the highest respect for law."[60]

∽ Agustín Aguayo

Agustín Aguayo was 35 years old when he joined the Army in 2003. Within a year, his beliefs had changed so much he felt "he could no longer, in good conscience, be a part of the armed forces," and he applied for conscientious objector status. While his application was being processed, he was sent to Iraq to serve as a medic. In Iraq, he refused to load his gun, even while he was on guard duty. The Army denied his conscientious objector application, but because it had been mishandled, Aguayo challenged the ruling, filing a *habeas corpus* appeal in federal court. His appeal was denied, and, one week later, on September 1, 2006, his unit redeployed to Iraq. Aguayo "made it clear to his chain of command that, as a conscientious objector, he would not participate in war in any form," and this time he refused to deploy.

After nearly three years of attempting to be recognized as a conscientious objector, Aguayo went AWOL, missing his unit's deployment. The next day, he turned himself in to the Military Police on his base in Germany. He was told by Army personnel that he would be going to Iraq, "even if they had to ... shackle, handcuff, and confine him until the deployment, and/or carry him on the plane." Aguayo felt he had no other option and went AWOL again from his base in Germany, flew to Mexico, and returned to the United States. On September 26, 2006, he turned himself in at Fort Irwin, California. On October 3, 2006, Aguayo was escorted in handcuffs back to Germany for court-martial.

On November 21, 2006, the U.S. Court of Appeals for the District of Columbia Circuit heard Aguayo's appeal in his case against the Secretary of the Army for refusing to recognize that he was a conscientious objector. This was the first military conscientious objector case to come before the DC Circuit Court since the Vietnam War. The Court of Appeals ruled against Aguayo's petition.

On March 6, 2007, in a court-martial in Germany, Army Specialist Agustín Aguayo was convicted of desertion and missing a military movement. He could have been sentenced to six years' imprisonment, but was instead sentenced to eight months' imprisonment and a Bad Conduct discharge. He had been in pretrial confinement from the time he voluntarily returned to military control in September 2006.[61] Aguayo was released in April 2007.

During the sentencing, his sergeant said he was sympathetic to Aguayo's beliefs, but "If ... twenty other guys ... do the same thing, ... I've got a problem." His civilian attorney, David Court, said that punishment would not change the mind of a soldier like Aguayo: "A military is strongest if soldiers are told, 'You do have a conscience.' Otherwise we have automatons." Aguayo is a soldier who became out of step with the military's mission and could not be threatened or pushed back into line. Aguayo asked, "How do you correct a person's mind? ... In the end, I had to obey a higher calling."[62] He has appealed the desertion conviction, as he was not absent from his unit for over thirty days.

∽
Agustín Aguayo's Statement

My beliefs and morals come from a transformation as a direct result of my combined religious/family upbringing, military experience, and new experiences I've created. As time progresses (it has been more than two and a half years since I became a conscientious objector), my beliefs have only become more firm and intense. I believe that participating in this deployment to Iraq would be fundamentally wrong, and, therefore, I cannot and will not participate. I believe that to do so, I would be taking part in organized killing and condoning war missions and operations, even though I object, on the basis of my religious training and belief, to participating in any war. I have to take a stand for my principles, values, and morals, and I must let my conscience be my guide. After all, I and no one else have to bear the consequences of my decision or the burden of neglecting my conscience.

Some people might think that a fear of death is the number one reason for my refusing to deploy. But that is not correct. I have to be true to myself and do what is right. Even though I deployed to Iraq as a noncombatant in 2004–2005, I still carry guilt from my participation. By doing guard duty, appearing to be armed, even without bullets, I gave the false impression that I would kill if need be. I am not willing to live a lie to satisfy any deployment operation. By helping countless soldiers for "sick call" as well as driving soldiers around on patrols, I helped them get physically better to be able to go out and do the very thing I am against—kill. This is something my conscience will not allow me to do. Although I myself did not pull the trigger, I now realize that what I did as a noncombatant nonetheless supported and enabled these missions.

In my last deployment, I witnessed how soldiers dehumanize the Iraqi people with words and actions. I saw countless innocent lives shortened due to the war. I still struggle with the senselessness of it all—Iraqi civilians losing their lives because they drove too close to a convoy or a checkpoint, and misunderstandings due to the language barrier leading to death. This is not acceptable to me. It makes no sense that to better the lives of these civilians, they must first endure great human loss imposed by others. That is immoral. This is clear and convincing evidence to me that all war is evil and harmful, not an aid in solving problems. The more time I spent in Iraq, the more evident it became to me that all wars are wrong. No human has the moral authority to decide when it is acceptable to end another's life. How can I be a perpetrator, culprit, and/or enabler of these operations? I cannot and will not. I would much rather suffer the consequences of missing a movement—prosecution by court-martial—than be part of any war activity.

I cannot carry that burden on my conscience. Therefore, this time I will not deploy to Iraq.[63]

✍ Ricky Clousing

Sergeant Ricky Clousing served in Iraq in 2004 and 2005 as a U.S. Army interrogator for the 82nd Airborne Division. Upon returning from Iraq, Clousing went AWOL from Fort Bragg, North Carolina. He left the following quote by Dr. Martin Luther King, Jr., on his bunk as he left Fort Bragg: "Cowardice asks the question, Is it safe? Expediency asks the question, Is it politic? But conscience asks the question, Is it right? And there comes a time when one must take a position that is neither safe, nor politic, nor popular, but because conscience tells one it is right."

Fourteen months later, on August 11, 2006, he went public with his opposition to the war during a press conference at the Veterans for Peace national conference in Seattle. Later that day, Clousing turned himself in to military police at Fort Lewis, Washington, where he was confined for two days before being ordered to Fort Bragg. Clousing was court-martialed on October 12, 2006, and pleaded guilty to being absent without leave. He was sentenced to three months' confinement, forfeiture of two-thirds pay while confined, and given a Bad Conduct discharge.[64]

At his sentencing hearing, Clousing continued to voice his concerns about the abuses of power that go without accountability and the everyday devastation of the occupation of Iraq. "My experiences in Iraq forced me to reevaluate my beliefs and ethics," he told the judge. "Ultimately, I felt like I could not serve."

The Army's 82nd Airborne Division opened two parallel investigations into disclosures made by Clousing about the abuse of power and lack of accountability of the U.S. military in Iraq, but it has not yet released the findings.

In response to charges related to his fourteen-month absence without leave, Clousing stated, "Since I left the Army, I have known that being court-martialed was a possibility I could face. I am at peace with my decision. I followed my conscience and, if need be, I will feel honored to join the ranks of others who have been prosecuted for doing the same."

Clousing did not claim to be a conscientious objector, as it is defined by the U.S. military. He is opposed to the war and occupation of Iraq based on his firsthand experience in country, which brought him to the conclusion that the Iraq War is a "war of aggression" that has "no legal basis to be fought."

Clousing was released from prison on December 22, 2006.[65]

Sergeant Ricky Clousing made the following statement at a press conference outside the Veterans for Peace convention in Seattle, Washington, on August 11, 2006.

~

Ricky Clousing's Statement

First, to my family, friends, brothers and sisters of the religious community, members of the press, and fellow citizens of this nation we are grateful to call home: thank you for your support here today before I turn myself over to military custody.

My name is Ricky Clousing. I am a sergeant in the United States Army, and I have served for three years. I have been absent from my unit since June 2005. Like many in uniform today, I enlisted after the events of September 11, wanting to defend the freedoms and privileges we enjoy here. After eighteen months of instruction, I completed my necessary training as an interrogator and was assigned to the 82nd

Airborne Division. As the invasion of Iraq unfolded, I felt confused about the premise behind such an attack. But in November of 2004 I deployed to Iraq in support of the first stage of elections to be held.

In Iraq I operated as an interrogator and was attached to tactical infantry units during daily patrol operations. As an interrogator, I spoke to Iraqis each day. This gave me an idea of what local civilians thought of coalition forces. Throughout my training, very appropriate guidelines for the treatment of prisoners were set. However, I witnessed our baseless incarceration of civilians. I saw civilians physically harassed. I saw an innocent Iraqi killed before me by U.S. troops. I saw the abuse of power that goes without accountability.

Being attached to a tactical infantry unit and being exposed to the brutalities of war, I began to second-guess my beliefs. I thought about these experiences and what they meant each day I was deployed and until I was back in garrison in April of 2005. Upon my return, I started to ask my unit the same questions I had been asking myself. Wearing the uniform demands subordination to your superiors and the orders passed down. But what if orders given violate morality, ethics, and even legality? If those orders go unquestioned down my chain of command, am I exempt from reevaluating them? My convictions, spiritually and politically, began to second-guess my ability to perform day-to-day functions as a soldier. I could not train or be trained under a false pretense of fighting for freedom.

Under the recommendation of my unit, I sought counsel from military chaplains and counselors, and as my feelings crystallized, I realized that I could not fulfill the duties expected of me. After months of questioning, I began considering the possibility of leaving. Each day, I felt haunted by my conscience that my association in uniform at this time was wrong, and my involvement, directly or indirectly, in this organization at this time was contradictory to my beliefs.

I stand here before you today about to surrender myself, which was always my intention. I do not know what to expect or the course of my future. We find ourselves in a pivotal era where we have traded humanity for patriotism, where we have traded our civil liberties for a sense of security. I stand before you sharing the same idea as Henry David

Thoreau: as a soldier, as an American, and as a human being, we mustn't lend ourselves to that same evil which we condemn.[66]

☙ Mark Wilkerson

Specialist Mark Wilkerson served in the U.S. Army's 4th Infantry Division, 720th Police Battalion in Iraq from March 2003 to March 2004. In November 2004, his request for conscientious objector status was denied by the Army. He subsequently refused redeployment back to Iraq on moral grounds and went AWOL for more than eighteen months. "I made the difficult decision to go AWOL and become a conscientious objector for political, spiritual, and personal reasons. After my experience in Iraq, I realized that I am not willing to kill, or be killed, or do anything else I consider morally wrong. There comes a time in a person's life when they must make the right moral decision for themselves, regardless of how popular that decision is in the eyes of others or what others feel about it."[67]

Wilkerson turned himself in to Fort Hood, Texas, on August 31, 2006, following a press conference in Crawford, Texas, at Camp Casey, Cindy Sheehan's antiwar protest encampment. On February 22, 2007, he was found guilty of desertion and missing a military movement, and sentenced to seven months' imprisonment and given a Bad Conduct discharge.[68] He was released from prison in July 2007.

☙

Mark Wilkerson's Statement

Today [August 31, 2006] is a big day for me. I am turning myself in from being absent without leave, or AWOL, from the military. I have been AWOL for a year and a half.

My name is Mark Wilkerson. My experience in the Army began in June, 2002, shortly after my high school graduation. I enlisted prior to September 11, but I found a new resolve to join after that tragic day. I thought that somehow, through my upcoming military experience, I would be able to avenge those people who had been killed on that day. After basic training, I ended up in Fort Hood, Texas, where in March 2003 I deployed to Iraq with the 720th Military Police Battalion. I was nervous and scared, but at that time I was supportive of my President's decision to go into Iraq, and I was optimistic about the good things that we could do there for the people of Iraq. I quickly learned that that wasn't going to happen.

I had many experiences in Iraq that made me question my mission and also made me change the way I viewed spirituality, relationships, our government, and my life in general. It was a complete life turnaround, which allowed me to come to the conclusion that military service was no longer the correct path for me to take. This revelation led me to apply as a conscientious objector immediately upon return from Iraq, in March 2004.

The military states that a conscientious objector is a person who objects to participation in all forms of war and whose belief is based on a religious, moral, or ethical belief system. I felt I met those requirements, though the military disagreed. I told myself I would never return to Iraq, but I would make sure I was discharged in the right and legal way. I told myself I would never go AWOL. In July, while my CO paper was still being processed, my unit was told we would be returning to Iraq in January 2005.

In November, my CO claim was denied, so I applied for a rebuttal, and was told it wouldn't be considered until my return from Iraq, more than a year away. So I made the difficult decision to go AWOL, for political, spiritual, and personal reasons. I am not willing to kill, or be killed, or do anything else I consider morally wrong, for reasons I don't believe in, and now, today, I am turning myself in to face the consequences of my actions.

I read a *USA Today* article that said that over 8,000 soldiers have gone AWOL during the Iraq War. I think it would be naive to assume that all 8,000 went AWOL in direct protest to the Iraq War, but I'm sure that many of them did. So this message is for those who are AWOL right now: you are not alone. Don't let anyone judge you for what you believe in.

As of August 27, there have been 2,628 U.S. soldiers killed in Iraq, on top of the over 19,000 wounded there. I honor and respect every soldier who has made the ultimate sacrifice for our country. I honor them and their families. May the soldiers who have been killed remind each and every one of us that life is short, and life is fragile, and life must be respected. I also respect every soldier who makes the decision to enlist in the military and to go to the wars in Iraq and Afghanistan, regardless of his personal opinions on war.

Let me remind you all as well that there are many other soldiers who should not be forgotten either: the large number who return from war with post-traumatic stress disorder, or PTSD, which is very hard to diagnose. Without treatment, many of these soldiers have a difficult time adjusting to their normal lives. Many soldiers affected with this disorder, this injury, don't come forward to make a claim, for one reason or another.

Again, I say to them: you are not alone. If you have a family member who is suffering, urge them to come forward and tell someone who can help. And I say this to every member of our Congress and our Senate, and even our President: *Don't leave any soldier behind.* Give them the help and support they need, because you sent them there.

I would like to thank everyone who has helped and supported me along this journey of the past year and a half—family, friends, fellow veterans. When I left the Army, I made what I felt was the right decision. I joined the military with honorable intentions, and I still feel honor in my heart. I love my country; I want no one to doubt that. I am unsure of what actions and punishments will be placed on me for my decision. I am scared, but I go with peace in my heart and hope for the future—not only my future, but the country's future as well.

This is a difficult and scary time for our country, but hopefully in the end, peace will rule this great land. John F. Kennedy once said that war will exist until that distant day when the conscientious objector enjoys the same reputation and prestige that the warrior does today. I look forward to that day.

There comes a time in a person's life when they must make the right moral decision for themselves, doubtless of how popular that decision is in others' eyes or what others feel about it. While I would not consider myself a very religious man, I do believe in the teachings of Jesus Christ. I would like to share two passages from the Bible. The first, from *Psalms*, Chapter 33, Verse 5: "Seek peace, and pursue it." The second, from *Matthew*, Chapter 5, Verse 9: "Blessed are the peacemakers, for they shall be called the sons of God." I believe that through my actions, I am doing my best to live by the values stated in those quotes.[69]

RESISTERS IN CANADA

During the Vietnam War, more than 50,000 American military resisters and deserters went to Canada. The resisters were generally draftees who went to avoid military service. The deserters were those who left the military and went for sanctuary. Pierre Trudeau, Prime Minister of Canada during the Vietnam War said, "Those who make a conscientious judgment that they must not participate in this war...have my complete sympathy, and indeed our political approach has been to give them access to Canada. Canada should be a refuge from militarism."[70]

At the time of the Vietnam War, U.S. citizens were able to apply for landed immigrant status at the Canadian border as they entered. They were interviewed, and, based on a point system that measured background, education, and other factors, border officials were able to make a decision on the spot. Trudeau's government even ordered the border police to refrain from asking questions about applicants' military status, so it would be easier for AWOL soldiers to cross safely into Canada.

In the 1980s, Canada's permanent residency law changed. Those requesting immigrant status must now apply at a Canadian embassy or consulate—outside of Canada—and it can be a lengthy process. U.S. military deserters cannot obtain immigrant status at the border or after they have entered the country. The only legal status available to them once they have arrived in Canada is as a refugee.

Since the Iraq War began, approximately 250 U.S military personnel have crossed the border into Canada. Thirty-five have identified themselves publicly. The rest are semi-underground, receiving help with housing, food, and work through the War Resisters Support Campaign. They have access to Canada's health care and social service systems and are eligible for work visas.

Twenty U.S. deserters have applied for refugee status, and, under possible pressure from the Bush administration, Canada's Immigration and Refugee Board has denied all twenty applications.[71] Jeremy Hinzman and Brandon Hughey's cases were heard by the Federal Court of Appeal, which dismissed their appeals on April 30, 2007, stating that they did not show that they had exhausted the means available to them in the U.S. to obtain conscientious objector status or a discharge. The Federal Court stated that their cases would more properly be made in the U.S., either within the military or through the U.S. courts. They have appealed their cases to the Supreme Court of Canada. Amnesty International and the International Human Rights Clinic are seeking intervener status in their cases.

The word *deserter* suggests cowardice, but these young men and women are anything but cowards. Following the dictates of conscience, they are now in legal jeopardy and immigration limbo. Being away from family and friends and living in a different country is a hardship, despite the help from Canadian supporters. Their conscientious and courageous efforts to choose among three difficult alternatives—serving in a war they find illegal and immoral, turning themselves in to authorities, or living in exile—deserve our respect.

One of the resisters in Canada is Private First Class Joshua Key, who served in Iraq: "I know that many Americans have their minds made up about people like me. They think we are cowards who just couldn't take it. I don't blame them. . . . I am not a coward and I never flinched from danger. The easiest thing would have been to keep on doing what I was told to do. Ever so slowly, as the jets raced and the illumination rounds burned and the houses fell down during the long Iraqi nights, my conscience returned. It could no longer be Army first, God second, and family third. It had to be the tiny voice inside me that would not sleep any longer. *I am not this man,* I told myself. *I cannot do these things any longer.*" Key said that a soldier's first obligation is to the "moral truth buried deep inside our own souls and that every person knows what is right and wrong and has the duty to choose right, regardless of what leaders tell us."[72]

✎ Jeremy Hinzman

During Army basic training, Jeremy Hinzman realized that everyone has a "strong, innate predisposition against killing, and the military breaks that down." He remembered that in target practice during basic training, "we started out with black circle targets. Then the circles grew shoulders and then the shoulders turned into torsos. Pretty soon they were human beings." Hinzman realized he "made the wrong career decision" when in basic training marching to the mess hall for a meal, everyone in his unit had to shout, "Trained to kill. Kill we will," and were threatened with push-ups if anyone did not show enough enthusiasm. He said he felt that the military was not merely training him to kill, but "to kill with a smile on my face." From that moment, Hinzman felt he had to get out of the Army.[73]

Yet, following basic training, Hinzman volunteered for airborne training and served in the U.S. Army's 82nd Airborne Division. Before deploying to Afghanistan in 2002, he had applied for conscientious objector status, and he was assigned to a noncombatant position—kitchen duty. "I had all this stuff internally that was telling me, I can't kill. I'll be happy to be Operation Human Shield, to be a pack mule and carry stuff, or be a combat medic and stick my neck out, no problem. If I die, that's the end. I mean we're all born with a death sentence and that's not what I have issues with. What I have issues with is taking other people's lives." He said he felt that he was living a lie. Joining the military voluntarily "doesn't mean that your ability to be a moral being should become static. Life is dynamic, and if you're confronted with doing something wrong, it's not right to abdicate your duty and obligation to be a moral being."[74] His application for CO status was denied.

After returning from Afghanistan, his unit was scheduled to be deployed to Iraq. Hinzman did not believe the Bush administration's reasons for the Iraq War; he thought it was only to benefit corporate America. In January 2004, at the age of 26, Hinzman went to Canada to seek asylum.

Canada's Immigration and Refugee Board denied Jeremy Hinzman refugee status, refusing to acknowledge him as a conscientious objector. The Immigration judge ruled: "I find that the claimants are not [Geneva] Convention refugees, as they have not established that they have a well-founded fear of persecution for a [Geneva] Convention ground in the U.S. I also find that they are not persons in need of protection, in that their removal to the U.S. would not subject them personally to a risk to their lives or to a risk of cruel and unusual treatment or punishment, and in that there are no substantial grounds to believe that their removal to the U.S. will subject them personally to a danger of torture."[75]

He has appealed his case to the Canadian Supreme Court.[76] Amnesty International considers that there is a significant risk that Hinzman would be imprisoned for one to five years for having left the armed forces without authorization, despite the fact that he had taken reasonable steps to obtain exemption from combatant duties on the ground of his conscientious objection. If he is forcibly returned and imprisoned, Amnesty International will adopt him as a prisoner of conscience.[77]

✎ Brandon Hughey

Army Specialist Brandon Hughey enlisted at age 17 so he'd be able to go to college. In December 2003, he was notified his unit would deploy to Iraq. Hughey believed President Bush had launched the war "based on lies" and refused "to let myself be a pawn in it...Just because I signed a contract doesn't mean I should throw out my moral principles." The day before his unit deployed, Hughey got a ride with a peace activist to Niagara Falls and entered Canada as a tourist.[78]

In Canada, he requested refugee status. "I feel that if a soldier is given an order that he knows to not only be illegal, but immoral as well, then it his responsibility to refuse that order. It is also my belief that if a soldier is refusing an order he knows to be wrong, it is not right for him to face persecution for it. If you were given an order to participate in an unlawful occupation that is resulting in the deaths of thousands of innocent people with no justifiable cause, would you be able to live with yourself if you carried out that order?" The Immigration and Refugee Board rejected his claim, saying that human rights abuses by coalition forces in Iraq are not systemic.

Like Jeremy Hinzman, Brandon Hughey's decision has been appealed to the Supreme Court of Canada. There are precedents in their favor. In the 1990s, the Canadian government gave refugee status to a Yemeni citizen who served in Saddam's army and to a soldier from Iraq. The Yemeni refused to participate in the invasion of Kuwait, and the Iranian refused to be party to chemical warfare. Both were denied refugee status at first, but the Canadian federal court reversed the decisions.[79]

✑ Joshua Key

Army combat engineer Private First Class Joshua Key deployed to Iraq in April 2003 and served seven months patrolling the streets of Fallujah, Ramadi, Al-Qa'im, and Al-Habbaniyah, blowing doors off Iraqi families' homes and rushing in on raids. He returned to Fort Carson, Colorado, in November 2003, on leave and decided not to go back to Iraq. "I left for Iraq with a purpose, but there were no weapons of mass destruction. The Iraqis had no military whatsoever. And I started to wonder. The atrocities that were happening to the innocent people of Iraq were the reason I deserted. I didn't want to be part of it anymore. I came home, and I deserted." In his book, *The Deserter's Tale,* Joshua Key describes American soldiers killing Iraqi civilians and committing other atrocities with impunity. He even witnessed Americans playing soccer with the heads of Iraqis.

Key said, "I am neither a coward nor a traitor.... I would not have deserted the U.S. Army, left my country, or chosen to speak out against the war in Iraq if American soldiers in my company had limited themselves to fighting enemy combatants. I left the war in Iraq because the American Army made no distinction between [combatants and civilians]."

In March 2005, at the age of 26, Joshua Key went to Canada with his wife and four young children. Two years later, in March 2007, three men claiming to be police visited the house in Toronto where he and his family had previously lived, seeking information about Key. Although Joshua Key faces charges of desertion in the U.S., Canada does not consider military offenses to be extraditable. Still, this incident had a chilling effect on Key and other deserters in Canada. The Canadian Immigration and Refugee Board rejected his application for refugee status, but Key is appealing the decision.[80]

∽ Patrick Hart

Sergeant Patrick Hart had served nine and a half years in the U.S. Army when he was sent to Iraq from April 2003 to March 2004. Photos taken by his fellow soldiers in Iraq began to disturb him. One showed a truck riddled with bullet holes when it failed to stop for a checkpoint. "They killed everyone inside, except for one." Another picture showed the sole survivor being treated for bullet wounds. There was a photo of a child, probably less than three years old, who had been burned by explosions or chemicals. Another set of photos showed corpses of mostly Iraqi soldiers, but some civilians, who had been burned to death or been killed by large-caliber machine guns. One dead Iraqi soldier's index finger had been shoved up his nose by American soldiers, and the caption read, "This is what happens when you're picking your nose instead of watching your sector." As Hart characterized it, "It's just the disregard for a human being."[81]

Two months after returning to the U.S., Patrick Hart heard British Member of Parliament (MP) George Galloway address the U.S. Senate, which had accused Galloway of being part of the UN Oil-for-Food scandal:

> I told the world that Iraq, contrary to your claims, did not have weapons of mass destruction. I told the world, contrary to your claims, that Iraq had no connection to al Qaeda. I told the world, contrary to your claims, that Iraq had no connection to the atrocity on 9/11/2001. I told the world, contrary to your claims, that the Iraqi people would resist a British and American invasion of their country and that the fall of Baghdad would not be the beginning of the end, but merely the end of the beginning. Senator, in everything I said about Iraq, I

turned out to be right and you turned out to be wrong and 100,000 people paid with their lives; 1,600 of them American soldiers sent to their deaths on a pack of lies; 15,000 of them wounded, many of them disabled forever on a pack of lies.[82]

Inspired by Galloway, Hart started thinking about desertion. He refused a second deployment to Iraq and went instead to Canada. His wife, Jill, opposed his decision and even cooperated with the Army to help find him. But after Hart's commanding officer said the Army would terminate their son Rian's medical care because Hart was AWOL, she and Rian joined Hart in Toronto.[83]

✎ Chris Magaoay

U.S. Marine Lance Corporal Christopher Magaoay of Maui, Hawai'i, refused to deploy with his unit to Iraq and went to Canada on March 7, 2006. Magaoay said he is not against war in general but against the war in Iraq, which he called a war of aggression, not sanctioned by the United Nations, and therefore illegal.

Magaoay found the instructions he received from his officers to be troubling. "The mentality is to shoot anyone who gets close to you and especially those who look like insurgents. I know that killing people just because they are of a different race is wrong no matter what the rules of engagement are. That is why I left." Magaoay said a senior officer told him not to take responsibility for any civilian deaths in Iraq, whether the Marines caused the deaths or not. "That just disgusted me. They wanted us to lie. The Marine Corps is supposed to be the most honorable service in the United States, and I wasn't expecting to hear them say this."[84]

Magaoay went to Canada with his wife, who is a Canadian citizen. He applied to obtain refugee status as a statement about the war in Iraq, but the Immigration Board denied his request and told him to apply for residency status through his wife.

∽ Darrell Anderson

Specialist Darrell Anderson joined the Army in January 2003, at the age of 20. A year later, he was sent to Iraq with the 1st Armored Division. Seven months into his deployment, he was wounded by a roadside bomb. After witnessing the abuse and killing of Iraqi civilians and being ordered to fire on an automobile containing Iraqi civilians, Anderson concluded that the war is wrong.

"[When I joined the Army,] I thought I was going to free Iraqi people. I thought I was going to do a good thing. I didn't know anything about the politics of it." During his first patrols in Baghdad, he thought, What are we doing here? Are we looking for weapons of mass destruction? No. Are we helping the people? No, they hate us. What are we working toward, apart from just staying alive? If this was my neighborhood and foreign soldiers were doing this, then what would I be doing? He was distressed at the racism and hatred of some of his fellow soldiers, but within a few months he found himself "cocking my weapon at innocent civilians without any sympathy or humanity."[85]

"I believed that if I returned to Iraq and followed military procedures and orders, that I would eventually kill innocent people. I believed it was my human right to choose not to do so, and my military duty to resist this war. I feel that by going to Canada and resisting, I made up for the things I did in Iraq. I feel I made up for the sins I committed in this war." In December 2004, while on holiday leave in Kentucky, Anderson decided to leave the Army. His parents drove him to Canada.

In Canada, Anderson appeared at peace rallies and gave interviews to international publications, attacking the Bush administration's policies. Despite family pressure for him to stay in Canada, Anderson felt he had to return home to "speak against President George W. Bush, even if it means a trial and going to jail." He said returning to the U.S. is the only way he can heal himself from the post-traumatic stress of being in Iraq.[86]

"I just couldn't live up in Canada anymore without work permits and health care and the support of my family, while dealing with post-traumatic stress from Iraq. I was working under the table as cheap labor in construction, cooking, just scraping by. I went to a psychiatrist a few times, but I just couldn't afford the transportation to get there anymore. And so, I wasn't living very well, but I had my freedom for the time I was there. And also I feel that I want to put on my uniform and stand on a military base and resist the war, because it was something that I wasn't strong enough to do before."[87]

On October 3, 2006, Anderson returned from Canada and turned himself into military custody. He was released from the military on October 6, 2006, after receiving an Other than Honorable discharge without facing court-martial.[88]

ᑫ **Ivan Brobeck**

Ivan Brobeck served seven months as a U.S. Marine in Iraq before deserting and going to Canada in April 2005. During his tour of duty, he witnessed the abuse of Iraqi detainees and the killing of civilians at military checkpoints. He said, "A majority of Marines know this war is pointless. But orders are orders. Going AWOL is always a hard decision because it means leaving everything and everyone you know."

After eight months in Canada, Brobeck surrendered to military authorities in Washington, DC, in November, 2006. On December 5, 2006, at his court-martial at Quantico Marine Base, Virginia, Brobeck pleaded guilty to unauthorized absence and missing movement. He was sentenced to eight months in a military brig, forfeiture of two-thirds pay, and a Bad Conduct discharge. Due to a pretrial agreement, Brobeck was required to serve only two months of the sentence, with the remaining time suspended. He was released on February 5, 2007.[89]

On November 6, 2006, the day Ivan Brobeck turned himself in to military authorities, he wrote a letter to President Bush and members of Congress:

> I was willing to join the military and risk my life for my coun-
> try and to fight for what is right just like others have done.
> ...When the U.S. was going to war with Iraq, I was confident
> that my country must be doing the right thing. I couldn't see
> a reason why they would lie to us.... I left for Iraq in March

of 2004. It wasn't until I got there that I found out what was really happening. I didn't need the news or to hear speeches to tell me that what was happening there was wrong. It was all as clear as day. The city I went to was called Mahmudiyah and had around 200,000 people. There was just a constant disrespect for the people, like pointing guns at the people just to get them to stop. There was also harsh treatment of detainees.

Checkpoints are where innocent civilians die. When manning a checkpoint, about fifty meters away is something called the TRP (target reference point). The TRP is usually marked by a cone or some sort of debris. If someone passes that line you have to open fire on the vehicle and the person inside.

I came back from Iraq in October of 2004. I was willing to stay in the military and put the events that happened in Iraq behind me. But when I heard rumors of us returning to Iraq, the stress and anxiety of what happened there started coming back to me. I was not willing to go back and fight a war that I did not believe was right, and I didn't want to put myself in a situation were I would possibly kill an innocent civilian. So, I went AWOL and hid out at a friend's house until I figured out what to do. While I was AWOL, my mom took me to a therapist who diagnosed me with PTSD.

Since I was not willing to return to Iraq, the only option I saw was to go to Canada. I have spent nearly two years there living, working, and married to my wife (who is six months pregnant).

Please, President Bush: do what is right. And do everything you can to bring our troops home from Iraq.[90]

✎ Kyle Snyder

Kyle Snyder joined the U.S. Army because he needed the money from the signing bonus ($5,000), college aid, and health coverage. "I joined the military when I was 19 years old. I wasn't a good kid. I didn't have a good background. I was in foster homes from 13 to 17, then when I was 17, I went through a government program called Job Corps. From

13 all the way up, I didn't have parental figures in my life. My parents divorced; my father was really abusive toward my mother and he was abusive toward me. I was put in Social Services when I was 13. I was an easy target for recruiters, plain and simple."[91]

Snyder was trained to be a construction engineer, but when he got to Iraq, he became a .50-caliber gunner escorting high-ranking officers. After seeing a new member of his unit shoot and cripple an Iraqi for life, Snyder requested an investigation of the shooting and was told not to question another soldier's decision to fire on Iraqi civilians. In a journal entry two months into his tour, he wrote, "Shots were fired at us right in the middle of downtown during broad daylight. Children's screams I will never forget. The smell of fresh blood. I need someone. How can I be loved if I am witness to such things almost weekly? I am a monster. Emotionless and like a machine." He adds, "I don't think I saw one [Iraqi] who was happy to see me or the other soldiers. It might have been that way in different cities, but not in Mosul. People would throw things at your convoy and give you these looks."[92]

While on leave from Iraq in April 2005, Snyder went AWOL to Canada. He petitioned the Canadian government for refugee status and waited more than a year for a hearing. Finally, on October 31, 2006, Snyder came back to the U.S. to turn himself in to Fort Knox, Kentucky. By prior agreement, he understood he would be discharged, as Darrell Anderson had been. But when he arrived at Fort Knox, he was ordered to return to his unit, which was about to deploy to Iraq for another tour. Facing either a court-martial or redeployment to Iraq, Snyder went AWOL again.

In December 2006, police in Alameda, California, attempted to arrest Snyder at a public gathering. The Alameda police told the *San Francisco Chronicle* the Army had requested his arrest. Kyle Snyder decided to return to Canada and marry his Canadian fiancée.

On February 23, 2007, police in Nelson, British Columbia, without a warrant, arrested Snyder in his home for unspecified immigration violations, and took him to jail. He was not read his rights or allowed to call his lawyer. The Nelson police told him he would be deported to the U.S., where he is wanted for unauthorized absence from the Army.

After calls to members of the Canadian Parliament, who then called the Canadian Citizenship and Immigration Department, immigration officials told the Nelson police they had no legal basis for holding Snyder. He was released after six hours. An immigration official in Vancouver said Snyder had been arrested at the request of the U.S. Army. Being AWOL from another country's military is not an extraditable offense in Canada.[93]

Kyle Snyder's Statement

It was a hard decision to leave Iraq and my friends, whom I had fought for and would have died for. But I told them in advance I was considering this decision. I went through a breakdown for one week after my plane went back to Kuwait without me.

Some people don't agree with what I've done and have sent me emails saying I should be hanged or shot. My real parents have rejected me. My father thinks I'm a disgrace, and my mother thinks my leaving Iraq was a sin and I should repent. It's been four and a half years since I've seen them. The first thing I would have done if I'd been discharged was to go to a Thanksgiving dinner with my family. But I don't want to see them when I'm in this position. However, my foster parents who actually raised me are really for me.

Eight thousand people are AWOL in the U.S., hiding in the shadows, and all they want to do is to be discharged and get on with their lives. One-third of all homeless people on the streets in the U.S. now are Viet Nam–era veterans. I don't want to see people my age living on the streets. I don't want to be part of the next generation of homeless people.

I don't regret going to Canada, and I don't regret coming back and becoming part of the war resistance movement. There's not a day that goes by without me thinking about the 500,000 Iraqis and 3,000 Americans who have died. I support the troops but oppose the war. I want my friends home so I don't have to question anymore. I don't believe in the Bush administration. One minute I'm looked at as a hero, and the next as a traitor. It's difficult for me to understand that kind of logic.[94]

BRITISH RESISTERS

M ore than 11,000 British soldiers have gone absent without leave since the Iraq War began. Almost 1,000 soldiers are currently AWOL, according to the British Ministry of Defence. Many of these have left the military, it seems, because they feel the invasion and occupation of Iraq are illegal.

✍ Ben Griffin

In 2006, after three months in Baghdad, Ben Griffin, an eight-year Army veteran and member of the elite SAS Parachute Regiment, told his commander that he would not fight beside American forces, because he had witnessed them commit "dozens of illegal acts." He said American soldiers viewed Iraqis as *untermenschen*—the Nazi word for persons regarded as subhuman. He said, "The American military's 'gung-ho and trigger-happy mentality' and tactics had completely undermined any chance of winning the hearts and minds of the Iraqi population.... Many innocent civilians were arrested in nighttime raids and interrogated by American soldiers, imprisoned in the notorious Abu Ghraib or handed over to the Iraqi authorities and 'most probably' tortured."

Griffin later told his SAS commanders that he could not take part in a war that he regarded as "illegal."[95] He believed that the Prime Minister and the Government had repeatedly lied over the war's conduct. "I did not join the British Army to conduct American foreign policy," he said. Expecting to be labeled a coward and to face a court-martial and imprisonment, he described refusing to fight as "the most difficult decision of my life."[96]

But rather than court-martial him, the British Army discharged Griffin "with a testimonial describing him as a balanced, honest, loyal, and determined individual who possesses the strength of character to have the courage of his convictions."[97]

✺ Malcolm Kendall-Smith

Flight Lieutenant Malcolm Kendall-Smith, a Royal Air Force (RAF) doctor, refused to return to Iraq for a third tour of duty on the grounds that the war was illegal. He had served two tours, but had "a change of mind" in July 2005 after reading the previously classified legal advice given to the British government before the decision to join the Americans in invading Iraq."[98] On April 13, 2006, Kendall-Smith was tried for "failing to comply with lawful orders."

A former university philosophy tutor with dual British and New Zealand citizenship, Kendall-Smith argued that the invasion of Iraq was "a moral equivalent" to a Nazi war crime and that "the ongoing presence of U.S.-led forces in Iraq was illegal." He told the military hearing that he had refused to serve "because he did not want to be complicit with an 'act of aggression' contrary to international law."[99]

Kendall-Smith was charged with disobeying a lawful order. The prosecution maintained that "the presence of U.S.-led forces in Iraq was legal, the prosecution declared, because they were there at the request of the country's democratically elected government."[100]

Judge Advocate Jack Bayliss told Kendall-Smith that the court-martial panel of five RAF officers "believed he had acted on moral grounds." However, he accused him of an "amazing arrogance" and said he intended to make an example of him. "Obedience of orders is at the heart of any disciplined force," he said. "Refusal to obey orders means that the force is not a disciplined force but a disorganized rabble. Those who wear the Queen's uniform cannot pick and choose which orders they will obey. Those who seek to do so must face the serious consequences."[101] Kendall-Smith was found guilty of failure to comply with five lawful orders and sentenced to eight months' incarceration, which was served in a civilian prison. "He was also ordered to pay £20,000 toward his defense costs."[102]

Flight Lieutenant Malcolm Kendall-Smith was released early from his prison sentence and placed under daily curfew. He was also banned from having contact with the media until the end of 2006.

Shortly after his conviction by the British military court-martial on April 13, 2006, Kendall-Smith made the following statement:

❦

Malcolm Kendall-Smith's Statement

I have been convicted and sentenced, a very distressing experience. But I still believe I was right to make the stand that I did and refuse to follow orders to deploy to Iraq—orders I believe were illegal. I am resigned to what may happen to me in the next few months. I shall remain resilient and true to my beliefs, which, I believe, are shared by so many others.

Iraq was the only reason I could not follow the order to deploy. As a commissioned officer, I am required to consider every order given to me. Further, I am required to consider the legality of such an order not only as to its effect on domestic but also international law. I was subjected, as was the entire population, to propaganda depicting force against Iraq to be lawful. I have studied in very great depth the various commentaries and briefing notes, including one prepared by the Attorney General, and in particular the main note to the Prime Minister dated 7 March 2003. I have satisfied myself that the actions of the armed forces with the deployment of troops were an illegal act—as indeed was the conflict. To comply with an order that I believe unlawful places me in breach of domestic and international law, something I am not prepared to do . . . To take the decision that I did caused great sadness, but I had no other choice.[103]

❦ Mohisin Khan

In 1999, Mohisin Khan enlisted in the British Air Force as a medical assistant, to serve nine years' active duty plus six years in the Royal Air Force Reserves. In January 2001, Khan applied for early release from active duty, and his request was granted. He became a reservist. In January 2003, Mohisin Khan was recalled to active military service as a part of the mobilization of reserves in the run-up to the war on Iraq.[104]

Khan refused, "because he did not want to fight against fellow Muslims." On October 7, 2004, he "lost his appeal in the High Court against his prosecution by the RAF for going absent without leave."

"The High Court of Justice ruled that the right to conscientious objection does not amount to a defense in law against punishment for absence without leave. The RAF punished Khan after his arrest with the loss of nine days' pay and seven days' privileges."[105]

6

Epilogue

*"Without debate, without criticism, no administration
and no country can succeed—and no republic can
survive."*[1]

–President John F. Kennedy

I n 1969, Pentagon analyst Daniel Ellsberg leaked a 7,000-page, top-
secret study of American decision-making in the war in Southeast
Asia. The study, called the Pentagon Papers, was published by the
New York Times in 1971. It revealed "patterns of official deception,"
including the secret bombing of Cambodia and Laos without congressional authorization.[2]

Although the Pentagon Papers did not cover the period of Richard
Nixon's presidency, the Nixon administration attempted to prosecute
Ellsberg for the release of "classified material relating to the national
defense, where national security would be gravely imperiled . . . [citing]
the 1917 Espionage Act, which forbids the publication of national defense secrets."[3] Nixon also had the office of Ellsberg's psychiatrist burglarized to try to find information that could undermine his credibility.[4]

Ellsberg was charged with espionage, theft, and conspiracy, and faced
115 years in prison if convicted. On May 11, 1973, after a five-month
trial, the judge dismissed the charges, citing "improper government
conduct," including illegal wiretapping.[5] In a secretly taped conversation that took place in the Oval Office the day the trial ended, Nixon
angrily told Chief of Staff H.R. Haldeman: "[O]n this national security thing, we have the rocky situation where the sonofabitching thief
is made a national hero and is going to get off on a mistrial. And the
New York Times gets a Pulitzer Prize for stealing documents. They're
trying to get at us with thieves. What in the name of God have we
come to?"[6]

The group that burglarized Ellsberg's psychiatrist's office were the same Cuban exiles later convicted of breaking into Democratic National Committee Headquarters at the Watergate Hotel in Washington, DC. A week after the Ellsberg trial ended, the Senate began hearings on the Watergate burglary. At the same time, the House of Representatives began to draft articles of impeachment that included the charge of abuse of power regarding the break-in into Ellsberg's psychiatrist's office.[7]

Every presidential administration needs to be held accountable for its actions. Voices of conscience like Daniel Ellsberg's play a crucial role in exposing abuses of power and even criminal actions. Dissent from within, including whistle-blowing, leaking documents, and publicly resigning in protest, is an essential component of our democracy. When a President uses executive privilege to withhold key information from the public, the legislature, and even the judiciary in violation of the intent of the Constitution and creates an atmosphere of extreme secrecy, who else but someone with inside knowledge can reveal the truth? In times of crisis, administrations might characterize whistle-blowing as dangerous to national security or "revealing state secrets." In many cases, so-called state secrets have turned out to be illegal actions by the government itself.

As we go to press, four and a half years into the war on Iraq, the Bush administration has yet to be held accountable for its actions, including conducting illegal warrantless domestic eavesdropping; using "enhanced interrogation techniques" that amount to torture; and imprisoning people indefinitely, here and abroad, without filing charges. We also need to know if any provocative actions have been taken inside Iran. Government employees are the ones who can inform us about these possibly illegal activities.

Security and secrecy are not synonymous, although some administrations act as though they are.[8] When government oversight fails, tragedies, such as a nation going to war on false premises, can occur. In 1964, President Lyndon B. Johnson used manipulated intelligence to convince Congress to pass the Gulf of Tonkin Resolution, which led to a massive escalation of the war in Vietnam.[9] The run-up to the war in Iraq is another example of the deadly consequence of government secrecy and the effort to suppress democracy.

In a 2004 *New York Times* Op-Ed, entitled "Truths Worth Telling," Daniel Ellsberg encouraged Bush administration officials to step forward and document how the White House misled the American public into supporting the Iraq War. In 1978, Senator Wayne Morse, one of only two senators who had voted against the Gulf of Tonkin Resolution, told Ellsberg that if he had leaked the Pentagon Papers in 1964—five years earlier than he did (and seven years before the *New York Times* published them)—that resolution would not have passed.

> That was hard to hear. But in 1964 it hadn't occurred to me to break my vow of secrecy. Though I knew that the war was a mistake, my loyalties then were to the Secretary of Defense and the President. *It took five years of war before I recognized the higher loyalty all officials owe to the Constitution, the rule of law, the soldiers in harm's way or their fellow citizens.*[10]

The road of dissent is not easy. Families can split over an act of conscience taken by a family member. Friends and colleagues can become former friends and former colleagues. Acts of conscience taken for the long-term good of our country—not for the benefit of one political party or President—are frequently castigated. Government employees, some of whom have worked for many administrations, Republican and Democratic, are too often called unpatriotic for their actions. Yet, like Ellsberg, many government insiders do take the difficult path of challenging an administration on its illegal actions, despite the adverse consequences they might face.

Acts of conscience like these not only hold the present administration accountable, they put future administrations on notice that there will always be some government insiders who, on behalf of their fellow citizens, will expose wrongdoings to try to prevent tragedies like the invasions of Vietnam and Iraq.

Appendix

United Nations Security Council Resolution 1441 on Iraq Disarmament Obligations
November 8, 2002

Holds Iraq in material breach of disarmament obligations and offers final chance to comply. Instructs weapons inspections to resume and repeats warning of "serious consequences" for continued violations.

The Security Council,

Recalling all its previous relevant resolutions, in particular its resolutions 661 (1990) of 6 August 1990, 678 (1990) of 29 November 1990, 686 (1991) of 2 March 1991, 687 (1991) of 3 April 1991, 688 (1991) of 5 April 1991, 707 (1991) of 15 August 1991, 715 (1991) of 11 October 1991, 986 (1995) of 14 April 1995, and 1284 (1999) of 17 December 1999, and all the relevant statements of its President,

Recalling also its resolution 1382 (2001) of 29 November 2001 and its intention to implement it fully,

Recognizing the threat Iraq's non-compliance with Council resolutions and proliferation of weapons of mass destruction and long-range missiles poses to international peace and security,

Recalling that its resolution 678 (1990) authorized Member States to use all necessary means to uphold and implement its resolution 660 (1990) of 2 August 1990 and all relevant resolutions subsequent to resolution 660 (1990) and to restore international peace and security in the area,

Further recalling that its resolution 687 (1991) imposed obligations on Iraq as a necessary step for achievement of its stated objective of restoring international peace and security in the area,

Deploring the fact that Iraq has not provided an accurate, full, final, and complete disclosure, as required by resolution 687 (1991), of all aspects of its programmes to develop weapons of mass destruction and ballistic missiles with a range greater than one hundred and fifty kilometres, and of all holdings of such weapons, their components and production facilities and locations, as well as all other nuclear programmes, including any which it claims are for purposes not related to nuclear-weapons-usable material,

Deploring further that Iraq repeatedly obstructed immediate, unconditional, and unrestricted access to sites designated by the United Nations Special Commission (UNSCOM) and the International Atomic Energy Agency (IAEA), failed to cooperate fully and unconditionally with UNSCOM and IAEA weapons inspectors, as required by resolution 687 (1991), and ultimately ceased all cooperation with UNSCOM and the IAEA in 1998,

Deploring the absence, since December 1998, in Iraq of international monitoring, inspection, and verification, as required by relevant resolutions, of weapons of mass destruction and ballistic missiles, in spite of the Council's repeated demands that Iraq provide immediate, unconditional, and unrestricted access to the United Nations Monitoring, Verification and Inspection Commission (UNMOVIC), established in resolution 1284 (1999) as the successor organization to UNSCOM, and the IAEA, and *regretting* the consequent prolonging of the crisis in the region and the suffering of the Iraqi people,

Deploring also that the Government of Iraq has failed to comply with its commitments pursuant to resolution 687 (1991) with regard to terrorism, pursuant to resolution 688 (1991) to end repression of its civilian population and to provide access by international humanitarian organizations to all those in need of assistance in Iraq, and pursuant to resolutions 686 (1991), 687 (1991), and 1284 (1999) to return or cooperate in accounting for Kuwaiti and third country nationals wrongfully detained by Iraq, or to return Kuwaiti property wrongfully seized by Iraq,

Recalling that in its resolution 687 (1991) the Council declared that a cease-fire would be based on acceptance by Iraq of the provisions of that resolution, including the obligations on Iraq contained therein,

Determined to ensure full and immediate compliance by Iraq without conditions or restrictions with its obligations under resolution 687 (1991) and other relevant resolutions and *recalling* that the resolutions of the Council constitute the governing standard of Iraqi compliance,

Recalling that the effective operation of UNMOVIC, as the successor organization to the Special Commission, and the IAEA is essential for the implementation of resolution 687 (1991) and other relevant resolutions,

Noting the letter dated 16 September 2002 from the Minister for Foreign Affairs of Iraq addressed to the Secretary-General is a necessary first step toward rectifying Iraq's continued failure to comply with relevant Council resolutions,

Noting further the letter dated 8 October 2002 from the Executive Chairman of UNMOVIC and the Director-General of the IAEA to General Al-Saadi of the Government of Iraq laying out the practical arrangements, as a follow-up to their meeting in Vienna, that are prerequisites for the resumption of inspections in Iraq by UNMOVIC and the IAEA, and *expressing* the gravest concern at the continued failure by the Government of Iraq to provide confirmation of the arrangements as laid out in that letter,

Reaffirming the commitment of all Member States to the sovereignty and territorial integrity of Iraq, Kuwait, and the neighbouring States,

Commending the Secretary-General and members of the League of Arab States and its Secretary-General for their efforts in this regard,

Determined to secure full compliance with its decisions,

Acting under Chapter VII of the Charter of the United Nations,

1. *Decides* that Iraq has been and remains in material breach of its obligations under relevant resolutions, including resolution 687 (1991), in particular through Iraq's failure to cooperate with United Nations inspectors and the IAEA, and to complete the actions required under paragraphs 8 to 13 of resolution 687 (1991);

2. *Decides,* while acknowledging paragraph 1 above, to afford Iraq, by this resolution, a final opportunity to comply with its disarmament obligations under relevant resolutions of the Council; and accordingly *decides* to set up an enhanced inspection regime with the aim of bringing to full and verified completion the disarmament process established by resolution 687 (1991) and subsequent resolutions of the Council;

3. *Decides* that, in order to begin to comply with its disarmament obligations, in addition to submitting the required biannual declarations, the Government of Iraq shall provide to UNMOVIC, the IAEA, and the Council, not later than 30 days from the date of this resolution, a currently accurate, full, and complete declaration of all aspects of its programmes to develop chemical, biological, and nuclear weapons, ballistic missiles, and other delivery systems such as unmanned aerial vehicles and dispersal systems designed for use on aircraft, including any holdings and precise locations of such weapons, components, sub-components, stocks of agents, and related material and equipment, the locations and work of its research, development and production facilities, as well as all other chemical, biological, and nuclear programmes, including any which it claims are for purposes not related to weapon production or material;

4. *Decides* that false statements or omissions in the declarations submitted by Iraq pursuant to this resolution and failure by Iraq at any time to comply with, and cooperate fully in the implementation of, this resolution shall

constitute a further material breach of Iraq's obligations and will be reported to the Council for assessment in accordance with paragraphs 11 and 12 below;

5. *Decides* that Iraq shall provide UNMOVIC and the IAEA immediate, unimpeded, unconditional, and unrestricted access to any and all, including underground, areas, facilities, buildings, equipment, records, and means of transport which they wish to inspect, as well as immediate, unimpeded, unrestricted, and private access to all officials and other persons whom UNMOVIC or the IAEA wish to interview in the mode or location of UNMOVIC's or the IAEA's choice pursuant to any aspect of their mandates; further *decides* that UNMOVIC and the IAEA may at their discretion conduct interviews inside or outside of Iraq, may facilitate the travel of those interviewed and family members outside of Iraq, and that, at the sole discretion of UNMOVIC and the IAEA, such interviews may occur without the presence of observers from the Iraqi Government; and *instructs* UNMOVIC and *requests* the IAEA to resume inspections no later than 45 days following adoption of this resolution and to update the Council 60 days thereafter;

6. *Endorses* the 8 October 2002 letter from the Executive Chairman of UNMOVIC and the Director-General of the IAEA to General Al-Saadi of the Government of Iraq, which is annexed hereto, and *decides* that the contents of the letter shall be binding upon Iraq;

7. *Decides further* that, in view of the prolonged interruption by Iraq of the presence of UNMOVIC and the IAEA and in order for them to accomplish the tasks set forth in this resolution and all previous relevant resolutions and notwithstanding prior understandings, the Council hereby establishes the following revised or additional authorities, which shall be binding upon Iraq, to facilitate their work in Iraq:

   – UNMOVIC and the IAEA shall determine the composition of their inspection teams and ensure that these teams are composed of the most qualified and experienced experts available;

   – All UNMOVIC and IAEA personnel shall enjoy the privileges and immunities, corresponding to those of experts on mission, provided in the Convention on Privileges and Immunities of the United Nations and the Agreement on the Privileges and Immunities of the IAEA;

   – UNMOVIC and the IAEA shall have unrestricted rights of entry into and out of Iraq, the right to free, unrestricted, and immediate movement to and from inspection sites, and the right to inspect any sites and buildings, including immediate, unimpeded, unconditional, and unrestricted access to Presidential Sites equal to that at other sites, notwithstanding the provisions of resolution 1154 (1998);

– UNMOVIC and the IAEA shall have the right to be provided by Iraq the names of all personnel currently and formerly associated with Iraq's chemical, biological, nuclear, and ballistic missile programmes and the associated research, development, and production facilities;

– Security of UNMOVIC and IAEA facilities shall be ensured by sufficient United Nations security guards;

– UNMOVIC and the IAEA shall have the right to declare, for the purposes of freezing a site to be inspected, exclusion zones, including surrounding areas and transit corridors, in which Iraq will suspend ground and aerial movement so that nothing is changed in or taken out of a site being inspected;

– UNMOVIC and the IAEA shall have the free and unrestricted use and landing of fixed- and rotary-winged aircraft, including manned and unmanned reconnaissance vehicles;

– UNMOVIC and the IAEA shall have the right at their sole discretion verifiably to remove, destroy, or render harmless all prohibited weapons, subsystems, components, records, materials, and other related items, and the right to impound or close any facilities or equipment for the production thereof; and

– UNMOVIC and the IAEA shall have the right to free import and use of equipment or materials for inspections and to seize and export any equipment, materials, or documents taken during inspections, without search of UNMOVIC or IAEA personnel or official or personal baggage;

8. *Decides further* that Iraq shall not take or threaten hostile acts directed against any representative or personnel of the United Nations or the IAEA or of any Member State taking action to uphold any Council resolution;

9. *Requests* the Secretary-General immediately to notify Iraq of this resolution, which is binding on Iraq; demands that Iraq confirm within seven days of that notification its intention to comply fully with this resolution; and *demands further* that Iraq cooperate immediately, unconditionally, and actively with UNMOVIC and the IAEA;

10. *Requests* all Member States to give full support to UNMOVIC and the IAEA in the discharge of their mandates, including by providing any information related to prohibited programmes or other aspects of their mandates, including on Iraqi attempts since 1998 to acquire prohibited items, and by recommending sites to be inspected, persons to be interviewed, conditions of such interviews, and data to be collected, the results of which shall be reported to the Council by UNMOVIC and the IAEA;

11. *Directs* the Executive Chairman of UNMOVIC and the Director-General of the IAEA to report immediately to the Council any interference by Iraq with inspection activities, as well as any failure by Iraq to comply with its disarmament obligations, including its obligations regarding inspections under this resolution;

12. *Decides* to convene immediately upon receipt of a report in accordance with paragraphs 4 or 11 above, in order to consider the situation and the need for full compliance with all of the relevant Council resolutions in order to secure international peace and security;

13. *Recalls,* in that context, that the Council has repeatedly warned Iraq that it will face serious consequences as a result of its continued violations of its obligations;

14. *Decides* to remain seized of the matter.

United States Congress Authorization for the Use of Military Force Against Iraq
October 2, 2002

Whereas in 1990 in response to Iraq's war of aggression against and illegal occupation of Kuwait, the United States forged a coalition of nations to liberate Kuwait and its people in order to defend the national security of the United States and enforce United Nations Security Council resolutions relating to Iraq;

Whereas after the liberation of Kuwait in 1991, Iraq entered into a United Nations sponsored cease-fire agreement pursuant to which Iraq unequivocally agreed, among other things, to eliminate its nuclear, biological, and chemical weapons programs and the means to deliver and develop them, and to end its support for international terrorism;

Whereas the efforts of international weapons inspectors, United States intelligence agencies, and Iraqi defectors led to the discovery that Iraq had large stockpiles of chemical weapons and a large scale biological weapons program, and that Iraq had an advanced nuclear weapons development program that was much closer to producing a nuclear weapon than intelligence reporting had previously indicated;

Whereas Iraq, in direct and flagrant violation of the cease-fire, attempted to thwart the efforts of weapons inspectors to identify and destroy Iraq's weapons of mass destruction stockpiles and development capabilities, which finally resulted in the withdrawal of inspectors from Iraq on October 31, 1998;

Whereas in 1998 Congress concluded that Iraq's continuing weapons of mass destruction programs threatened vital United States interests and international peace and security, declared Iraq to be in "material and unacceptable breach of its international obligations" and urged the President "to take appropriate action, in accordance with the Constitution and relevant laws of the United States, to bring Iraq into compliance with its international obligations" (Public Law 105–235);

Whereas Iraq both poses a continuing threat to the national security of the United States and international peace and security in the Persian Gulf region and remains in material and unacceptable breach of its international obliga-

tions by, among other things, continuing to possess and develop a significant chemical and biological weapons capability, actively seeking a nuclear
weapons capability, and supporting and harboring terrorist organizations;

Whereas Iraq persists in violating resolutions of the United Nations Security Council by continuing to engage in brutal repression of its civilian population thereby threatening international peace and security in the region, by
refusing to release, repatriate, or account for non-Iraqi citizens wrongfully
detained by Iraq, including an American serviceman, and by failing to return
property wrongfully seized by Iraq from Kuwait;

Whereas the current Iraqi regime has demonstrated its capability and willingness to use weapons of mass destruction against other nations and its own
people;

Whereas the current Iraqi regime has demonstrated its continuing hosti-
lity toward, and willingness to attack, the United States, including by attempting in 1993 to assassinate former President Bush and by firing on many
thousands of occasions on United States and Coalition Armed Forces engaged
in enforcing the resolutions of the United Nations Security Council;

Whereas members of al Qaida, an organization bearing responsibility
for attacks on the United States, its citizens, and interests, including the attacks
that occurred on September 11, 2001, are known to be in Iraq;

Whereas Iraq continues to aid and harbor other international terrorist
organizations, including organizations that threaten the lives and safety of
American citizens;

Whereas the attacks on the United States of September 11, 2001, under-
scored the gravity of the threat posed by the acquisition of weapons of mass
destruction by international terrorist organizations;

Whereas Iraq's demonstrated capability and willingness to use weapons of
mass destruction, the risk that the current Iraqi regime will either employ those
weapons to launch a surprise attack against the United States or its Armed
Forces or provide them to international terrorists who would do so, and the
extreme magnitude of harm that would result to the United States and its citizens from such an attack, combine to justify action by the United States to
defend itself;

Whereas United Nations Security Council Resolution 678 authorizes the
use of all necessary means to enforce United Nations Security Council Resolution 660 and subsequent relevant resolutions and to compel Iraq to cease
certain activities that threaten international peace and security, including
the development of weapons of mass destruction and refusal or obstruction of

United Nations weapons inspections in violation of United Nations Security Council Resolution 687, repression of its civilian population in violation of United Nations Security Council Resolution 688, and threatening its neighbors or United Nations operations in Iraq in violation of United Nations Security Council Resolution 949;

Whereas Congress in the Authorization for Use of Military Force Against Iraq Resolution (Public Law 102–1) has authorized the President "to use United States Armed Forces pursuant to United Nations Security Council Resolution 678 (1990) in order to achieve implementation of Security Council Resolutions 660, 661, 662, 664, 665, 666, 667, 669, 670, 674, and 677";

Whereas in December 1991, Congress expressed its sense that it "supports the use of all necessary means to achieve the goals of United Nations Security Council Resolution 687 as being consistent with the Authorization of Use of Military Force Against Iraq Resolution (Public Law 102–1)," that Iraq's repression of its civilian population violates United Nations Security Council Resolution 688 and "constitutes a continuing threat to the peace, security, and stability of the Persian Gulf region," and that Congress, "supports the use of all necessary means to achieve the goals of United Nations Security Council Resolution 688";

Whereas the Iraq Liberation Act (Public Law 105–338) expressed the sense of Congress that it should be the policy of the United States to support efforts to remove from power the current Iraqi regime and promote the emergence of a democratic government to replace that regime;

Whereas on September 12, 2002, President Bush committed the United States to "work with the United Nations Security Council to meet our common challenge" posed by Iraq and to "work for the necessary resolutions," while also making clear that "the Security Council resolutions will be enforced, and the just demands of peace and security will be met, or action will be unavoidable";

Whereas the United States is determined to prosecute the war on terrorism and Iraq's ongoing support for international terrorist groups combined with its development of weapons of mass destruction in direct violation of its obligations under the 1991 cease-fire and other United Nations Security Council resolutions make clear that it is in the national security interests of the United States and in furtherance of the war on terrorism that all relevant United Nations Security Council resolutions be enforced, including through the use of force if necessary;

Whereas Congress has taken steps to pursue vigorously the war on terrorism through the provision of authorities and funding requested by the President to take the necessary actions against international terrorists and terrorist organizations, including those nations, organizations or persons who planned, authorized, committed or aided the terrorist attacks that occurred on September 11, 2001, or harbored such persons or organizations;

Whereas the President and Congress are determined to continue to take all appropriate actions against international terrorists and terrorist organizations, including those nations, organizations or persons who planned, authorized, committed or aided the terrorist attacks that occurred on September 11, 2001, or harbored such persons or organizations;

Whereas the President has authority under the Constitution to take action in order to deter and prevent acts of international terrorism against the United States, as Congress recognized in the joint resolution on Authorization for Use of Military Force (Public Law 107–40); and

Whereas it is in the national security of the United States to restore international peace and security to the Persian Gulf region;

Now, therefore, be it resolved by the Senate and House of Representatives of the United States of America in Congress assembled,

SEC. 1. SHORT TITLE.
This joint resolution may be cited as the "Authorization for the Use of Military Force Against Iraq."

SEC. 2. SUPPORT FOR UNITED STATES DIPLOMATIC EFFORTS.
The Congress of the United States supports the efforts by the President to—
> (a) strictly enforce through the United Nations Security Council all relevant Security Council resolutions applicable to Iraq and encourages him in those efforts; and
> (b) obtain prompt and decisive action by the Security Council to ensure that Iraq abandons its strategy of delay, evasion and noncompliance and promptly and strictly complies with all relevant Security Council resolutions.

SEC. 3. AUTHORIZATION FOR USE OF UNITED STATES ARMED FORCES.
> (a) AUTHORIZATION. The President is authorized to use the Armed Forces of the United States as he determines to be necessary and appropriate in order to

(1) defend the national security of the United States against the continuing threat posed by Iraq; and

(2) enforce all relevant United Nations Security Council Resolutions regarding Iraq.

(b) PRESIDENTIAL DETERMINATION. In connection with the exercise of the authority granted in subsection (a) to use force the President shall, prior to such exercise or as soon there after as may be feasible, but no later than 48 hours after exercising such authority, make available to the Speaker of the House of Representatives and the President pro tempore of the Senate his determination that

(1) reliance by the United States on further diplomatic or other peaceful means alone either (A) will not adequately protect the national security of the United States against the continuing threat posed by Iraq or (B) is not likely to lead to enforcement of all relevant United Nations Security Council resolutions regarding Iraq, and

(2) acting pursuant to this resolution is consistent with the United States and other countries continuing to take the necessary actions against international terrorists and terrorist organizations, including those nations, organizations or persons who planned, authorized, committed or aided the terrorists attacks that occurred on September 11, 2001.

(c) WAR POWERS RESOLUTION REQUIREMENTS.

(1) SPECIFIC STATUTORY AUTHORIZATION.—Consistent with section 8(a)(1) of the War Powers Resolution, the Congress declares that this section is intended to constitute specific statutory authorization within the meaning of section 5(b) of the War Powers Resolution.

(2) APPLICABILITY OF OTHER REQUIREMENTS.—Nothing in this resolution supersedes any requirement of the War Powers Resolution.

SEC. 4. REPORTS TO CONGRESS.

(a) The President shall, at least once every 60 days, submit to the Congress a report on matters relevant to this joint resolution, including actions taken pursuant to the exercise of authority granted in section 2 and the status of planning for efforts that are expected to be required after such actions are completed, including those actions described in section 7 of Public Law 105–338 (the Iraq Liberation Act of 1998).

(b) To the extent that the submission of any report described in subsection (a) coincides with the submission of any other report on matters relevant to this joint resolution otherwise required to be submitted to Congress pursuant to the reporting requirements of Public Law 93–148 (the War Powers Resolution), all such reports may be submitted as a single consolidated report to the Congress.

(c) To the extent that the information required by section 3 of Public Law 102–1 is included in the report required by this section, such report shall be considered as meeting the requirements of section 3 of Public Law 102–1.

Downing Street Memos

"Cabinet Office paper: Conditions for military action"
The paper, known as DSM II or pre-DSM, was produced by the Cabinet Office on July 21, 2002. It is incomplete because the last page is missing.

PERSONAL SECRET UK EYES ONLY

IRAQ: CONDITIONS FOR MILITARY ACTION (A Note by Officials)

Summary
Ministers are invited to:
(1) Note the latest position on US military planning and timescales for possible action.
(2) Agree that the objective of any military action should be a stable and law-abiding Iraq, within present borders, co-operating with the international community, no longer posing a threat to its neighbours or international security, and abiding by its international obligations on WMD.
(3) Agree to engage the US on the need to set military plans within a realistic political strategy, which includes identifying the succession to Saddam Hussein and creating the conditions necessary to justify government military action, which might include an ultimatum for the return of UN weapons inspectors to Iraq. This should include a call from the Prime Minister to President Bush ahead of the briefing of US military plans to the President on 4 August.
(4) Note the potentially long lead times involved in equipping UK Armed Forces to undertake operations in the Iraqi theatre and agree that the MOD should bring forward proposals for the procurement of Urgent Operational Requirements under cover of the lessons learned from Afghanistan and the outcome of SR2002.
(5) Agree to the establishment of an ad hoc group of officials under Cabinet Office Chairmanship to consider the development of an information campaign to be agreed with the US.

Introduction
1. The US Government's military planning for action against Iraq is proceeding apace. But, as yet, it lacks a political framework. In particular, little thought has been given to creating the political conditions for military action, or the aftermath and how to shape it.

2. When the Prime Minister discussed Iraq with President Bush at Crawford in April he said that the UK would support military action to bring about regime change, provided that certain conditions were met: efforts had been made to construct a coalition/shape public opinion, the Israel–Palestine Crisis was quiescent, and the options for action to eliminate Iraq's WMD through the UN weapons inspectors had been exhausted.

3. We need now to reinforce this message and to encourage the US Government to place its military planning within a political framework, partly to forestall the risk that military action is precipitated in an unplanned way by, for example, an incident in the No Fly Zones. This is particularly important for the UK because it is necessary to create the conditions in which we could legally support military action. Otherwise we face the real danger that the US will commit themselves to a course of action which we would find very difficult to support.

4. In order to fulfil the conditions set out by the Prime Minister for UK support for military action against Iraq, certain preparations need to be made, and other considerations taken into account. This note sets them out in a form which can be adapted for use with the US Government. Depending on US intentions, a decision in principle may be needed soon on whether and in what form the UK takes part in military action.

The Goal

5. Our objective should be a stable and law-abiding Iraq, within present borders, co-operating with the international community, no longer posing a threat to its neighbours or to international security, and abiding by its international obligations on WMD. It seems unlikely that this could be achieved while the current Iraqi regime remains in power. US military planning unambiguously takes as its objective the removal of Saddam Hussein's regime, followed by elimination of Iraqi WMD. It is however, by no means certain, in the view of UK officials, that one would necessarily follow from the other. Even if regime change is a necessary condition for controlling Iraqi WMD, it is certainly not a sufficient one.

US Military Planning

6. Although no political decisions have been taken, US military planners have drafted options for the US Government to undertake an invasion of Iraq. In a 'Running Start,' military action could begin as early as November of this year, with no overt military build-up. Air strikes and support for opposition groups in Iraq would lead initially to small-scale land operations,

with further land forces deploying sequentially, ultimately overwhelming Iraqi forces and leading to the collapse of the Iraqi regime. A 'Generated Start' would involve a longer build-up before any military action were taken, as early as January 2003. US military plans include no specifics on the strategic context either before or after the campaign. Currently the preference appears to be for the 'Running Start.' CDS will be ready to brief Ministers in more detail.

7. US plans assume, as a minimum, the use of British bases in Cyprus and Diego Garcia. This means that legal base issues would arise virtually whatever option Ministers choose with regard to UK participation.

The Viability of the Plans

8. The Chiefs of Staff have discussed the viability of US military plans. Their initial view is that there are a number of questions which would have to be answered before they could assess whether the plans are sound. Notably these include the realism of the 'Running Start,' the extent to which the plans are proof against Iraqi counterattack using chemical or biological weapons and the robustness of US assumptions about the bases and about Iraqi (un)willingness to fight.

UK Military Contribution

9. The UK's ability to contribute forces depends on the details of the US military planning and the time available to prepare and deploy them. The MOD is examining how the UK might contribute to US-led action. The options range from deployment of a Division (ie Gulf War sized contribution plus naval and air forces) to making available bases. It is already clear that the UK could not generate a Division in time for an operation in January 2003, unless publicly visible decisions were taken very soon. Maritime and air forces could be deployed in time, provided adequate basing arrangements could be made. The lead times involved in preparing for UK military involvement include the procurement of Urgent Operational Requirements, for which there is no financial provision.

The Conditions Necessary for Military Action

10. Aside from the existence of a viable military plan we consider the following conditions necessary for military action and UK participation: justification/legal base; an international coalition; a quiescent Israel–Palestine; a positive risk/benefit assessment; and the preparation of domestic opinion.

Justification

11. US views of international law vary from that of the UK and the international community. Regime change per se is not a proper basis for military action under international law. But regime change could result from action that is otherwise lawful. We would regard the use of force against Iraq, or any other state, as lawful if exercised in the right of individual or collective self-defence, if carried out to avert an overwhelming humanitarian catastrophe, or authorised by the UN Security Council. A detailed consideration of the legal issues, prepared earlier this year, is at Annex A. The legal position would depend on the precise circumstances at the time. Legal bases for an invasion of Iraq are in principle conceivable in both the first two instances but would be difficult to establish because of, for example, the tests of immediacy and proportionality. Further legal advice would be needed on this point.

12. This leaves the route under the UNSC resolutions on weapons inspectors. Kofi Annan has held three rounds of meetings with Iraq in an attempt to persuade them to admit the UN weapons inspectors. These have made no substantive progress; the Iraqis are deliberately obfuscating. Annan has downgraded the dialogue but more pointless talks are possible. We need to persuade the UN and the international community that this situation cannot be allowed to continue ad infinitum. We need to set a deadline, leading to an ultimatum. It would be preferable to obtain backing of a UNSCR for any ultimatum and early work would be necessary to explore with Kofi Annan and the Russians, in particular, the scope for achieving this.

13. In practice, facing pressure of military action, Saddam is likely to admit weapons inspectors as a means of forestalling it. But once admitted, he would not allow them to operate freely. UNMOVIC (the successor to UNSCOM) will take at least six months after entering Iraq to establish the monitoring and verification system under Resolution 1284 necessary to assess whether Iraq is meeting its obligations. Hence, even if UN inspectors gained access today, by January 2003 they would at best only just be completing setting up. It is possible that they will encounter Iraqi obstruction during this period, but this more likely when they are fully operational.

14. It is just possible that an ultimatum could be cast in terms which Saddam would reject (because he is unwilling to accept unfettered access) and which would not be regarded as unreasonable by the international community. However, failing that (or an Iraqi attack) we would be most unlikely to achieve a legal base for military action by January 2003.

An International Coalition

15. An international coalition is necessary to provide a military platform and desirable for political purposes.

16. US military planning assumes that the US would be allowed to use bases in Kuwait (air and ground forces), Jordan, in the Gulf (air and naval forces) and UK territory (Diego Garcia and our bases in Cyprus). The plans assume that Saudi Arabia would withhold co-operation except granting military over-flights. On the assumption that military action would involve operations in the Kurdish area in the North of Iraq, the use of bases in Turkey would also be necessary.

17. In the absence of UN authorisation, there will be problems in securing the support of NATO and EU partners. Australia would be likely to participate on the same basis as the UK. France might be prepared to take part if she saw military action as inevitable. Russia and China, seeking to improve their US relations, might set aside their misgivings if sufficient attention were paid to their legal and economic concerns. Probably the best we could expect from the region would be neutrality. The US is likely to restrain Israel from taking part in military action. In practice, much of the international community would find it difficult to stand in the way of the determined course of the US hegemon. However, the greater the international support, the greater the prospects of success.

A Quiescent Israel–Palestine

18. The Israeli re-occupation of the West Bank has dampened Palestinian violence for the time being but is unsustainable in the long-term and stoking more trouble for the future. The Bush speech was at best a half step forward. We are using the Palestinian reform agenda to make progress, including a resumption of political negotiations. The Americans are talking of a ministerial conference in November or later. Real progress towards a viable Palestinian state is the best way to undercut Palestinian extremists and reduce Arab antipathy to military action against Saddam Hussein. However, another upsurge of Palestinian/Israeli violence is highly likely. The co-incidence of such an upsurge with the preparations for military action against Iraq cannot be ruled out. Indeed Saddam would use continuing violence in the Occupied Territories to bolster popular Arab support for his regime.

Benefits/Risks

19. Even with a legal base and a viable military plan, we would still need to ensure that the benefits of action outweigh the risks. In particular, we need

to be sure that the outcome of the military action would match our objective as set out in paragraph 5 above. A post-war occupation of Iraq could lead to a protracted and costly nation-building exercise. As already made clear, the US military plans are virtually silent on this point. Washington could look to us to share a disproportionate share of the burden. Further work is required to define more precisely the means by which the desired endstate would be created, in particular what form of Government might replace Saddam Hussein's regime and the timescale within which it would be possible to identify a successor. We must also consider in greater detail the impact of military action on other UK interests in the region.

Domestic Opinion

20. Time will be required to prepare public opinion in the UK that it is necessary to take military action against Saddam Hussein. There would also need to be a substantial effort to secure the support of Parliament. An information campaign will be needed which has to be closely related to an overseas information campaign designed to influence Saddam Hussein, the Islamic World and the wider international community. This will need to give full coverage to the threat posed by Saddam Hussein, including his WMD, and the legal justification for action.

Timescales

21. Although the US military could act against Iraq as soon as November, we judge that a military campaign is unlikely to start until January 2003, if only because of the time it will take to reach consensus in Washington. That said, we judge that for climatic reasons, military action would need to start by January 2003, unless action were deferred until the following autumn.

22. As this paper makes clear, even this timescale would present problems. This means that:

   (a) We need to influence US consideration of the military plans before President Bush is briefed on 4 August, through contacts between the Prime Minister and the President and at other levels;

http://www.timesonline.co.uk/tol/news/world/article531957.ece

Text of the Downing Street Memo
July 23, 2002

As originally reported in the London Sunday Times,
May 1, 2005

SECRET AND STRICTLY PERSONAL—UK EYES ONLY

DAVID MANNING
From: Matthew Rycroft
Date: 23 July 2002
S 195 /02
cc: Defence Secretary, Foreign Secretary, Attorney-General, Sir Richard Wilson, John Scarlett, Francis Richards, CDS, C, Jonathan Powell, Sally Morgan, Alastair Campbell

IRAQ: PRIME MINISTER'S MEETING, 23 JULY
Copy addressees and you met the Prime Minister on 23 July to discuss Iraq.

This record is extremely sensitive. No further copies should be made. It should be shown only to those with a genuine need to know its contents.

John Scarlett summarised the intelligence and latest JIC assessment. Saddam's regime was tough and based on extreme fear. The only way to overthrow it was likely to be by massive military action. Saddam was worried and expected an attack, probably by air and land, but he was not convinced that it would be immediate or overwhelming. His regime expected their neighbours to line up with the US. Saddam knew that regular army morale was poor. Real support for Saddam among the public was probably narrowly based.

C reported on his recent talks in Washington. There was a perceptible shift in attitude. Military action was now seen as inevitable. Bush wanted to remove Saddam, through military action, justified by the conjunction of terrorism and WMD. But the intelligence and facts were being fixed around the policy. The NSC had no patience with the UN route, and no enthusiasm for publishing material on the Iraqi regime's record. There was little discussion in Washington of the aftermath after military action.

CDS said that military planners would brief CENTCOM on 1–2 August, Rumsfeld on 3 August and Bush on 4 August.

The two broad US options were:

(a) Generated Start. A slow build-up of 250,000 US troops, a short (72 hour) air campaign, then a move up to Baghdad from the south. Lead time of 90 days (30 days preparation plus 60 days deployment to Kuwait).

(b) Running Start. Use forces already in theatre (3 x 6,000), continuous air campaign, initiated by an Iraqi casus belli. Total lead time of 60 days with the air campaign beginning even earlier. A hazardous option.

The US saw the UK (and Kuwait) as essential, with basing in Diego Garcia and Cyprus critical for either option. Turkey and other Gulf states were also important, but less vital. The three main options for UK involvement were:

(i) Basing in Diego Garcia and Cyprus, plus three SF squadrons.

(ii) As above, with maritime and air assets in addition.

(iii) As above, plus a land contribution of up to 40,000, perhaps with a discrete role in Northern Iraq entering from Turkey, tying down two Iraqi divisions.

The Defence Secretary said that the US had already begun "spikes of activity" to put pressure on the regime. No decisions had been taken, but he thought the most likely timing in US minds for military action to begin was January, with the timeline beginning 30 days before the US congressional elections.

The Foreign Secretary said he would discuss this with Colin Powell this week. It seemed clear that Bush had made up his mind to take military action, even if the timing was not yet decided. But the case was thin. Saddam was not threatening his neighbours, and his WMD capability was less than that of Libya, North Korea or Iran. We should work up a plan for an ultimatum to Saddam to allow back in the UN weapons inspectors. This would also help with the legal justification for the use of force.

The Attorney-General said that the desire for regime change was not a legal base for military action. There were three possible legal bases: self-defence, humanitarian intervention, or UNSC authorisation. The first and second could not be the base in this case. Relying on UNSCR 1205 of three years ago would be difficult. The situation might of course change.

The Prime Minister said that it would make a big difference politically and legally if Saddam refused to allow in the UN inspectors. Regime change and WMD were linked in the sense that it was the regime that was producing the WMD. There were different strategies for dealing with Libya and Iran.

If the political context were right, people would support regime change. The two key issues were whether the military plan worked and whether we had the political strategy to give the military plan the space to work.

On the first, CDS said that we did not know yet if the US battleplan was workable. The military were continuing to ask lots of questions.

For instance, what were the consequences, if Saddam used WMD on day one, or if Baghdad did not collapse and urban warfighting began? You said that Saddam could also use his WMD on Kuwait. Or on Israel, added the Defence Secretary.

The Foreign Secretary thought the US would not go ahead with a military plan unless convinced that it was a winning strategy. On this, US and UK interests converged. But on the political strategy, there could be US/UK differences. Despite US resistance, we should explore discreetly the ultimatum. Saddam would continue to play hard-ball with the UN.

John Scarlett assessed that Saddam would allow the inspectors back in only when he thought the threat of military action was real.

The Defence Secretary said that if the Prime Minister wanted UK military involvement, he would need to decide this early. He cautioned that many in the US did not think it worth going down the ultimatum route. It would be important for the Prime Minister to set out the political context to Bush.

Conclusions:

(a) We should work on the assumption that the UK would take part in any military action. But we needed a fuller picture of US planning before we could take any firm decisions. CDS should tell the US military that we were considering a range of options.

(b) The Prime Minister would revert on the question of whether funds could be spent in preparation for this operation.

(c) CDS would send the Prime Minister full details of the proposed military campaign and possible UK contributions by the end of the week.

(d) The Foreign Secretary would send the Prime Minister the background on the UN inspectors, and discreetly work up the ultimatum to Saddam.

He would also send the Prime Minister advice on the positions of countries in the region especially Turkey, and of the key EU member states.

(e) John Scarlett would send the Prime Minister a full intelligence update.

(f) We must not ignore the legal issues: the Attorney-General would consider legal advice with FCO/MOD legal advisers.

(I have written separately to commission this follow-up work.)

MATTHEW RYCROFT

(Rycroft was a Downing Street foreign policy aide)

To read the other Downing Street Memos, listed below, visit www.downingstreetmemo.com/memos.html

Foreign Secretary Jack Straw's Memo

March 25, 2002, memo from Jack Straw (UK Foreign Secretary) to Tony Blair in preparation for Blair's visit to Bush's Crawford ranch, covering Iraq–al Qaeda linkage, legality of invasion, weapons inspectors, and postwar considerations.

British Foreign Office Political Director Peter Ricketts' Letter

March 22, 2002, memo from Peter Ricketts (Political Director, UK Foreign and Commonwealth Office) to Jack Straw (UK Foreign Secretary) providing Ricketts's advice for the Prime Minister on issues of the threat posed by Iraq, connections to al Qaeda, postwar considerations, and working with the UN.

British Ambassador Christopher Meyer's Letter

March 18, 2002, memo from Christopher Meyer (UK ambassador to the U.S.) to David Manning (UK Foreign Policy Adviser) recounting Meyer's meeting with Paul Wolfowitz (U.S. Deputy Secretary of Defense).

Chief Foreign Policy Adviser David Manning's Memo

March 14, 2002, memo from David Manning (UK Foreign Policy Adviser) to Tony Blair recounting Manning's meetings with his U.S. counterpart Condoleezza Rice (National Security Adviser), and advising Blair for his upcoming visit to Bush's Crawford ranch.

Iraq Options

March 8, 2002, memo from Overseas and Defence Secretariat Cabinet Office outlining military options for implementing regime change.

Iraq: Legal Background

March 8, 2002, memo from UK Foreign and Commonwealth Office (office of Jack Straw, Foreign Secretary) to Tony Blair advising him on the legality of the use of force against Iraq.

Notes

Prologue

1. April 16, 1967, Ebenezer Baptist Church, Atlanta, Georgia.

2. His Holiness the 14th Dalai Lama, "Non-Violence, the Appropriate and Effective Response to Human Conflicts," on the Commemoration of the First Anniversary of September 11, 2001, www.dalailama.com/page.44.htm.

3. "Decoding Mr. Bush's Denials," editorial, *New York Times*, November 15, 2005.

1—How We Got Into Iraq

1. "President Bush Announces Major Combat Operations in Iraq Have Ended," remarks by the President from the *USS Abraham Lincoln*, May 1, 2003.

2. The President's Address to the Nation, January 10, 2007.

3. May 30, 2007.

4. G. Burnham, R. Lafta, S. Doocy, L. Roberts, "Mortality after the 2003 invasion of Iraq: a cross-sectional cluster sample survey," *Lancet*, October 21, 2006, 1421.

5. Damien Cave, "Report Finds Dire Humanitarian Crisis in Iraq," *New York Times*, July 30, 2007.

6. Nancy Benac, "Poll: Americans Oppose Iraq Troop Surge," Associated Press, January 11, 2007; "Poll: 60% Oppose Iraq Troop Escalation," *Honolulu Advertiser*, January 19, 2007.

7. The first Gulf War started on January 17, 1991, and ended just six weeks later, on February 28. One month later, on April 3, the UN Security Council passed Resolution 687, stating that Iraq must agree not to make, acquire, or use any weapons of mass destruction. ("Security Council Resolutions Concerning Iraq," excerpt from White House background paper "A Decade of Deception and Defiance," U.S. Dept of State website, November 8, 2002.)

8. George Bush and Brent Scowcroft, *A World Transformed* (New York: Knopf, 1998).

9. Ron Suskind, *The Price of Loyalty: George W. Bush, the White House, and the Education of Paul O'Neill* (New York: Simon & Schuster, 2004).

10. "Clarke's Take On Terror" *60 Minutes,* CBS, March 21, 2004.

11. John Barry and Mark Hosenball, "What Went Wrong," *Newsweek*, February 9, 2004, p. 31.

12. U.S. Department of Defense. "Secretary Rumsfeld Contrasts Iraq and North Korea," January 20, 2003. www.defenselink.mil/releases/release.aspx?releaseid=3605; George W. Bush, March 16, 2003.

13. *Late Edition with Wolf Blitzer,* CNN, September 8, 2002.

14. "President Bush Outlines Iraqi Threat: Remarks by the President on Iraq" at the Cincinnati Museum Center, October 7, 2002.

15. Craig Unger, "The War They Wanted, The Lies They Needed," *Vanity Fair*, July 2006, p. 95.

16. Linda Feldmann, "The impact of Bush linking 9/11 and Iraq," *Christian Science Monitor*, March 14, 2003.

17. Ibid.

18. Bruce Morton, "Selling an Iraq-al Qaeda connection: Some critics blame TV news for making Baghdad new enemy," CNN, March 11, 2003.

19. Feldmann, "Impact of Bush linking 9/11 and Iraq."

20. James Bovard, "War Lies and the 2004 Election," *Freedom Daily*, July 23, 2007.

21. Suskind, *The Price of Loyalty*.

22. William Rivers Pitt, "The Writing on the Latrine Walls," truthout.org, August 9, 2004.

23. Suskind, *The Price of Loyalty*.

24. William R. Clark, *Petrodollar Warfare: Oil, Iraq and the Future of the Dollar* (Gabriola Island, BC: New Society Publishers, 2005); "U.S. Dollar vs. the Euro: Another Reason for the Invasion of Iraq," Project Censored, 2004; Hazel Henderson, "Iraq, the Dollar and the Euro," *Globalist*, June 2, 2003; "U.N. to let Iraq Sell Oil for Euros, Not Dollars," CNN, October 30, 2000; Charles Recknagel, "Iraq: Baghdad Moves to Euro," Radio Free Europe, November 1, 2000.

25. For a thorough discussion of the factors that led the U.S. into Iraq, see Stephen Kinzer, *Overthrow: America's Century of Regime Change from Hawaii to Iraq* (New York: Times Books, 2006).

26. "Clarke's Take on Terror" *60 Minutes*, CBS, March 21, 2004.

27. Jacob Goodwin, "Did DoD lawyers blow the chance to nab Atta?," GSN: Government Security News, August 2005.

28. "Clarke's Take on Terror." See Clarke's *Against All Enemies: Inside America's War on Terror* (New York: Free Press, 2004).

29. Kinzer, *Overthrow*, 288–89.

30. Walter Pincus, "CIA Learned in '02 that Bin Laden Had No Iraq Ties, Report Says," *Washington Post*, September 15, 2006.

31. Interview, *Frontline*, PBS, June 20, 2006.

32. "President Bush Announces Major Combat Operations in Iraq Have Ended."

33. "The Dark Side," *Frontline*, PBS, June 20, 2006; Michael Scheuer, CIA 1982–2004; Senator Bob Graham (D-FL), Senate Select Committee on Intelligence, 2001–2003.

34. John Nichols, Robert W. McChesney, et al., *Tragedy and Farce: How the American Media Sell Wars, Spin Elections, and Destroy Democracy* (New York: New Press, 2005), 66.

35. "The Dark Side."

36. "Newsmaker: Hans Blix," *News Hour,* PBS, March 17, 2004.

37. Craig Unger, "The War They Wanted, The Lies They Needed," *Vanity Fair,* July 2006, 95.

38. Jesse Nunes, "Pentagon report debunks prewar Iraq-Al Qaeda connection," *Christian Science Monitor,* April 6, 2007; R. Jeffrey Smith, "Hussein's Prewar Ties To Al-Qaeda Discounted," *Washington Post,* April 6, 2007; "U.S. military: Al-Zarqawi was alive after bombing," CNN, June 9, 2006; "Profile: Abu Musab al-Zarqawi," *BBC News,* November 10, 2005.

39. Weisman, "Iraq's Alleged Al-Qaeda Ties Disputed Before War."

40. "Blair 'knew Iraq WMD claim wrong,'" CNN, October 5, 2003,

41. David Cracknell, "Blair 'Knew Iraq Had No WMD,'" *Times* (London), October 5, 2003.

42. Jason Allardyce and Brian Brady, "Cook: Blair knew Iraq had no WMD," *Scotsman,* October 5, 2003.

43. Glenn Frankel, "From Memos, Insights into Ally's Doubts on Iraq War: British Advisers Foresaw Variety of Risks, Problems," *Washington Post,* June 28, 2005.

44. Warren Hoge, "Blair Doubted Iraq Had Arms, Ex-Aide Says," *New York Times,* October 6, 2003; "WMD pressure builds up for Blair," *BBC News,* January 24, 2004.

45. Michael Smith, "Secret papers show Blair was warned of Iraq chaos," *Daily Telegraph* (UK), September 18, 2004.

46. Walter Pincus, "Memo: U.S. Lacked Full Postwar Iraq Plan: Advisers to Blair Predicted Instability," *Washington Post,* June 12, 2005.

47. Ibid.

48. Smith, "Secret papers show Blair warned of Iraq chaos."

49. Michael Smith, "The Leak that Changed Minds on the Iraq War," *Sunday Times* (London), June 12, 2005.

50. Michael Smith, "Ministers were told of need for Gulf war 'excuse,'" *Sunday Times* (London), June 12, 2005.

51. Ibid. See also "BBC/Blair Battle Timeline," "NOW" website, www.PBS.org, February 3, 2006; and Michael Smith, "Blair Planned Iraq War from Start," *Sunday Times* (London), May 1, 2005.

52. Smith, "Ministers told of need for Gulf war 'excuse.'"

53. Smith, "Blair Planned Iraq War from Start."

54. "The secret Downing Street memo," *Sunday Times,* May 1, 2005, www.times online.co.uk/tol/news/uk/article387374.ece

55. "Bush makes historic speech aboard warship," CNN, May 1, 2003.

56. Michael Smith, "General admits to secret air war," *Sunday Times* (London), June 26, 2005; Smith, "Leak that Changed Minds on Iraq War"; Michael Smith, "The Real News in the Downing Street Memos," *Los Angeles Times,* June 23, 2005.

57. Michael Smith, "British bombing raids were illegal, says Foreign Office," *Times* (London), June 19, 2005.

58. Nichols, McChesney, et al., *Tragedy and Farce.*

59. Michael Smith, "The Downing Street Memo," *Washington Post* online chat, June 16, 2005.

60. Nichols, McChesney, et al., *Tragedy and Farce,* 78.

61. Ibid., 79; Matthew Clark, "Why has 'Downing Street memo' story been a 'dud' in US?," *Christian Science Monitor,* May 17, 2005.

62. Nichols, McChesney, et al., *Tragedy and Farce,* 79.

63. Smith, "Leak that Changed Minds on Iraq War."

64. Smith, "Real News in Downing Street Memos"; Smith, "British bombing raids were illegal."

65. "President Signs Iraq Resolution," October 16, 2002,

66. Richard Norton-Taylor and Vikram Dodd, "Kelly panic led Blair to intervene," *Guardian* (UK), August 15, 2003.

67. Colin Brown and Francis Elliott, "No. 10 says sorry to MI6 for 'dodgy' Iraq dossier," *Telegraph,* August 6, 2003.

68. Richard Norton-Taylor, "WMD claims were 'totally implausible,'" *Guardian,* June 20, 2005; Carne Ross, written transcript to the Butler Inquiry, June 9, 2004, http://news.independent.co.uk/uk/politics/article2076142.ece.

69. Stephen Moss, "Diplomat at large," *Guardian,* June 20, 2005; Norton-Taylor, "WMD claims 'totally implausible'"; "Written evidence submitted by Mr. Carne Ross: Testimony to House of Commons Foreign Affairs Committee: Commentary on FCO White Paper 'Active Diplomacy,'" www.publications.parliament.uk/pa/cm200506/cmselect/cmfaff/uc1720-i/1720m02.htm; "Foreign Affairs—Minutes of Evidence," taken before the Foreign Affairs Committee, House of Commons, November 8, 2006.

70. Norton-Taylor, "WMD claims 'totally implausible'"; Ross, written transcript to the Butler Inquiry; testimony to House of Commons.

71. Jason Deans, Julia Day, and Ciar Byrne, "MoD man reveals dossier 'disquiet,'" *Guardian,* August 11, 2003.

72. Richard Norton-Taylor, "Of course Dr Kelly was no Walter Mitty," *Guardian,* August 7, 2003.

73. Ciar Byrne, Matthew Tempest, and Julia Day, "Bombshell hits government's claims," *Guardian,* September 3, 2003; Norton-Taylor and Dodd, "Kelly panic led Blair to intervene."

74. Don Van Natta, Jr., "Bush Was Set on Path to War, British Memo Says," *New York Times,* March 27, 2006.

75. Philippe Sands, "Why did attorney general support such a weak and dismal argument?" *Guardian,* February 23, 2005; "Iraq: Legal Background," prepared by the Foreign & Commonwealth Office Legal Department, March 8, 2002.

76. Bill Vann, "US repudiates International Criminal Court," May 7, 2002, www.wsws. org/articles/2002/may2002/icc-m07.shtml.

77. Richard Norton-Taylor, "Revealed: the rush to war," *Guardian,* February 23, 2005.

78. Richard Norton-Taylor, "Whitehall united in doubt on war," *Guardian,* February 27, 2004; Raymond Whitaker and Robert Verkaik, "Revealed: Attorney General changed his advice on legality of Iraq war," *Independent* (UK), February 29, 2004; John Kampfner, "The law chief who bowed to Blair," *New Statesman,* November 22, 2004.

79. Kampfner, "Law chief who bowed to Blair."

80. Simon Walters, "Proof Blair was told war could be ruled illegal," *Daily Mail* (London), April 24, 2005.

81. Richard Norton-Taylor, "Blair-Bush deal before Iraq war revealed in secret memo," *Guardian,* February 3, 2006.

82. Ibid.

83. Van Natta, "Bush Was Set on Path to War."

84. Ibid.

85. Norton-Taylor, "Blair-Bush deal before Iraq war revealed."

86. Ibid.

87. Bob Herbert, "A Single Conscience v. the State," *New York Times,* January 19, 2004.

88. Martin Bright, Ed Vulliamy, and Peter Beaumont, "Revealed: US dirty tricks to win vote on Iraq war," *Observer* (UK), March 2, 2003; Martin Bright, Gaby Hinsliff, Antony Barnett, Paul Harris, Jo Tuckman, and Ed Vulliamy, "Whistleblower," *Observer,* February 29, 2004.

89. Van Natta, "Bush Was Set on Path to War."

90. Herbert, "Single Conscience v. the State."

91. Bright, Vulliamy, and Beaumont, "Revealed"; Bright, Hinsliff, et al., "Whistleblower."

92. March 6, 2003.

93. Michael Smith, "Blair Planned Iraq War from Start," *Sunday Times* (London), May 1, 2005.

94. Norton-Taylor, "Blair-Bush deal before Iraq war revealed."

95. Joby Warrick, "Warnings on WMD 'Fabricator' Were Ignored, Ex-CIA Aide Says," *Washington Post,* June 25, 2006.

96. Ibid.; "Former aide: Powell WMD speech 'lowest point in my life,'" CNN, August 23, 2005.

97. "Dark Side."

98. Robert Scheer, "Now Powell Tells Us," *Nation,* April 11, 2006.

99. Sarah Baxter, "Powell tried to talk Bush out of war," *Sunday Times* (London), July 8, 2007.

100. Kampfner, "Law chief who bowed to Blair."

101. "How to legitimize a war in 10 days," *Pretoria News* (South Africa), May 2, 2005.

102. Kampfner, "Law chief who bowed to Blair."

103. Walters, "Proof Blair told war could be ruled illegal."

104. John Kampfner, "The Blundering Actions of a Desperate Man," *Independent,* April 29, 2005.

105. Philippe Sands, *Lawless World: America and the Making and Breaking of Global Rules from FDR's Atlantic Charter to George W. Bush's Illegal War* (New York: Viking, 2005), 186.

106. Martin Bright and Peter Beaumont, "Britain spied on UN allies over war vote: Security Council members 'illegally targeted' by GCHQ after plea from U.S. security agency," *Observer,* February 8, 2004.

107. "How to legitimize a war in 10 days."

108. Richard Norton-Taylor, "Blair's evasions will catch up with him," *Guardian,* April 25, 2005; "How to legitimize a war in 10 days."

109. Raymond Whitaker and Andy McSmith, "The Whistleblower, the loose cannon and the case for war," *Independent,* February 29, 2004.

110. Bright, Hinsliff, et al., "Whistleblower."

111. Andrew Sparrow, "Cook and Meacher could be in the next wave of rebellion," *Telegraph,* March 11, 2003.

112. James Cusick, "US Told UK Attorney General to Alter Legal Advice on Iraq War," *Sunday Herald* (Edinburgh), February 29, 2004.

113. Clare Dyer, "Leading lawyers back FO adviser who quit over ruling," *Guardian,* March 25, 2005; Nigel Morris, "Lawyer was paid 50,000 pounds to give advice on Iraq invasion," *Independent,* March 22, 2005.

114. Morris, "Lawyer paid 50,000 pounds"; Simon Jenkins, "Just do what the PM wants," *Times* (London), March 25, 2005.

115. Kampfner, "Law chief who bowed to Blair."

116. Philippe Sands, "Why did attorney general support such a weak and dismal argument?" *Guardian,* February 23, 2005.

117. Kampfner, "Blundering Actions of a Desperate Man."

118. Jenkins, "Just do what PM wants"; "Blair's case for war questioned: Iraq, Tony and the Truth," *BBC News,* March 21, 2005.

119. Kampfner, "Law chief who bowed to Blair."

120. Norton-Taylor, "Revealed: rush to war."

121. Kampfner, "Blundering Actions of a Desperate Man"; Bernard Hibbitts, "New leaked document shows UK AG reservation on Iraq war legality," *Jurist,* April 27, 2005.

122. Norton-Taylor, "Revealed: rush to war."

123. Tam Dalyell, "Robin Cook: Former Foreign Secretary who resigned from the Cabinet in protest against war in Iraq," *Independent,* August 8, 2005.

124. Bright, Hinsliff, et al., "Whistleblower."

125. Elizabeth Wilmshurst's resignation letter, March 18, 2003.

126. "The Judgment: The Nazi Regime in Germany," Yale Law School Avalon Project, www.yale.edu/lawweb/avalon/imt/proc/judnazi.htm#common.

127. "Truth, Consequences and the Road to War," *Newsweek,* February 9, 2004, 30.

128. "Security Council Resolutions Concerning Iraq," excerpt from White House background paper "A Decade of Deception and Defiance," U.S. Dept. of State website, November 8, 2002, www.state.gov/p/nea/rls/01fs/14906.htm.

129. "Blair wins war backing amid revolt," *BBC News,* March 19, 2003.

130. Matthew Tempest, "Cook resigns from cabinet over Iraq," *Guardian,* March 17, 2003.

131. "Blair wins war backing amid revolt."

132. Colin Brown, "Cook: 'Blair admitted to me that Saddam had no usable WMD,'" *Telegraph,* October 5, 2003.

133. "Blair 'knew Iraq WMD claim wrong.'"

134. "Clare Short remains as resignations mount," *Guardian,* March 18, 2003.

135. Norton-Taylor and Dodd, "Kelly panic led Blair to intervene."

136. "BBC/Blair Battle Timeline," NOW website, www.PBS.org, February 3, 2006.

137. Norton-Taylor and Dodd, "Kelly panic led Blair to intervene."

138. "Timeline: The David Kelly affair," www.CNN.com, January 28, 2004.

139. Barry and Hosenball, "What Went Wrong."

140. David Rose, "MI6 chief to quit after split on Iraq," *Observer,* August 3, 2003.

141. Norton-Taylor, "Whitehall united in doubt."

142. Patrick E. Tyler, "Britain Drops Charges in Leak of U.S. Memo," *New York Times,* February 26, 2004.

143. Norton-Taylor, "Whitehall united in doubt."

144. Editorial, *Sunday Times* (London), February 29, 2004.

145. Norton-Taylor, "Whitehall united in doubt."

146. "Truth, Consequences and Road to War," 26.

147. Julian Borger, "The Inspector's Final Report," *Guardian,* March 3, 2004.

148. Moss, "Diplomat at large"; Norton-Taylor, "WMD claims 'totally implausible,'"; "Written evidence submitted by Ross: Testimony to Foreign Affairs Committee."

149. Kampfner, "Blundering Actions of a Desperate Man."

150. Brian Jones, "Burying the Butler report," *Guardian,* March 31, 2005.

151. Robin Cook, "Britain's worst intelligence failure and Lord Butler says no one is to blame," *Independent,* July 15, 2004.

152. Craig Murray, "SUBJECT: US/Uzbekistan: Promoting Terrorism," telegram to Foreign Office, September 16, 2002.

153. Anthony Kuhn, "Britain's Straw Faces a Challenge over Iraq," interview with Craig Murray, *Weekend Edition*, NPR, May 1, 2005.

154. Goldsmith had testified days before the war began, on March 13, 2003, that he met with Blair's two closest aides. The leaked testimony quoted Goldsmith as saying, "They shortly, of course, set out my view."

155. Richard Norton-Taylor and Michael White, "Transcripts show No 10's hand in war legal advice," *Guardian*, February 24, 2005.

156. Joshua Rozenberg and George Jones, "Goldsmith disproves Iraq war advice claim," *Telegraph*, February 26, 2005.

157. Richard Norton-Taylor, "War Resignation Letter Censored," *Guardian*, March 24, 2005.

158. Hannah K. Strange, "Pressure mounts in UK over Iraq war legal advice," *Washington Times*, March 24, 2005.

159. Toby Helm, "John Major calls on Blair to publish Goldsmith's war advice," *Telegraph*, March 1, 2004.

160. Norton-Taylor, "Blair-Bush deal before Iraq war revealed."

161. Kampfner, "Law chief who bowed to Blair."

2—Diplomats Who Resigned

1. George C. Harris, "The Rule of Law and the War on Terror: The Professional Responsibilities of Executive Branch Lawyers in the Wake of 9/11," *Journal of National Security Law & Policy*, 2005, Vol. 1, pp. 409-453.

2. "Channeling Dissent from the Foreign Service," *Morning Edition*, NPR, October 14, 2004.

3. Steve Kashkett, "Prisoners of Conscience," *Foreign Service Journal*, May 2007.

4. John Brown, "Why I Resigned," *Foreign Service Journal*, September 2003; John Brady Kiesling, Letter of Resignation, February 23, 2003; and Mary A. Wright, Letter of Resignation to Secretary of State Colin Powell, *Government Executive*, May 15, 2003.

5. Shane Harris, "The Unquiet Americans," *Government Executive*, May 15, 2003.

6. Ibid.

7. Kiesling, Letter of Resignation.

8. Kiesling, "U.S. Diplomacy and Other Sacrifices, *Foreign Service Journal*, March 2004.

9. Ibid.

10. Ibid.

11. Stephen Lapyrouse, "An Interview with John H. Brown," *American Diplomacy*, January 24, 2007.

12. Brown, "Why I Resigned."

13. Wright, Letter of Resignation.

14. Ann Wright, "Why Dissent Is Important and Resignation Honorable," *Foreign Service Journal,* September 2003.

15. Ibid.

16. Ibid.

17. Ibid.

3—Coalition-of-the-Willing Dissenters

1. Quoted in *Hartford Courant,* March 20, 2003.

2. "Top Secret Document Reveals U.S. Spying on U.N. Delegates," Institute for Public Accuracy, March 3, 2003.

3. "Prominent Americans Support British Whistleblower," Institute for Public Accuracy, January 29, 2004.

4. Nick Cohen, "Beware smoking Guns," *Observer,* February 29, 2004.

5. "New York Times Column Today Shines Light on British Whistleblower," Institute for Public Accuracy, January 19, 2004.

6. Martin Bright, Gaby Hinsliff, Antony Barnett, Paul Harris, Jo Tuckman, and Ed Vulliamy, "Whistleblower," *Observer,* February 29, 2004.

7. Katharine Gun, "The truth must out," *Observer,* September 19, 2004.

8. Norman Solomon, "For Telling the Truth," *Baltimore Sun,* December 14, 2003.

9. Martin Bright and Peter Beaumont, "Britain Spied on UN Allies over War Vote," *Observer,* February 8, 2004.

10. Bob Herbert, "A Single Conscience v. the State," *New York Times,* January 19, 2004.

11. Text of NSC memo, *Observer,* March 2, 2003.

12. Bright and Beaumont, "Britain Spied on UN Allies."

13. Megan Lane, "The rise of the whistle-blower," BBC News Online Magazine, February 26, 2004.

14. Herbert, "Single Conscience v. the State."

15. Neil Tweedie, "The U.S. Spymaster, the whistleblower, and the secret email she exposed," *Telegraph,* February 26, 2004.

16. "International War Whistleblowers Tell Why They Exposed Their Governments," *Democracy Now!,* Pacifica, September 9, 2004.

17. Lane, "Rise of the whistle-blower."

18. Herbert, "Single Conscience v. the State."

19. Patrick Radden Keefe, "The Leak Was Me," *New York Review of Books,* June 10, 2004.

20. Tweedie, "U.S. Spymaster, whistleblower, and secret email."

21. Ibid.

22. "New Support for British Whistleblower Katharine Gun," Institute for Public Accuracy, February 12, 2004.

23. "Prominent Americans Support British Whistleblower."

24. Ibid.

25. "New Developments in Case of U.S. Spying on U.N. Security Council: Former British Cabinet Minister Decries Prosecution of Whistleblower," *Democracy Now!*, Pacifica, December 17, 2003.

26. Mark Oliver, "GCHQ whistleblower cleared," *Guardian*, February 25, 2004.

27. "UK 'Spied on UN's Kofi Annan,'" *BBC News*, February 26, 2004.

28. Ibid.

29. Ewen MacAskill, Richard Norton-Taylor, and Julian Borger, "The Spy Who Blew the Whistle," *World Press Review*, April 2004.

30. Bright, Hinsliff, et al., "Whistleblower."

31. Institute for Public Accuracy, February 2004.

32. "Prominent Americans Support British Whistleblower."

33. Gun, "Truth must out."

34. Chris Strohm, "Whistleblowers urge workers to disclose classified information," *Government Executive*, September 9, 2004.

35. Gun, "Truth must out."

36. Ibid.

37. Katharine Gun, "Iran: Time to Leak," www.TomPaine.com, March 20, 2006.

38. Cook's Letter of Resignation to Prime Minister Tony Blair, March 17, 2003, http://politics.guardian.co.uk/labour/story/0,,916145,00.html.

39. Tam Dalyell, "Robin Cook: Former Foreign Secretary who resigned from the Cabinet in protest against war in Iraq," *Independent*, August 8, 2005.

40. Steve Crawshaw, "Cook's Enduring Legacy," *Tablet*, August 13, 2005; David Edwards, "Robin Cook's 'Ethical' Foreign Policy," ZNet/Foreign Policy, August 26, 2005.

41. Joan Smith, "Britain Still Needs an Ethical Foreign Policy," *Independent*, August 10, 2005.

42. "Cook loses Foreign Office," *BBC News*, June 8, 2001.

43. See John Kampfner, *Blair's Wars* (London: Free Press, 2004); James Naughtie, *The Accidental American: Tony Blair and the Presidency* (New York: MacMillan, 2004).

44. Richard Ingrams, "The genuine article," *Observer*, August 14, 2005.

45. Tony Blair's response to Robin Cook regarding his resignation, http://politics.guardian.co.uk/labour/story/0,9061,916148,00.html.

46. Crawshaw, "Cook's Enduring Legacy"; "Heart disease caused Cook's death," *BBC News,* August 9, 2005.

47. Torcuil Crichton, "Robin Cook: A Tribute," *Sunday Herald* (Scotland), August 7, 2005.

48. Bright, Hinsliff, et al., "Whistleblower."

49. Elizabeth Wilmshurst's Letter of Resignation.

50. "Adviser admits resigning over war," *BBC News,* February 27, 2004.

51. "Blair could go to prison," *Guardian,* March 1, 2004.

52. Bright, Hinsliff, et al., "Whistleblower."

53. Paul Waugh, "Lawyer Who Quit over Iraq to Testify at Antiwar Trial," *Independent,* March 10, 2004.

54. "Adviser admits resigning over war."

55. "Elizabeth Wilmshurst, Rules of engagement," *Guardian,* October 14, 2004.

56. Amy Goodman, "Clare Short on Why She Quit Tony Blair's Government in Protest of the Iraq War & How British Intelligence Spied on UN Chief Kofi Annan," interview, *Democracy Now!,* Pacifica, February 15, 2005.

57. Rahul Mahajan, "We Think the Price Is Worth It," *Extra!,* November 2001, http://www.fair.org/index.php?page=1084.

58. Goodman, "Clare Short on Why She Quit."

59. Patrick Wintour, "Short Spearheads Rebellion with Threat to Quit over War," in Guardian, March 10, 2003.

60. "Clare Short remains as resignations mount," *Guardian,* March 18, 2003.

61. Goodman, "Clare Short on Why She Quit."

62. Catherine Deveney, "The Honourable Member," *Scotsman,* September 18, 2005.

63. "Clare Short Quits Post over Iraq," BBC, May 12, 2003.

64. Clare Short, "Resignation Statement," *BBC News,* May 12, 2003.

65. Raymond Whitaker and Andy McSmith, "The Whistleblower, the loose cannon and the case for war," *Independent,* February 29, 2004.

66. Goodman, "Clare Short on Why She Quit."

67. Deveney, "Honourable Member."

68. Sarah Left and Matthew Tempest, "No. 10 did not summarize Iraq advice," *Guardian,* February 25, 2005.

69. Deveney, "Honourable Member."

70. Nicholas Wood, "Rebellious Diplomat Finds Work as Envoy of the Voiceless," *New York Times,* March 3, 2007.

71. Stephen Moss, "Diplomat at large" *Guardian,* June 20, 2005.

72. Wolf Blitzer, *Situation Room,* CNN, May 4, 2007.

73. Richard Norton-Taylor, "WMD claims were 'totally implausible,'" *Guardian,* June 20, 2005.

74. Moss, "Diplomat at large."

75. Jamie Doward, "11th-hour bid to halt Iraq war revelations," *Observer,* January 28, 2007.

76. "UK Iraq Policy a 'rank disaster,'" *BBC News,* November 8, 2006; Anne Penketh and Andy McSmith, "Whistleblower that Ministers Tried to Muzzle," *Independent,* December 15, 2006; Wood, "Rebellious Diplomat Finds Work."

77. Carne Ross, written transcript to the Butler Inquiry, June 9, 2004, http://news.independent.co.uk/uk/politics/article2076142.ece.

78. Doward, "11th-hour bid to halt Iraq war revelations"; Norton-Taylor, "WMD claims 'totally implausible,'"; Ross, Butler Inquiry transcript.

79. Penketh and McSmith, "Whistleblower Ministers Tried to Muzzle."

80. Ibid.; Norton-Taylor, "WMD claims 'totally implausible.'"

81. "Foreign Affairs—Minutes of Evidence," taken before Foreign Affairs Committee, House of Commons, November 8, 2006, www.publications.parliament.uk/pa/cm200607/cmselect/cmfaff/167/6110801.htm.

82. "Written evidence submitted by Mr. Carne Ross: Testimony to House of Commons Foreign Affairs Committee: Commentary on FCO White Paper "Active Diplomacy," November 6, 2006, www.publications.parliament.uk/pa/cm200506/cmselect/cmfaff/uc1720-i/1720m02.htm.

83. "Foreign Affairs—Minutes of Evidence."

84. Ned Temko, "Foreign Office tries to gag ex-envoy," *Observer,* November 26, 2006.

85. Penketh and McSmith, "Whistleblower Ministers Tried to Muzzle."

86. Temko, "Foreign Office tries to gag ex-envoy"; Colin Brown and Andy McSmith, "Diplomat's suppressed document lays bare the lies behind Iraq war," *Independent,* December 15, 2006.

87. Doward, "11th-hour bid to halt Iraq war revelations."

88. "UK Iraq Policy 'rank disaster'"; Brown and McSmith, "Diplomat's suppressed document lays bare lies."

89. Brown and McSmith, "Diplomat's suppressed document lays bare lies."

90. Blitzer, *Situation Room,* May 4, 2007.

91. "Foreign Affairs–Minutes of Evidence."

92. "How Beckett's answers raise more questions on Iraq," *Guardian,* December 20, 2006; Wood, "Rebellious Diplomat Finds Work."

93. Moss, "Diplomat at large."

94. www.independentdiplomat.com.

95. Moss, "Diplomat at large."

96. Blitzer, *Situation Room,* May 4, 2007.

97. Nick Paton Walsh, "US Looks Away as New Ally Tortures Islamists," *Guardian,* May 26, 2003.

98. Ibid.; Craig Murray, "What drives support for this torturer?" *Guardian,* May 16, 2005; "Uzbekistan: Country Reports on Human Rights Practices," U.S. State Department report, February 2001, http://www.state.gov/g/drl/rls/hrrpt/2001/eur/8366.htm.

99. Nick Paton Walsh, "Uzbekistan kicks US out of military base," *Guardian,* August 1, 2005.

100. David Leigh, Nick Paton Walsh, and Ewen MacAskill, "Ambassador accused after criticising US," *Guardian,* October 18, 2003.

101. Don Van Natta, Jr., "US Recruits a Rough Ally to Be a Jailer," *New York Times,* May 1, 2005.

102. Amy Goodman, interview with Craig Murray, *Democracy Now!,* Pacifica, January 19, 2006.

103. Van Natta, "US Recruits Rough Ally"; Nick Paton Walsh, "The Envoy Who Said Too Much," *Guardian,* July 15, 2004; Goodman, interview with Craig Murray.

104. Walsh, "Uzbekistan kicks U.S. out."

105. Craig Murray, "The Uses of Torture," speech at York University, February 24, 2005.

106. "UN Visits Uzbekistan and Finds Torture to be 'Systemic,'" Human Rights Watch, http://www.hrw.org/update/2003/01.html#9.

107. Craig Murray, "The Banality of Evil," speech at Massachusetts Institute of Technology, June 15, 2006.

108. Craig Murray, *Murder in Samarkand: A British Ambassador's Controversial Defiance of a Tyrannical Regime Within the War on Terror* (Edinburgh: Mainstream, 2006).

109. Johann Hari, "The blood of the Uzbeks, the hypocrisy of the West, and the last great oil grab," *Independent,* May 18, 2005.

110. Nick Paton Walsh, "Envoy in Human Rights Row Dismissed," *Guardian,* October 15, 2004.

111. "'Torture intelligence' criticized," *BBC News,* October 11, 2004.

112. Walsh, "Envoy Who Said Too Much."

113. Gedye, "The Envoy Silenced After Telling Undiplomatic Truths," *Guardian,* October 16, 2004; Joan Smith, "Our Man in Tashkent," *Independent,* April 4, 2004.

114. Gedye, "Envoy Silenced After Telling Undiplomatic Truths."

115. Leigh, Walsh, and MacAskill, "Ambassador accused after criticising US"; Gedye, "Envoy Silenced After Telling Undiplomatic Truths."

116. Murray, *Murder in Samarkand,* 68.

117. Annex 2 in EUROPEAN PARLIAMENT, "Temporary Committee on the alleged use of European countries by the CIA for the transport and illegal detention of

prisoners, WORKING DOCUMENT No. 5 on the testimony by Craig Murray, former British Ambassador," June 1, 2006. www.europarl.europa.eu/comparl/tempcom/tdip/working_docs/pe374341_en.pdf

118. Annex 1 in EUROPEAN PARLIAMENT, June 1, 2006.

119. Murray, "Uses of Torture"; "Pick Your Cotton Carefully," Environmental Justice Foundation, www.ejfoundation.org/page141.html.

120. Murray, "Uses of Torture."

121. Hari, "Blood of the Uzbeks."

122. Susana Raby, "Craig Murray Interview," *Sunday Times,* May 28, 2006.

123. Walsh, "Envoy Who Said Too Much"; Evan Williams, "Uzbekistan," transcript, March 29, 2005, www.abc.net.au/foreign/content/2005/s1335846.htm; Gedye, "Envoy Silenced After Telling Undiplomatic Truths."

124. Murray, "Banality of Evil."

125. Ibid.

126. Murray, "Uses of Torture."

127. Ibid.

128. Raby, "Craig Murray Interview."

129. Ibid.; Goodman, interview with Craig Murray.

130. President Bush's White House Address to the Nation, March 17, 2003.

131. Leigh, Walsh, and MacAskill, "Ambassador accused after criticising US."

132. Annex 2 in EUROPEAN PARLIAMENT, June 1, 2006.

133. Leigh, Walsh, and MacAskill, "Ambassador accused after criticising US."

134. Goodman, interview with Craig Murray.

135. Walsh, "Envoy Who Said Too Much."

136. Hari, "Blood of the Uzbeks."

137. Walsh, "Envoy Who Said Too Much."

138. Gedye, "Envoy Silenced After Telling Undiplomatic Truths."

139. Leigh, Walsh, and MacAskill. "Ambassador accused after criticising US."

140. Walsh, "Envoy Who Said Too Much."

141. Leigh, Walsh, and MacAskill. "Ambassador accused after criticising US"; Raby, "Craig Murray Interview."

142. Murray, *Murder in Samarkand.*

143. Annex 3 in EUROPEAN PARLIAMENT, June 1, 2006.

144. Raby, "Craig Murray Interview."

145. Van Natta, "US Recruits Rough Ally."

146. Gedye, "Envoy Silenced After Telling Undiplomatic Truths"; Ewen MacAskill, "Ex-envoy to face discipline charges, says FO," *Guardian,* October 22, 2004.

147. Goodman, interview with Craig Murray.

148. Sanchia Berg, "Ambassador speaks out," *BBC News,* October 15, 2004.

149. "Uzbeks Protest at British Envoy's Sacking," *Scotsman,* October 29, 2004.

150. Gedye, "Envoy Silenced After Telling Undiplomatic Truths."

151. Ibid.

152. Philip Stephens, "The price of turning a diplomatic blind eye," *Financial Times,* October 19, 2004.

153. David Leigh, "Whitehall Unconfidential: The Censors are on the Run" *Guardian,* January 6, 2006.

154. Paul Reynolds, "Confessions of a British diplomat," BBC, October 15, 2004.

155. R. Jeffrey Smith and Glenn Kessler, "U.S. Opposed Calls at NATO for Probe of Uzbek Killings—Officials Feared Losing Air Base Access," *Washington Post,* June 14, 2005.

156. Monica Eng, "Ex-ambassador skewers CIA," *Chicago Tribune,* May 21, 2006; Walsh, "Uzbekistan kicks U.S. out."

157. Ibid.

158. Murray, "Banality of Evil."

159. Goodman, interview with Craig Murray.

160. Murray, "Banality of Evil."

161. Walsh, "Envoy Who Said Too Much."

162. Goodman, interview with Craig Murray.

163. Murray, "Uses of Torture."

164. Murray, *Murder in Samarkand.*

165. "Transcript: A Mighty Heart, [Interview with] Michael Winterbottom, Director," *Washington Post,* June 15, 2007.

166. U.S. State Department website, August 2005, www.state.gov/r/pa/ei/bgn/3167.htm.

167. "Journalist duo could face jail time," *Copenhagen Post,* April 27, 2006.

168. "Danish furore over Iraq secrets," *BBC News World Edition,* April 15, 2004.

169. Bo Elkjær, "The Lies of the War—the War of the Lies," *Ekstra Bladet,* October 5, 2003. According to the Danish Peace Academy, in November 2005: "Bo Elkjær shared the Cavling Prize for 2003 with two other journalists for their exposure of the Danish government's collusion in the invasion of Iraq. The Danish original of this account, titled 'Løgnen om krigen—krigen om løgnen,' was published as a supplement to the Danish daily newspaper, *Ekstra Bladet,* on October 5, 2003."

170. "International War Whistleblowers Tell Why They Exposed Their Governments," interview with Amy Goodman, *Democracy Now!,* Pacifica, September 9, 2004.

171. Ibid.

172. "Danish Official Jailed for Leaking Report on Iraq WMDs," *Democracy Now!* December 1, 2004.

173. Ibid.

174. "Danish furore over Iraq secrets."

175. Ibid.

176. Niall Green, "Danish Whistleblower Charged after accusing Prime Minister of Exaggerating Iraqi WMD," www.wsws.org, April 24, 2004.

177. "Open Letter to the Danish Government and Public: 11 Former and Current US and UK Government Employees Issue Letter Supporting Danish Whistle-blower Frank Grevil," September 22, 2004. www.freerepublic.com/focus/fnews/1451334/posts.

178. Green, "Danish Whistleblower Charged."

179. Ibid.

180. Reporters without Borders, "Denmark—Annual report 2007," www.rsf.org/article.php3?id_article=20811; "Danish State Secrets," ABC Radio National (Australia), May 18, 2006, www.abc.net.au/rn/mediareport/stories/2006/1642694.htm#.

181. Reporters without Borders, "Denmark—Annual report 2007."

182. Jeff Fleischer, "Inside the Axis of Deceit," *Mother Jones,* August 16, 2004.

183. Elkjær, "Lies of the War."

184. Fleischer, "Inside Axis of Deceit."

185. Ibid.

186. Ray McGovern, "One Person Can Make a Difference," commondreams.org, October 15, 2003.

187. Rod McGuirk, "Australian probe faults weak prewar intelligence on Iraq," *Boston Globe,* July 23, 2004.

188. "Wilkie: my judgment is vindicated," *The Age,* July 23, 2004.

189. Elkjær, "Lies of the War."

190. "Wilkie: my judgment is vindicated."

191. Elkjær, "Lies of the War."

192. Fleischer, "Inside Axis of Deceit."

193. "McKew death threats familiar: Wilkie," Yahoo News, March 3, 2007.

4—U.S. Whistleblowers

1. Jesselyn Radack. "A Legal Defense of Russell Tice, the Whistleblower who Revealed the President's Authorization of NSA's Warrantless Domestic Wiretapping" Findlaw.com, January 27, 2006.

2. ACLU, "Government Engaging in Pattern of Cover-up; Whistleblowers Silenced at the Expense of Our Safety" January 26, 2005, www.aclu.org/safefree/general/18827res20050126.html.

3. In 1971, Daniel Ellsberg leaked what became known as the Pentagon Papers, 7,000 pages of classified documents that detailed many years of government deception about American involvement in Vietnam. This leak helped to bring about a quicker end to the U.S. war in Vietnam.

4. Daniel Ellsberg, *Democracy Now!*, Pacifica, July 2, 2007.

5. "Buying the War," *Bill Moyers Journal*, PBS, April 25, 2007.

6. "Ashcroft: Critics of new terror measures undermine effort," CNN, December 7, 2001. Ashcroft was speaking to the Senate Judiciary Committee.

7. *The Works of Theodore Roosevelt: The Great Adventure* (New York: Collier, 1926), vol. 19, 289.

8. Thom Hartmann, "Reclaiming the Issues: Why Is Bush Spying on Democrats?!?" Common Dreams, www.commondreams.org, July 10, 2006.

9. Quoted in Nichols and McChesney, *Tragedy and Farce*, 36.

10. Talk given at BookExpo America, June 2, 2007.

11. Michael Parenti, *Superpatriotism* (San Francisco: City Lights Books, 2004).

12. Alec Russell, "War on Iraq was illegal, says Annan" *Telegraph*, September 16, 2004.

13. Catherine Rampell, "Whistleblowers Tell of Cost of Conscience," *USA Today*, November 24, 2006.

14. Ibid.

15. Sherrie Gossett, "NSA Accused of Psychologically Abusing Whistleblowers," www.CNSNews.com, January 25, 2006; Daniel Zwerdling, "U.S. Military Whistleblowers Face Retribution," *All Things Considered*, NPR, May 21, 2004.

16. Martin Luther King, Jr., Letter from a Birmingham Jail, 1963.

17. "Prominent Americans Support British Whistleblower," Institute for Public Accuracy, January 29, 2004.

18. William G. Weaver, J.D., Ph.D., Testimony to the House Committee on Oversight and Government Reform re: Whistleblower Protection Enhancement Act of 2007, February 13, 2007, www.fas.org/sgp/congress/2007/021307weaver.pdf.

19. Laurie Abraham, "Anatomy of a Whistleblower," *Mother Jones*, January 2004.

20. *Democracy Now!*, Pacifica, July 2, 2007.

21. Zwerdling, "U.S. Military Whistleblowers Face Retribution"; Gossett, "NSA Accused of Psychologically Abusing Whistleblowers."

22. C. Fred Alford, "Whistle-blower narratives: the experience of choiceless choice," *Social Research*, Spring 2007, 223.

23. Quoted on the jacket of Myron Peretz Glazer and Penina Migdal Glazer, *The Whistleblowers: Exposing Corruption in Government and Industry* (New York: Basic Books, 1989).

24. Rampell, "Whistleblowers Tell of Cost of Conscience."

25. Jesselyn Radack, "Why the 'Paul Revere Freedom to Warn' Act Should Be Passed, to Better Protect National Security Whistleblowers: The Lessons of Deep Throat, the Plame Leak, and the Lindh Case," www.FindLaw.com, June 13, 2005.

26. Jesselyn Radack, "A Legal Defense of Russell Tice, the Whistleblower who Revealed the President's Authorization of NSA's Warrantless Domestic Wiretapping," www.FindLaw.com, January 27, 2006.

27. Ibid.

28. Daniel Schulman, "Office of Special Counsel's War On Whistleblowers," *Mother Jones*, May 2007.

29. *Democracy Now!*, Pacifica, July 2, 2007.

30. Adam Zagorin and Timothy J. Burger, "Beyond the Call of Duty," *Time*, October 24, 2004; "Bunnatine Greenhouse," www.pbs.org/now/shows/315/whistleblowers.html

31. Michael Shnayerson, "The Spoils of War," *Vanity Fair*, March 7, 2005.

32. Ibid.

33. Eric Herring and Glen Rangwala. *Iraq in Fragments: The Occupation and Its Legacy* (Ithaca: Cornell University Press, 2006), 249.

34. Shnayerson, "Spoils of War."

35. Ibid.

36. Erik Eckholm, "Top Army Official Calls for a Halliburton Inquiry," *New York Times*, October 25, 2004.

37. Shnayerson, "Spoils of War."

38. Bunnatine Greenhouse, letter to the acting Secretary of the Army, October 21, 2003. www.publicintegrity.org/docs/halliburton/Attorney_Letter.pdf

39. Eckholm, "Top Army Official Calls for Halliburton Inquiry."

40. Ibid.

41. Shnayerson, "Spoils of War."

42. Erik Eckholm, "A Watchdog Follows the Money in Iraq," *New York Times*, November 15, 2004.

43. Ibid.

44. Ibid.

45. Shnayerson, "Spoils of War."

46. Griff Witte, "Halliburton Contract Critic Loses Her Job," *Washington Post*, August 29, 2005.

47. Eckholm, "Top Army Official Calls for Halliburton Inquiry."

48. Ibid.

49. Erik Eckholm, "Army Contract Official Critical of Halliburton Pact is Demoted," *New York Times,* August 29, 2005.

50. Neely Tucker, "A Web of Truth: Whistle-Blower or Troublemaker, Bunny Greenhouse Isn't Backing Down," in *Washington Post,* October 19, 2005.

51. Tucker, "A Web of Truth."

52. Shnayerson, "Spoils of War."

53. Ibid.

54. Ibid.

55. Abraham, "Anatomy of a Whistleblower."

56. *Radack v. U.S. Department of Justice,* August 9, 2005, https://ecf.dcd.uscourts.gov/cgi-bin/show_public_doc?2004cv1881–10.

57. "Whistleblower Charges Justice Dept. with Misconduct in Chertoff's Prosecution of John Walker Lindh," *Democracy Now!,* Pacifica, January 13, 2005.

58. *Jesselyn A. Radack v. United States Department of Justice,* 2006 WL 2024978 (July 17, 2006 D.D.C.), www.nobc.org/cases/0706.asp

59. Michael Isikoff, "The Lindh E-mails," *Newsweek,* June 24, 2002.

60. "Whistleblower Charges Justice Dept. with Misconduct."

61. Abraham, "Anatomy of a Whistleblower."

62. *Radack v. U.S. Department of Justice.*

63. Gregg Leslie, "Justice and the whistleblower," *News Media & the Law,* Summer 2003, 4.

64. *Radack v. U.S. Department of Justice.*

65. Leslie, "Justice and the whistleblower."

66. "Whistleblower Charges Justice Dept. with Misconduct."

67. *Radack v. U.S. Department of Justice.*

68. Ibid.

69. Radack, "Why 'Paul Revere Freedom to Warn' Act Should Be Passed."

70. Michael Isikoff, "The Lindh E-mails," *Newsweek,* June 24, 2002.

71. "Whistleblower Charges Justice Dept. with Misconduct."

72. Jesselyn Radack, "Whistleblowing in Washington," *Reform Judaism,* Spring 2006.

73. Abraham, "Anatomy of a Whistleblower."

74. Ibid.

75. Radack, "Whistleblowing in Washington."

76. "Jesselyn Radack Was the Justice Department Official Who Knew Too Much," www.buzzflash.com, February 16, 2007.

77. "About the Contributors," *University of Colorado Law Review,* Volume 77 Issue 1, Winter 2006.

78. Radack, "Why 'Paul Revere Freedom to Warn' Act Should Be Passed."

79. Radack, "Whistleblowing in Washington."

80. Radack, "Why 'Paul Revere Freedom to Warn' Act Should Be Passed."

81. Brian Friel, "State Department Official Blasts Government Agencies," *Government Executive*, October 12, 2001.

82. Ibid.

83. Bob Drogin, Eric Lichtblau and Greg Krikorian. "CIA, FBI Disagree on Urgency of Aug. 27 Cable Warning of Terrorists Entering U.S." *Los Angeles Times*, October 28, 2001.

84. Ibid.

85. Ibid.

86. Ibid.

87. Ibid.

88. Ibid.

89. Shawn Zeller, "The Brave New World of Visa Processing," *Foreign Service Journal*, September 2004.

90. Teri Schultz, "State Department Head of Consular Affairs Retires," *Fox News*, July 11, 2002.

91. Ibid.

92. Mary A. Ryan, "Statement of Mary A. Ryan to the National Commission on Terrorist Attacks Upon the United States," January 26, 2004.

93. Christopher Deliso, "An Interview with Sibel Edmonds: FBI Whistleblower Talks to Antiwar.com," July 1, 2004.

94. 2006 PEN/Newman's Own First Amendment Award Video about Sibel Edmonds, www.pen.org/page.php/prmID/172.

95. David Rose, "An Inconvenient Patriot," *Vanity Fair*, August 15, 2005; Anne E. Kornblut, "Translator in eye of storm on retroactive classification," *Boston Globe*, July 5, 2004.

96. Kornblut, "Translator in eye of storm."

97. Ed Bradley, "Lost in Translation," interview with Sibel Edmonds, *60 Minutes*, CBS, October 25, 2002.

98. Ibid.

99. Ibid.

100. Rose, "An Inconvenient Patriot"; James V. Grimaldi, "2 FBI Whistle-Blowers Allege Lax Security, Possible Espionage," *Washington Post*, June 19, 2002.

101. Rose, "An Inconvenient Patriot."

102. Ibid.

103. Bradley, "Lost in Translation."

104. Ibid.

105. Ibid.

106. Ibid.

107. Ibid.

108. Ibid.

109. Sibel Edmonds, Letter to the National Committee on Terrorist Attacks on the United States, August 1, 2004, www.justacitizen.org/articles_documents/Letter_to_Kean.pdf.

110. Bradley, "Lost In Translation."

111. "Sibel Edmonds: A Patriot Silenced, Unjustly Fired but Fighting Back to Help Keep America Safe," ACLU website, January 26, 2005, www.aclu.org/safefree/general/18828res20050126.html.

112. Kevin Bohn, "FBI translator suit dismissed over security issues," CNN, July 7, 2004.

113. Bradley, "Lost In Translation."

114. "Sibel Edmonds: A Patriot Silenced."

115. Bohn, "FBI translator suit dismissed."

116. Ibid.

117. Ibid.

118. Ibid.

119. "Sibel Edmonds: A Patriot Silenced."

120. Bradley, "Lost In Translation."

121. Ibid.

122. Bohn, "FBI translator suit dismissed."

123. Ibid.

124. Tom Regan, "National security whistle-blowers call for boycott of hearing," *Christian Science Monitor,* November 30, 2005; William Fisher, "Security Whistle-blowers Demand End to Retaliation," Inter Press Service, May 12, 2005.

125. Radack, "Legal Defense of Russell Tice."

126. Glenn A. Fine, "A Review of the FBI's Actions in Connection With Allegations Raised by Contract Linguist Sibel Edmonds," Office of the Inspector General, Department of Justice, January 2005.

127. 2006 PEN/Newman's Own First Amendment Award Video about Sibel Edmonds, www.pen.org/page.php/prmID/172.

128. "Translator Fired from FBI for Blowing Whistle on Intelligence Failures to Receive 2006 PEN/Newman's Own First Amendment Award," www.pen.org/viewmedia.php/prmMID/633/prmID/172.

129. Rose, "An Inconvenient Patriot."

130. Jesselyn Radack, "A Legal Defense of Russell Tice, the Whistleblower Who Revealed the President's Authorization of NSA's Warrantless Domestic Wiretapping," *Findlaw, Legal News and Commentary,* January 27, 2006.

131. James Risen and Eric Lichtblau, "Bush Lets U.S. Spy on Callers without Courts," *New York Times,* December 16, 2005.

132. Risen and Lichtblau, "Bush Lets U.S. Spy on Callers."

133. Ibid.

134. "NSA Whistleblower Warns Domestic Spying Program is a Sign the U.S. is decaying into a 'Police State,'" *Democracy Now!,* Pacifica, January 3, 2006.

135. *Radack v. U.S. Department of Justice,* August 9, 2005, https://ecf.dcd.uscourts.gov/cgi-bin/show_public_doc?2004cv1881-10; and James Risen and Eric Lichtblau, "Justice Deputy Resisted Parts of Spy Program," *New York Times,* January 1, 2006.

136. Brian Ross, "NSA Whistleblower Alleges Illegal Spying," *ABC News,* January 10, 2006.

137. "NSA Whistleblower Warns," *Democracy Now!*

138. David Jackson, "Judge: NSA Warrantless Wiretapping Unconstitutional," *USA Today,* August 17, 2006.

139. "Democrats Capitulate to President Bush as Congress Gives Government Broad New Powers to Conduct Warrantless Surveillance on American Citizens," *Democracy Now!,* Pacifica, August 6, 2007.

140. "NSA Whistleblower Warns" *Democracy Now!*

141. Ibid.

142. Radack, "Legal Defense of Russell Tice."

143. "NSA Whistleblower Warns," *Democracy Now!*

144. Ibid.

145. Ibid.

146. Ibid.

147. Radack, "Legal Defense of Russell Tice."

148. Risen and Lichtblau, "Justice Deputy Resisted Parts of Spy Program."

149. Ibid.

150. Dan Eggen and Paul Kane, "Gonzales Hospital Episode Detailed: Ailing Ashcroft Pressured on Spy Program, Former Deputy Says," *Washington Post,* May 16, 2007.

151. Ibid.

152. Jackson, "Warrantless Wiretapping Unconstitutional."

153. *ACLU v. NSA.* August 17, 2006, www.mied.uscourts.gov/eGov/taylorpdf/06%2010204.pdf

154. Jackson, "Warrantless Wiretapping Unconstitutional."

155. Adam Liptak, "Appeals Court Rejects Lawsuit on Surveillance" *New York Times,* July 6, 2007.

156. Ibid.

157. Ellen Nakashima and Joby Warrick, "House Approves Wiretap Measure: White House Bill Boosts Warrantless Surveillance," *Washington Post,* August 5, 2007.

158. James Risen, "Bush Signs Law to Widen Reach for Wiretapping," *New York Times,* August 6, 2007; "Democrats Capitulate to President Bush," *Democracy Now!;* "Fact Sheet: The Protect America Act of 2007: President Bush Signs Legislation Modernizing Foreign Intelligence Law To Better Protect America," August 6, 2007, www.whitehouse.gov/news/releases/2007/08/20070806-5.html.

159. Romesh Ratnesar and Michael Weisskopf, "How the FBI Blew the Case," *Time,* May 26, 2002.

160. Ibid.

161. Greg Gordon, "Coleen Rowley retires from the FBI," *Minneapolis Star Tribune,* January 1, 2005.

162. Ratnesar and Weisskopf, "How FBI Blew Case."

163. Ibid.

164. Gordon, "Coleen Rowley retires from FBI."

165. Ratnesar and Weisskopf, "How FBI Blew Case."

166. Ibid.

167. Richard Lacayo and Amanda Ripley, "Persons of the Year 2002: Cynthia Cooper, Colleen Rowley and Sherron Watkins," *Time,* December 22, 2002.

168. Ibid.

169. Gordon, "Coleen Rowley retires from FBI."

170. Coleen Rowley, February 26, 2003, letter to FBI director Mueller, quoted in *Minneapolis Star Tribune,* March 6, 2003.

171. Gordon, "Coleen Rowley retires from FBI."

172. Ibid.

173. Ibid.

174. Ibid.

175. "Coleen Rowley," biography, Huffington Post, www.huffingtonpost.com/coleen-rowley.

176. Gordon, "Coleen Rowley retires from FBI."

177. "Coleen Rowley," biography, Huffington Post.

178. Coleen Rowley's Memo to FBI Director Robert Mueller, May 21, 2002, www.time.com/time/nation/article/0,8599,249997,00.html.

179. And both of the violations originally cited in vain by the Minneapolis agents disputing the issue with FBIHQ personnel are among those on which Moussaoui is currently indicted.

180. Just minutes after I saw the first news of the World Trade Center attack(s), I was standing outside the office of Minneapolis ASAC M. Chris Briesse, waiting for him to finish a phone call, when he received a call on another line from this SSA. Since I figured I knew what the call might be about and wanted to ask, in light of the unfolding events and the apparent urgency of the situation, if we should now immediately attempt to obtain a criminal search warrant for Moussaoui's laptop and personal property, I took the call. I said something to the effect that, in light of what had just happened in New York, it would have to be the "hugest coincidence" at this point if Moussaoui was not involved with the terrorists. The SSA stated something to the effect that I had used the right term, "coincidence" and that this was probably all just a coincidence and we were to do nothing in Minneapolis until we got their (HQ's) permission because we might "screw up" something else going on elsewhere in the country.

181. Certainly Rule 41 of the Federal Rules of Criminal Procedure, which begins, "Upon the request of a federal law enforcement officer or an attorney for the government," does not contain this requirement. Although the practice that has evolved is that FBI agents must secure prior approval for any search or arrest from the United States Attorneys Office, the Federal Rule governing Search and Seizure clearly envisions law enforcement officers applying, on their own, for search warrants.

182. During the early aftermath of September 11th, when I happened to be recounting the pre–September 11th events concerning the Moussaoui investigation to other FBI personnel in other divisions or in FBIHQ, almost everyone's first question was "Why?—Why would (an) FBI agent(s) deliberately sabotage a case?" (I know I shouldn't be flippant about this, but jokes were actually made that the key FBIHQ personnel had to be spies or moles, like Robert Hansen, who were actually working for Osama bin Laden to have so undercut Minneapolis' effort.)

Our best real guess, however, is that, in most cases avoidance of all "unnecessary" actions/decisions by FBIHQ managers (and maybe to some extent field managers as well) has, in recent years, been seen as the safest FBI career course. Numerous high-ranking FBI officials who have made decisions or have taken actions which, in hindsight, turned out to be mistaken or just turned out badly (i.e., Ruby Ridge, Waco, etc.) have seen their careers plummet and end. This has in turn resulted in a climate of fear which has chilled aggressive FBI law enforcement action/decisions.

In a large hierarchal bureaucracy such as the FBI, with the requirement for numerous superiors' approvals/oversight, the premium on career enhancement, and the chilling factor of recent, extreme public and congressional criticism/oversight, I think you will see at least the makings of the most likely explanation. Another factor, not to be underestimated, probably explains the SSA and other FBIHQ personnel's reluctance to act, and so far I have heard no FBI official even allude to this problem: that FBI Headquarters is staffed with a number of short-term careerists* who, like the SSA in question, must only serve an 18-month, just-time-to-get-your-ticket-punched minimum. It's no wonder very little expertise can be acquired by a Headquarters unit! And no wonder FBIHQ is mired in mediocrity! (That may be a little strong, but it would definitely be fair to say that there is unevenness in competency among Headquarters personnel.)

(It's also a well-known fact that the FBI Agents Association has complained for years about the disincentives facing those entering the FBI management career path, with the result that very few of the FBI's best and brightest choose to go into management. Instead, the ranks of FBI management are filled with many who were failures as street agents. Along these lines, let me ask why it has suddenly become necessary for the Director to "handpick" the FBI management?)

It's quite conceivable that many of the HQ personnel who so vigorously disputed Moussaoui's ability/predisposition to fly a plane into a building were simply unaware of all the various incidents and reports worldwide of al Qaeda terrorists attempting or plotting to do so.

*By the way, just in case you did not know it, let me furnish you Merriam-Webster's definition of *careerism:* "the policy or practice of advancing one's career often at the cost of one's professional or personal integrity." Maybe that sums up the whole problem!

183. For example, at one point, the Supervisory Special Agent at FBIHQ posited that the French information could be worthless because it only identified Zacarias Moussaoui by name and he, the SSA, didn't know how many people by that name existed in France. A Minneapolis agent attempted to surmount this problem by quickly phoning the FBI's Legal Attaché (Legat) in Paris, so that a check could be made of the French telephone directories. Although the Legat in France did not have access to all the French telephone directories, he was quickly able to ascertain that there was only one Zacarias Moussaoui listed in the Paris directory. It is not known if this sufficiently answered the question, for the SSA continued to find new reasons to stall.

184. Another factor that cannot be underestimated as to the HQ Supervisor's apparent reluctance to do anything was (and is) the ever-present risk of being "written up" for an Intelligence Oversight Board (IOB) "error." In the year(s) preceding the September 11th acts of terrorism, numerous alleged IOB violations on the part of FBI personnel had to be submitted to the FBI's Office of Professional Responsibility (OPR) as well as to the IOB. I believe the chilling effect on all levels of FBI agents assigned to intelligence matters and on their managers hampered us from aggressive investigation of terrorists.

Since one generally only runs the risk of IOB violations when one does something, the safer course is to do nothing. Ironically, in this case, a potentially huge IOB violation arguably occurred due to FBIHQ's failure to act; that is, FBIHQ's failure to inform the Department of Justice Criminal Division of Moussaoui's potential criminal violations (which, as I've already said, were quickly identified in Minneapolis as violations of Title 18 United States Code Section 2332b [Acts of terrorism transcending national boundaries] and Section 32 [Destruction of aircraft or aircraft facilities]). This failure would seem to run clearly afoul of the Attorney General directive contained in the "1995 Procedures for Contacts

Between the FBI and the Criminal Division Concerning Foreign Intelligence and Foreign Counterintelligence Investigations" which mandatorily require the FBI to notify the Criminal Division when "facts or circumstances are developed' in an FI or FCI investigation "that reasonably indicate that a significant federal crime has been, is being, or may be committed."

I believe that Minneapolis agents actually brought this point to FBIHQ's attention on August 22, 2001, but HQ personnel apparently ignored the directive, ostensibly due to their opinion of the lack of probable cause. But the issue of whether HQ personnel deliberately undercut the probable cause can be sidestepped at this point because the Directive does not require probable cause. It requires only a "reasonable indication," which is defined as "substantially lower than probable cause." Given that the Minneapolis Division had accumulated far more than "a mere hunch" (which the directive would deem insufficient), the information ought to have, at least, been passed on to the "Core Group" created to assess whether the information needed to be further disseminated to the Criminal Division. However, to date I have never heard that any potential violation of this directive has been submitted to the IOB or to the FBI's OPR (though I don't know for sure that none has been submitted). It should also be noted that, when making determinations of whether items need to be submitted to the IOB, it is my understanding that NSLU normally used/uses a broad approach, erring, when in doubt, on the side of submitting potential violations.

185. For starters, if prevention rather than prosecution is to be our new main goal (an objective I totally agree with), we need more guidance on when we can apply the Quarles "public safety" exception to *Miranda's* Fifth Amendment requirements. We were prevented from even attempting to question Moussaoui on the day of the attacks, when, in theory, he could have possessed further information about other co-conspirators. (Apparently no government attorney believes there is a "public safety" exception in a situation like this?!)

186. Joseph Wilson, "What I Didn't Find in Africa," *New York Times,* July 6, 2003.

187. Craig Unger, "The War They Wanted, The Lies They Needed," *Vanity Fair,* July 2006, 95.

188. "The Dark Side," *Frontline,* PBS, June 20, 2006.

189. "News War: Secrets, Sources, and Spin," *Frontline,* PBS, February 14, 2007.

190. Wilson, "What I Didn't Find in Africa."

191. Ray McGovern, "Why Cheney Lost It When Joe Wilson Spoke Out," www.truthout.org, March 7, 2007.

192. Amy Goldstein, "Bush Commutes Libby's Prison Sentence," *Washington Post,* July 3, 2007.

193. Carol Leonnig, "Plame's Suit Against Top Officials Dismissed," *Washington Post,* July 20, 2007.

194. Jason Leopold and Matt Renner, "Plame Suit Dismissed by Controversial GOP Loyalist," www.truthout.org, July 19, 2007.

5—Opposition Within the Military

1. Lieut. Gen. Greg Newbold, "Why Iraq Was a Mistake," *Time,* April 9, 2006.

2. Lieut. Gen. Brent Scowcroft, "Don't Attack Saddam," *Wall Street Journal,* August 15, 2002.

3. Ibid.

4. Ibid.

5. Ibid.

6. Gen. Anthony Zinni, "They've Screwed Up," *60 Minutes,* CBS, May 21, 2004.

7. Tom Clancy and Tony Zinni, *Battle Ready* (New York: Putnam, 2004).

8. Richard J. Whalen, "Revolt of the Generals," *Nation,* October 16, 2006.

9. David Margolick, "The Night of the Generals," *Vanity Fair,* April 2007.

10. Newbold, "Why Iraq Was a Mistake."

11. Ibid.

12. Ibid.

13. Ibid.

14. Newbold, quoted in Margolick, "Night of the Generals."

15. Maj. Gen. (Ret.) Paul D. Eaton, "A Top-Down Review for the Pentagon," *New York Times,* March 19, 2006.

16. Ibid.

17. Margolick, "Night of the Generals"; Thom Shanker, "Army Career Behind Him, General Speaks Out on Iraq," *New York Times,* May 13, 2007; William Branigin, "Three Retired Officers Demand Rumsfeld's Resignation," *Washington Post,* September 25, 2006.

18. Margolick, "Night of the Generals."

19. Whalen, "Revolt of the Generals."

20. John Barry, Michael Hirsh and Michael Isikoff, "The Roots of Torture," *Newsweek International,* May 24, 2007.

21. Mark Denbeaux, "The Guantanamo Detainees: The Government's Story." Seton Hall University Law School.

22. Mark Huband, "US officer predicts Guantánamo releases," *Financial Times,* October 4, 2004.

23. "Truthdigger of the Week: Lt. Cmdr. Charles Swift," December 16, 2006. www.truthdig.com/report/item/20061216_truthdigger_charles_swift.

24. Brooks Egerton, "Moral decision jeopardizes Navy Lawyer's career," *Dallas Morning News,* May 18, 2007; "Navy lawyer convicted of leaking Guantanomo names," CNN, May 18, 2007; see also couragetoresist.org.

25. Dawn Bryan, "Abu Ghraib whistleblower's ordeal," *BBC News,* August 5, 2007; "Exposing The Truth Of Abu Ghraib: Anderson Cooper Interviews Whistleblower Joe Darby," *60 Minutes,* CBS, June 24, 2007.

26. Joe Darby, as told to Wil S. Hylton, "Prisoner of Conscience," *Gentleman's Quarterly*, www.men.style.com/gq/features/full?id=content_4785.

27. Michelle Norris, "Abu Ghraib Whistleblower Speaks Out," *All Things Considered*, NPR, August 15, 2006.

28. Tara McKelvey, *Monstering: Inside America's Policy of Secret Interrogations and Torture in the Terror War* (New York: Carroll & Graf, 2007), 6.

29. Ibid, 7.

30. Samuel Provance, "Testimony to the U.S. House of Representatives' Committee on Governmental Reform National Security subcommittee," February 13, 2006.

31. Dean Paton, "Backstory: Dissent of an Officer," *Christian Science Monitor*, February 2, 2007.

32. Charles E. Anderson, "Breaking Ranks: Troops Call for Iraq Withdrawal," www.truthout.org, January 14, 2007.

33. Eaton, "Top-Down Review."

34. Medea Benjamin, "Camilo Mejía Goes to Prison for His Stance against the War in Iraq," www.commondreams.org, May 24, 2004; "Support Sg.t Camilo Mejía! First Iraqui War Vet to refuse further military service," June 4, 2004, www.notinourname.net/troops/mejia-17mar04.htm

35. Ibid.

36. Camilo Mejía, "Regaining My Humanity," www.freecamilo.com/words.htm, reprinted with permission; "Support Sgt. Mejía!"

37. Chet Barfield, "He Won't Board Ship Transporting Troops," *San Diego Union-Tribune*, December 6, 2004.

38. Marjorie Cohn, "Navy Judge Finds War Protest Reasonable," www.zmag.org/content/showarticle.cfm?ItemID=7918, May 22, 2005; "War Resister Pablo Paredes Denied Conscientious Objector Status," *Democracy Now!*, Pacifica, April 26, 2005.

39. Ibid.

40. Pablo Paredes, "Statement to the Court," www.tomjoad.org/paredes_statement.htm, May 12, 2005.

41. David Zucchimo, "Breaking Ranks to Shun War," *Los Angeles Times*, February 7, 2005; see also Sean Harder, "Soldier Who Refused Combat Fighting Discharge," *Savannah Morning News*, October 3, 2006.

42. Ibid.

43. Sgt. Kevin Benderman, with Monica Benderman, *Letters from Fort Lewis Brig: A Matter of Conscience* (Guilford, Conn.: The Lyons Press, 2007). Used with permission.

44. Chris McGann, "Marine: I Refuse to Kill," *Seattle Post-Intelligencer*, April 2, 2003.

45. Joe Garofoli, "Between Anti-War Hero and Military Villain," *San Francisco Chronicle*, March 14, 2004.

46. McGann, "Marine: I Refuse to Kill."

47. Amnesty International urgent Action, February 2005, ACT 60/004/2005; AMR 51/071/2005, May 10, 2005. http://web.amnesty.org/library/index/ENGAMR 510712005?open&of=ENG-USA; Amnesty International Prisoner of Conscience, March 10, 2005, www.amnesty.org.

48. Abdullah Webster, "Abdullah Webster's Statement after Release from Prison," Amnesty International Media Briefing, News Service No. 125, May 13, 2005.

49. Scott Fleming, "In Good Conscience: An Interview With Reservist Turned Conscientious Objector Aidan Delgado," *LiP Magazine*, Spring 2005, www.alternet.org/waroniraq/20935.

50. "Conscientious Objector Witnessed Abuse, Killing of Iraqi Detainees at Abu Ghraib," *Democracy Now!*, Pacifica, December 17, 2004; Fleming, "In Good Conscience."

51. Fleming, "In Good Conscience."

52. Guillermo Contreras, "Soldier Loses Court Battle," *San Antonio Express News*, November 11, 2005; Statement of SPC Katherine Jashinski, www.courageto resist.org/x/content/view/17/2/, November 17, 2005.

53. U.S. Department of Justice, "Court Upholds Army's Denial of Texas National Guard Soldier's Conscientious Objector Application," March 8, 2006, www.usdoj.gov/usao/txw/press_releases/2006/Jashinski.pdf.

54. "Free Katherine," www.myspace.com/freekatherine; "Katherine Jashinski Released" www.couragetoresist.org/x/content/blogcategory/27/42/

55. Statement of SPC Katherine Jashinski, www.couragetoresist.org/x/content/view/17/2/, November 17, 2005.

56. Randy Furst, "Melanie McPherson, Minnesota Reservist, Charged with Desertion," *Minneapolis Star Tribune*, October 12, 2006.

57. "Soldier Gets Three Months in Military Prison for Deserting Unit the Day Before Deployment," Associated Press, February 5, 2007; "Soldier found guilty of desertion, not AWOL," *Deseret News*, February 6, 2007.

58. Furst, "Minnesota Reservist Charged with Desertion."

59. Jeremy Brecher and Brendan Smith, "Watada, the War and the Law," *Nation*, July 10, 2006; Dean Paton, "Backstory: Dissent of an officer," *Christian Science Monitor*, February 2, 2007; Hal Bernton, "Officer at Fort Lewis calls Iraq war illegal, refuses order to go," *Seattle Times*, June 7, 2006; "Army Lieutenant Becomes First Commissioned Officer to Refuse Deployment to Iraq," *Democracy Now!*, Pacifica, June 8, 2006; "Conduct Unbecoming an Officer and a Gentlemen: Lieutenant Ehren Watada Charged Again for Refusing to Deploy to Iraq," *Democracy Now!*, Pacifica, September 19, 2006; "Army moves forward with court martial of Lt. Ehren Watada, February 5: Update," November 11, 2006. www.couragetoresist.org/x/content/view/143/39/; Mike Barber, "Mistrial Could Be End of Watada Case," *Seattle Post-Intelligencer*, February 8, 2007.

60. Transcribed by Veterans For Peace, Greater Atlanta Chapter 125, www.vfp125.org/watadaspeech.html.

61. "Prisoner of Conscience: Agustín Aguayo," Amnesty International Urgent Action, March 8, 2007; www.aguayodefense.org/; "Court hears appeal of imprisoned conscientious objector Agustin Aguayo," www.couragetoresist.org/x/content/view/146/36/.

62. Mary Wiltenburg, "US Army Struggles With Soldier Who Won't Pull the Trigger," *Christian Science Monitor,* August 14, 2007.

63. Agustín Aguayo, "Declaration to the U.S. District Court in Washington, DC," August 10, 2006.

64. Laurie Goodstein, "A Soldier Hoped to Do Good, But Was Changed By War," *New York Times,* October 12, 2006.

65. Ibid.

66. Ricky Clousing, "Statement of Sgt. Ricky Clousing," www.couragetoresist.org/x/content/blogcategory/21/37/, August 11, 2006.

67. Diana Welch, "Soldier of Morality: Spc. Mark Wilkerson Learns that it's a Lot Easier to Get into the Army than it is to Get Out," *Austin Chronicle,* September 8, 2006; www.couragetoresist.org/x/ content/view/111/41; www.couragetoresist.org/x/content/view/253/41/.

68. Angela K. Brown, "AWOL Soldier Sentenced to Seven Months," *Guardian Unlimited* (UK), February 22, 2007.

69. Mark Wilkerson, "Statement by Mark Wilkerson" at Camp Casey, Crawford, Texas, www.couragetoresist.org/x/content/view/112/4/, August 21, 2006.

70. www.couragetoresist.org/x/content/view/69/27.

71. Lee Zaslofsk, War Resisters Support Campaign–Canada, email to Ann Wright, March 26, 2007.

72. Joshua Key, as told to Lawrence Hill, *The Deserter's Tale: The Story of an Ordinary Soldier Who Walked away from the War in Iraq* (New York: Atlantic Monthly Press, 2007), 229.

73. Frida Berrigan, "Soldier of Misfortune," in *The Progressive,* November 18, 2004.

74. Tracy McNicoll, "An Illegal, Immoral Order: An American Soldier Explains Why He Is Refusing to Fight in Iraq," *Newsweek,* March 30, 2005.

75. Peter Koch, "Brave Hart," in *Art Voice,* March 9, 2006.

76. War Resisters Support Campaign Canada, www.resisters.ca/resisters_stories.

77. "Jeremy Hinzman—Conscientious Objector Seeking Refuge Status in Canada," Amnesty International, *Amnesty News,* May 13, 2005.

78. Tony Jones, "US Deserters Head to Canada Over Iraq," Australian Broadcasting Corporation, December 4, 2004.

79. Josh Robinson, "Deserter's Bid for Asylum," *Toronto Sun,* June 3, 2005; Gerry Condon, "U.S. War Resisters in Canada, *Z Magazine Online,* July/August 2005.

80. Key, *Deserter's Tale.*

81. Koch, "Brave Hart."

82. "Galloway v. U.S. Senate," London *Times,* May 18, 2005.

83. Koch, "Brave Hart."

84. Claudine San Nicolas, "AWOL Marine with Maui Ties Flees to Canada," *Maui News,* May 1, 2006.

85. Gary Young, "We Shall Not Be Moved," *Guardian,* August 26, 2006; "War Resister Darrell Anderson Returns from Canada to Face Possible Charges," *Democracy Now!,* Pacifica, October 3, 2006; www.couragetoresist.org/x/content/blog category/26/40.

86. Phingo Gomba, "Deserter Defies Mom in Return to U.S.," *Toronto Star,* September 8, 2006.

87. "War Resister Darrell Anderson Returns from Canada," *Democracy Now!*

88. "Darrell Anderson, Iraq Veteran and War Resister, Released from Army," www. couragetoresist.org/x/content/view/125/40.

89. "Iraq veteran and war resister, Ivan Brobeck, released from military brig!" www. couragetoresist.org/ivanbrobeck.

90. Ivan Brobeck, Letter to President Bush, www.couragetoresist.org/ivanbrobeck/ index.php?option=com_content&task=view&id=17&Itemid=33, November 6, 2007.

91. Karen Button, "Refusing to Fight: an interview with war resister Kyle Snyder," www.Uruknet.info, August 9, 2006.

92. Mike Howell, "Soldiers of Misfortune," *Vancouver Courier,* March 17, 2006.

93. Gerry Condon, "Iraq War resister arrested in Canada, then released; US Army requested the illegal apprehension," www.couragetoresist.org/x/content/blog category/20/34/, February 28, 2007.

94. Mark Gabrish Conlan, "Kyle Snyder, War Resister, Speaks to Peace & Justice Coalition," Zenger's Newsmagazine, www.zengersmag.blogspot.com/2006/12/kyle-snyder-war-resister-speaks-to.html.

95. Sean Rayment, "SAS soldier quits Army in disgust at 'illegal' American tactics in Iraq," *Sunday Telegraph,* November 3, 2006.

96. Ibid.

97. Ibid.

98. Michael Evans, "RAF doctor refused a third tour of duty in 'illegal' war," *Times* (London), March 16, 2006.

99. "RAF doctor jailed over Iraq refusal," *Guardian,* April 13, 2006.

100. Ibid.

101. Ibid.

102. Kim Sengupta, "Prisoner of conscience: RAF doctor who refused Iraq service is jailed," *Independent,* April 14, 2006.

103. Ibid.

104. "Britain: Muslim Iraq war objector loses appeal," www.wri-irg.org/pubs/upd-0411.htm.

105. "Britain: Muslim Iraq war objector loses appeal."

6—Epilogue

1. President John F. Kennedy, "The President and the Press: Address before the American Newspaper Publishers Association," Waldorf-Astoria Hotel, New York City, April 27, 1961.

2. "Q-and-A with Daniel Ellsberg: Connecting Students to the World," Institute of International Studies, UC Berkeley, High School Students' E-Mail Exchange with Daniel Ellsberg, May 1999; Bill Katovski. *Patriots Act: Voices of Dissent and the Risk of Speaking Out.* (Guilford, Conn.: The Lyons Press, 2006).

3. "News War: Secrets, Sources & Spin," *Frontline*, PBS, February 13, 2007. www.pbs.org/wgbh/pages/frontline/newswar/etc/script2.html.

4. Katovski, *Patriots Act.*

5. "Pentagon Papers: Case Dismissed," in *Time*, May 21, 1973.

6. Daniel Ellsberg, *Secrets: A Memoir of Vietnam and the Pentagon Papers.* (New York: Penguin Books, 2003), 457.

7. Katovski, *Patriots Act.*

8. "Secret Government," *Now*, PBS, April 5, 2002.

9. Joel Beinin, "Ashcroft and Lieberman Suppress Debate? An Obligation to Question Prevailing Wisdom," *Los Angeles Times.* Dec. 30, 2001.

10. Daniel Ellsberg, "Truths Worth Telling," *New York Times,* September 28, 2004. Italics added.

Postscript

1. David S. Cloud, " Ex-Commander Says Iraq Effort is a Nightmare," *New York Times,* October 13, 2007.

2. The War as We Saw It," *New York Times,* August 19, 2007.

3. "The Real Iraq We Knew," *Washington Post,* October 16, 2007.

4. Ellen Nakashima. "A Story of Surveillance," *Washington Post,* November 7, 2007.

5. Naomi Wolf, "Ten Steps to Close Down an Open Society," *HuffingtonPost.com,* April 24, 2007.

Bibliography

Alford, C. Fred. *Whistleblowers: Broken Lives and Organizational Power.* Ithaca, NY: Cornell University Press, 2002.

Benderman, Sgt. Kevin. *Letters from Fort Lewis Brig: A Matter of Conscience.* Guilford, Conn.: The Lyons Press, 2007.

Blix, Hans. *Disarming Iraq: The Search for Weapons of Mass Destruction.* New York: Pantheon, 2004.

Chang, Nancy, *Silencing Political Dissent: How Post-September 11 Anti-Terrorism Measures Threaten Our Civil Liberties.* New York: Seven Stories Press, 2002.

Chomsky, Noam. *Hegemony or Survival: America's Quest for Global Dominance.* New York: Owl Books, 2004.

Clark, William R. *Petrodollar Warfare: Oil, Iraq and the Future of the Dollar.* Gabriola Island, BC: New Society Publishers, 2005.

Clarke, Richard A. *Against All Enemies: Inside America's War on Terror.* New York: The Free Press, 2004.

Cook, Robin. *The Point of Departure: Diaries from the Front Bench.* New York: Pocket Books, 2004.

Delgado, Aidan. *The Sutras of Abu Ghraib: Notes from a Conscientious Objector.* Boston: Beacon Press, 2007.

Ellsberg, Daniel. *Secrets: A Memoir of Vietnam and the Pentagon Papers.* New York: Penguin Books, 2003.

Engelhardt, Tom. *Mission Unaccomplished: TomDispatch Interviews with American Iconoclasts and Dissenters.* New York: Nation Books, 2006.

Everest, Larry. *Oil, Power & Empire: Iraq and the U.S. Global Agenda.* Monroe, Maine: Common Courage Press, 2004.

Glazer, Myron Peretz, and Penina Migdal Glazer. *Whistleblowers: Exposing Corruption in Government and Industry.* New York: Basic Books, 1991.

Goodman, Amy, and David Goodman. *Static: Government Liars, Media Cheerleaders, and the People Who Fight Back.* New York: Hyperion, 2007.

Grey, Stephen. *Ghost Plane: The True Story of the CIA Torture Program.* New York: St. Martin's Press, 2006.

Hedges, Chris, and Laila Al-Arian. *Collateral Damage: America's War against Iraqi Civilians.* New York: Nation Books, 2007.

Hersh, Seymour M. *Chain of Command: The Road from 9/11 to Abu Ghraib.* New York: HarperCollins, 2004.

Isikoff, Michael, and David Corn. *Hubris: The Inside Story of Spin, Scandal, and the Selling of the Iraq War.* New York: Three Rivers Press, 2007.

Johnson, Chalmers. *Nemesis: The Last Days of the American Republic.* New York: Metropolitan Books, 2007.

Juhasz, Antonia. *The Bush Agenda: Invading the World, One Economy at a Time.* New York: Regan Books, 2006.

Kampfner, John. *Blair's Wars.* London: Free Press, 2004.

Katovsky, Bill. *Patriots Act: Voices of Dissent and the Risk of Speaking Out.* Guilford, Conn.: The Lyons Press, 2006.

Key, Joshua, and Lawrence Hill. *The Deserter's Tale: The Story of an Ordinary Soldier Who Walked Away from the War in Iraq.* New York: Atlantic Monthly Press, 2007.

Kiesling, John Brady. *Diplomacy's Lessons: Realism for an Unloved Superpower.* Washington, DC: Potomac Books, 2006.

Kinzer, Stephen. *Overthrow: America's Century of Regime Change from Hawaii to Iraq.* New York: Times Books, 2006.

Knapke, Margaret, ed. *From Warriors to Resisters: U.S. Veterans on Terrorism.* 2nd ed. Yellow Springs, Ohio: fxBear, 2005.

Lappé, Frances Moore, *Democracy's Edge: Choosing to Save Our Country by Bringing Democracy to Life.* San Francisco: Jossey-Bass, 2005.

Laufer, Peter. *Mission Rejected: U.S. Soldiers Who Say No to Iraq.* White River Junction, Vt.: Chelsea Green, 2006.

McKelvey, Tara. *Monstering: Inside America's Policy of Secret Interrogations and Torture in the Terror War.* New York: Carroll & Graf, 2007.

Mejía, Camilo. *Road from Ar Ramadi: The Private Rebellion of Staff Sergeant Mejía.* New York: The New Press, 2007.

Murray, Craig. *Dirty Diplomacy: The Rough-and-Tumble Adventures of a Scotch-Drinking, Skirt-Chasing, Dictator-Busting and Thoroughly Unrepentant Ambassador Stuck on the Frontline of the War Against Terror.* New York: Scribner, 2007.

Nichols, John, and Robert W. McChesney. *Tragedy and Farce: How the American Media Sell Wars, Spin Elections, and Destroy Democracy.* New York: New Press, 2005.

Palast, Greg. *Armed Madhouse: From Baghdad to New Orleans—Sordid Secrets and Strange Tales of a White House Gone Wild.* New York: Plume, 2007.

Parenti, Michael. *Superpatriotism.* San Francisco: City Lights Books, 2004.

Peters, Charles, and Taylor Branch. *Blowing the Whistle: Dissent in the Public Interest.* New York: Praeger, 1972.

Radack, Jesselyn. *The Canary in the Coal Mine: Blowing the Whistle in the Case of the "American Taliban" John Walker Lindh.* Washington, DC: Patriot Truthteller, 2006.

Ritter, Scott. *Iraq Confidential: The Untold Story of the Intelligence Conspiracy to Undermine the UN and Overthrow Saddam Hussein.* New York: Nation Books, 2006.

Ross, Carne. *Independent Diplomat: Dispatches from an Unaccountable Elite.* Ithaca, NY: Cornell University Press, 2007.

Sands, Philippe. *Lawless World: America and the Making and Breaking of Global Rules from FDR's Atlantic Charter to George W. Bush's Illegal War.* New York: Viking Press, 2005.

Sarat, Austin, ed. *Dissent in Dangerous Times.* Ann Arbor: University of Michigan Press, 2005.

Savage, Charlie. Takeover: *The Return of the Imperial Presidency and the Subversion of American Democracy.* Boston: Little, Brown and Co., 2007.

Scheuer, Michael. *Imperial Hubris: Why the West Is Losing the War on Terror.* Washington, DC: Potomac Books, 2005.

Short, Clare. *An Honourable Deception?: New Labour, Iraq, and the Misuse of Power.* New York: The Free Press, 2005.

Suskind, Ron. *The Price of Loyalty: George W. Bush, the White House, and the Education of Paul O'Neill.* New York: Simon & Schuster, 2004.

Wilkie, Andrew. *Axis of Deceit: The Story of the Intelligence Officer Who Risked All to Tell the Truth about WMD and Iraq.* Melbourne, Australia: Black, Inc, 2004.

Wilson, Joseph. *The Politics of Truth: A Diplomat's Memoir: Inside the Lies that Led to War and Betrayed My Wife's CIA Identity.* New York: Carroll & Graf, 2004.

Woodward, Bob. *Bush at War.* New York: Pocket Books, 2003.

Zinn, Howard. *A Power Governments Cannot Suppress.* San Francisco: City Lights Books, 2006.

Resources for Education and Action

**Organizations Supporting Government Oversight
and Individual Rights**

American Civil Liberties Union: Defends and preserves individual rights and liberties. www.aclu.org

Coalition for Civil Rights and Democratic Liberties: Registers ordinary Americans' discontent about sacrificing freedom in the name of freedom. www.cradl.org/Index.htm

Fund for Constitutional Government: Funds organizations and journalists working for open, accountable government. www.fcgonline.org

Government Accountability Project: Defends whistleblowers and empowers citizen activists. www.whistleblower.org

National Security Whistleblowers Coalition: Provides fellowship for national security whistleblowers, advocates reform, and educates the public. www.nswbc.org

National Whistleblower Center: Works to ensure that disclosures are fully heard and whistleblowers defended. www.whistleblowers.org

Project on Government Oversight: Investigates, exposes, and seeks to remedy systematic abuses of power, mismanagement, and subservience by the government to special interests. www.pogo.org

Truth-Telling Project: Encourages whistle-blowing in the national interest. www.truthtellingproject.org

Groups Working for Peace and Justice

After Downing Street: Coalition of 200 groups pressuring Congress and media to investigate whether the President has committed impeachable offenses in connection with Iraq. www.afterdowningstreet.org

CODEPINK: Women for Peace: Works for positive social change through creative protest and nonviolent direct action. www.codepink4peace.org

Friends Committee on National Legislation: Lobbies for social and economic justice, peace, and good government. www.fcnl.org

Institute for Public Accuracy: Helps progressive perspectives receive media exposure. www.accuracy.org

Not In Our Name: Works to resist the U.S. government's course of war and repression waged in the name of fighting terrorism. www.notinourname.net

United for Peace and Justice: 1,300 groups joined together to oppose the Iraq War. www.unitedforpeace.org

Voices for Creative Nonviolence: Draws on the experiences of those who challenged U.S. and UN-imposed economic sanctions against the Iraqi people from 1990–2003 and confronts U.S. warmaking though nonviolent action. www.vcnv.org

War Resisters League: Strives nonviolently to remove all causes of war. www.warresisters.org

World Can't Wait: Organizes to stop the disastrous course of the Bush administration. worldcantwait.org

Groups Supporting Active-Duty Military, Veterans, Recruits, and their Families

Center on Conscience and War: Works to defend and extend the rights of conscientious objectors. www.centeronconscience.org

Central Committee for Conscientious Objectors: Supports and promotes individual and collective resistance to war. www.objector.org

Citizen Soldier: Works for GI rights. www.citizen-soldier.org

Courage to Resist: Supports resistance to illegal war and occupation. www.couragetoresist.org

GI Rights Hotline: Provides information to servicemembers about military discharges, grievance and complaint procedures, and other civil rights. 800-394-9544. http://girights.objector.org

Gold Star Families for Peace: Family members of those killed in war working to end the occupation of Iraq. www.gsfp.org

Iraq Veterans Against the War: Veterans and active-duty servicemen and women of the Global War on Terror working to bring their brothers and sisters home. www.ivaw.org

Military Families Speak Out: Relatives and loved ones of those in the military working to end the war in Iraq. www.mfso.org

National Lawyers Guild Military Law Task Force: Assists those working on military law issues. www.nlgmltf.org

Project on Youth and Non-Military Opportunities: Provides young people with alternative viewpoints about enlistment. www.projectyano.org

Service Women's Action Network: Mentors women considering military service, addresses problems facing women in uniform, and promotes their healing after service. www.servicewomen.org

Thank You, Lieutenant: News and updates about Lieutenant Ehren Watada's refusal to deploy to Iraq. www.thankyoult.org

Veterans for Peace: Veterans raising public awareness of the true costs and consequences of militarism and war, seeking effective, peaceful alternatives. www.veteransforpeace.org

War Resisters Support Campaign: Supports U.S. soldiers seeking asylum in Canada. www.resisters.ca

News and Information

In an era when commercial values overwhelm democratic values and corporate media prevails over public interest, these networks and programs encourage independent, diverse viewpoints.

Broadcast Media

Air America Radio: Informative, opinionated, progressive talk radio. www.airamerica.com

Bill Moyers Journal (PBS): Weekly analysis of vital issues in politics, arts and letters, science, religion, and media. www.pbs.org/moyers/journal

C-SPAN TV: Public access to the political process. www.c-span.org

Democracy Now! (Pacifica): Daily news offering access to people and perspectives rarely heard on corporate-sponsored media. www.democracynow.org

Free Speech TV: Programs that reflect diversity, provide underrepresented perspectives, and shine the spotlight on citizens working for progressive social change. www.freespeech.org

Frontline (PBS): Engaging documentaries that explore and illuminate critical issues of our times. www.pbs.org/wgbh/pages/frontline

Independent Media Center: Network of collectively run independent media organizations and journalists. www.indymedia.org

Link TV: In-depth programs offering a global perspective, giving voice to the voiceless, and encouraging action. www.linktv.org

NOW (PBS): Documentary segments and interviews with original thinkers, offering viewers the context to explore their relationship with the world. www.pbs.org/now

Public Access TV: Community-run cable stations that provide opportunities for locally based programming.

Print Media

Mother Jones: Bimonthly magazine committed to social justice through investigative reporting. www.motherjones.com

The Nation: Weekly magazine that brings a critical spirit to political and social issues (Founded 1865). www.thenation.com

Ode: Monthly magazine of people and ideas changing our world for the better. www.odemagazine.com

The Progressive: Monthly magazine of social, intellectual, and institutional progress (Founded 1909). www.progressive.org

Project Censored: Annual list of stories that were overlooked, under-reported, or self-censored by major U.S. media. www.projectcensored.org

Utne Reader: Bimonthly magazine bringing the best of alternative media. www.utne.com

Yes! : Quarterly magazine supporting active engagement in creating a just, sustainable, compassionate world. www.yesmagazine.org

Internet News Sources

In addition to the above-listed broadcast and print media, the following sources are exclusively online. Follow links on these sites for even more alternatives to mainstream media.

www.alternet.org
www.buzzflash.com
www.commondreams.org
www.dahrjamailiraq.com
www.huffingtonpost.com
www.michaelmoore.com
www.tomdispatch.com
www.truthdig.com
www.truthout.org

Acknowledgments

Ann Wright

I spent virtually my entire adult life working in the federal government, in the U.S. military, and the diplomatic corps. I am very appreciative that since my resignation in March 2003 in opposition to the war on Iraq, in four short years, colleagues in the fields of peace and social justice have included me in their fold.

I want to acknowledge the men and women in government service who took stands of conscience on the war on Iraq and other policies of the Bush administration, particularly Brady Kiesling and John Brown, the two other U.S. diplomats who resigned in opposition to the war in Iraq.

I am deeply appreciative of the tremendous dedication of my co-author, Susan Dixon, who organized the volumes of materials I had collected and then volunteered, while teaching a university course titled "The Geography of War and Peace" and working on her Ph.D. dissertation, to coauthor the book when I became too involved with a busy speaking schedule to write the entire book myself.

I thank Glenn Paige, author of *Nonkilling Global Political Science* and president of the Center for Global Nonviolence in Honolulu, for suggesting to publisher Arnie Kotler that he approach me about writing a book about those who had taken acts of conscience. And many thanks to Arnie Kotler, owner of Koa Books, who felt the stories of these voices of conscience should be told and had the patience to work with two busy first-time authors to get the project done.

Two voices of conscience greatly influenced this book. I want to thank Tex Harris, a retired U.S. diplomat who in the 1970s bravely told the U.S. government (which didn't want to hear) through dissent-channel cables the story of those "disappeared" by the military junta in Argentina.

And we can never thank enough Dan Ellsberg for risking going to prison for xeroxing, hiding, and eventually convincing a congressman to go with him to the *New York Times* to publish the Pentagon

Papers. I respect so much Dan's example of truth telling. One's best hope is that somehow the voices of conscience portrayed in this book will have, in some small way, the same effect that the Pentagon Papers had thirty-five years ago—bringing a war to an end.

I also want to acknowledge Ray McGovern, retired CIA analyst who uses his tremendous skills in writing and speaking to educate the public on the duplicity of the Bush administration.

As a new peace activist, I want to thank for their insights, humor, and guidance Medea Benjamin, Jodie Evans, Gael Murphy, and Diane Wilson and the CODEPINK: Women for Peace, who individually and collectively are some of the most creative, energetic peace activists in the world.

Helping Cindy Sheehan and Gold Star Families for Peace challenge George Bush for twenty-six hot days in the ditches of Crawford, Texas, in August 2005, and at subsequent holidays every time President Bush returns to his estate in Crawford, has been one of the most moving and exhilarating experiences of my life.

I appreciate greatly fellow Veterans for Peace, who believe in peace, not war, and are some of the most dedicated activists we have. Their Arlington West installations are remarkable displays of the costs of war that have touched the hearts of hundreds of thousands.

I have tremendous admiration for members of Iraq Veterans Against the War, veterans of the Iraq and Afghanistan wars who speak so forcefully about their experiences and work to end the war, and for proper treatment for veterans when they return.

And thanks to the parents, brothers, sisters, wives, and husbands of Military Families Speak Out, who talk against the war despite their loved ones' serving in the military.

To Amy Goodman and the staff of *Democracy Now!*, the daily source of news and interviews with people whose important stories seldom are covered in any other media, thank you for keeping us educated!

And, finally, to all the peace activists who vigil every week in their home towns, participate in regional and national peace rallies and marches, practice civil disobedience, and are willing to be arrested to protest an illegal and immoral war, and other important social justice issues, I am honored to be one of you. I dedicate this book to each of you, who display your conscience with every action, every day!

Susan Dixon

To the innumerable victims of this war and to those who tried to prevent it.

Huge thanks to Ann Wright: for inviting me to be part of this incredible project, for giving up the career she loved to follow her conscience, for living a life of integrity, and for being a constant source of inspiration.

Thanks to Arnie Kotler and Koa Books for believing in the importance of this work;

to Irene Calis, my collaborator in FSU, for her love, passion, and sense of justice. As Sweet Honey and the Rock sings, "We who believe in freedom cannot rest...";

to my amazing friends from Trinity College, especially Becky Holt and Michelle Monti, for their love, laughter, and support;

to Susan (Gundersen) Scott for lifelong friendship and legal advice on this book;

to the University of Hawai'i at Manoa for giving me incredible opportunities during my graduate studies. I've been lucky to work with some amazing professors there including Les Sponsel, Krisna Suryanata, and Terence Wesley-Smith.

Thanks especially to Mary McDonald, my adviser at UH, for her generosity, optimism, patience, and unwavering belief in my abilities: I wouldn't be where I am today without you, Mary;

to Kevin Chang and Kalama Cabigon of Kupa'aina for donating their time and talent over the years to share their music with my students and me;

to Sarah Hadmack for her comments and suggestions on the manuscript;

to Rieko Wagoner, my Japanese professor at Trinity, who believed in me early on;

to massage therapist Kristen Chir, for repeatedly fixing my muscles after I stared at a computer screen far too long while working on this book;

to Karen Williams for reminding me to follow my bliss, giving me unconditional love, and for sharing her lifelong ability to see buffalo.

In addition to Karen, I want to thank Amy Eagan and Jill Oliveira-Berry, without whom none of this would have been possible.

Thanks especially to my family for their love and encouragement: to my brother, Dave Dixon, for all of his wise advice over the years and for making me laugh; to my sister, Polly Ann Strovink, and to my mom, Martha Dixon, for being a part of this writing process from the beginning, for their excellent comments and suggestions for this manuscript, and especially for encouraging me to follow my dreams.

To Shelley Hartling, for editing multiple drafts of this manuscript, for love and laughter, for her music and poetry, and for wanting to make the world a better place.

And, finally, thanks to my dad, who taught me every day about love and integrity by the way he lived his life. He trusted and encouraged me to find my own way even when he didn't understand it.

Postscript

The publication of this book has been delayed for four months. When I joined the State Department, I signed a waiver that if I ever wrote a book on international relations or foreign affairs, I would submit the manuscript to the State Department for review, to ensure that I had not inadvertently revealed classified information. I emailed the manuscript to the State Department at the end of July 2007. It took the State Department, Department of Defense, FBI, and Department of Justice four months to review this book. During those four months, many events occurred that we would have liked to include in the book. We are using this Postscript to highlight a few of these events.

More military officers, including former U.S. ground commander in Iraq Lieutenant General Ricardo Sanchez, have spoken out on their concerns on the war on Iraq. On October 12, 2007, retired General Sanchez told a group of military reporters and editors that the Bush administration's handling of the war has been incompetent and warned that the United States was "living a nightmare with no end in sight." He blamed the Bush administration for a "catastrophically flawed, unrealistically optimistic war plan" and called the surge strategy a "desperate" move that will not achieve long-term stability. He said, "After more than fours years of fighting, America continues its desperate struggle in Iraq without any concerted effort to devise a strategy that will achieve victory in that war-torn country or in the greater conflict against extremism." In September, Sanchez told those attending a veterans meeting that there is a "crisis in national political leadership."[1]

Active-duty sergeants from the U.S. Army's 82nd Airborne Division publicly commented on the war in Iraq in a *New York Times* Op-Ed on August 19, 2007, entitled, "The War as We Saw It." They said, "In the end, we need to recognize that our presence may have released Iraqis from the grip of a tyrant, but that it has also robbed them of their self-respect. They will soon realize that the best way to regain dignity is to call us what we are—an army of occupation—and force our withdrawal. Until that happens, it would be prudent for us to increasingly let Iraqis take center stage in all matters, to come up with a nuanced policy in which we assist them from the margins but let them resolve their differences as they see fit. This suggestion is not meant to be defeatist, but rather to highlight our pursuit of incompatible policies to absurd ends without recognizing the incongruities. We need not talk about our morale. As committed soldiers, we will see this mission through."[2]

Shortly after the Op-Ed appeared, two of the seven sergeants were killed in Iraq when their vehicle flipped, and a third sergeant was shot in the head, reportedly by insurgent gunfire, sustaining a traumatic brain injury.

Twelve former active-duty U.S. Army Captains also spoke out. They wrote in the *Washington Post* on October 16, 2007, in "The Real Iraq We Knew": "There is one way we might be able to succeed in Iraq. To continue an operation of this intensity and duration, we would have to abandon our volunteer military for compulsory service. Short of that, our best option is to leave Iraq immediately. A scaled withdrawal will not prevent a civil war, and it will spend more blood and treasure on a losing proposition. America, it has been five years. It's time to make a choice."[3]

More information on the extent of the Bush administration's eavesdropping on American citizens emerged in the autumn of 2007. In early November 2007, former AT&T technician Mark Klein revealed that the National Security Agency set up secret internet and telephone rooms in the major communications companies—all major companies except Qwest—to sweep up incredible volumes of data from American citizens. Klein said that the subjects of the surveillance program were American citizens, not overseas terrorists. A class action lawsuit as well as thirty-seven other lawsuits alleging that the communications companies illegally worked with the NSA has been filed in federal court. Litigants are demanding that Congress deny the Bush administration's request for immunity for the corporations' cooperation with the NSA.[4]

Political intimidation and curtailment of civil liberties of opponents of the Bush administration increased during the four months this book was being reviewed by the U.S. Government. I found myself denied entry to Canada, because I am now listed on the FBI's National Crime Information Center database (created to track violent gangs, terrorist groups, foreign fugitives, parole violators and sex offenders) for peaceful, nonviolent misdemeanor convictions from protesting the war in Iraq. While many Canadian parliamentarians are outraged that their government is using a tainted FBI database to deny entry to peace activists from the United States, to date we have been unable to stir Congress to find out who ordered that the names of peace activists be placed on the database, when the order was given, and for what reason. For me to enter Canada—after the one-year ban on my entry is lifted—I must be "criminally rehabilitated" before they will even consider my application for a Temporary Resident Permit, which is essentially a visa for one who has been previously denied entry. It appears that the Harper government in Canada is working with the Bush administration to silence dissent against the war by curtailing the freedom to travel.

The role of dissent and the measures taken by governments against opposition were admirably discussed by Naomi Wolf in her book, *The End of America: A Letter of Warning to a Young Patriot,* published in September 2007 by Chelsea Green. Wolf urges us to critically evaluate the Bush administration's approach to national security and dissent after 9/11 in terms of how the measures have affected our civil liberties. She calls the evaluation "Ten Steps to Close Down an Open Society."[5] She writes that a government intent on stifling dissent and opposition will:

1. Invoke a terrifying internal and external enemy.
2. Create a prison system outside the rule of law for troublemakers.
3. Develop paramilitary groups to intimidate citizens.
4. Set up an internal surveillance system.
5. Harass citizens groups.
6. Engage in arbitrary detention and release.
7. Target key individuals.
8. Control the press.
9. Equate dissent with treason.
10. Suspend the rule of law.

We hope that the stories of the women and men in this book, *Dissent: Voices of Conscience,* will give you courage to stand up and speak out against governmental abuses, especially those listed in Wolf's Ten Steps. The future of our country depends on your actions.

Do not be silent!

Index

About the Authors

Ann Wright grew up in Bentonville, Arkansas, and attended the University of Arkansas, where she received a master's and a law degree. She also has a master's degree in national security affairs from the U.S. Naval War College. After college, she spent thirteen years in the U.S. Army and sixteen additional years in the Army Reserves, retiring as a Colonel. She is airborne-qualified.

In 1987, Col. Wright joined the Foreign Service and served as U.S. Deputy Ambassador in Sierra Leone, Micronesia, Afghanistan, and Mongolia. She received the State Department's Award for Heroism for her actions during the evacuation of 2,500 people from the civil war in Sierra Leone. She was on the first State Department team to go to Afghanistan and helped reopen the Embassy there in December 2001. Her other overseas assignments include Somalia, Kyrgyzstan, Grenada, Micronesia, and Nicaragua. On March 19, 2003, the eve of the U.S. invasion of Iraq, Ann Wright cabled a letter of resignation to Secretary of State Colin Powell, stating that without the authorization of the UN Security Council, the invasion and occupation of a Muslim, Arab, oil-rich country would be a disaster. Since then, she has been writing and speaking out for peace. She fasted for a month, picketed at Guantánamo, served as a juror on an international impeachment commission, and has been arrested numerous times for peaceful, nonviolent protest of Bush's policies, particularly the war on Iraq. She lives in Honolulu.

Susan Dixon grew up in Connecticut and received a bachelor's degree in Asian studies from Trinity College in Hartford. She earned a master's degree in geography from the University of Hawai'i at Manoa, where she is a doctoral candidate. She teaches  on the geography of peace and war as well as on political activism and nonviolence. She has won a three-year fellowship from the National Science Foundation and the Frances Davis Award for Excellence in Undergraduate Teaching at the University of Hawai'i. She spent her senior year in college on a yearlong academic study abroad program focusing on "The World Politics of Peace and Conflict." This International Honors Program was led by Johan Galtung, who is widely considered the founder of peace studies as a science. Dixon has also taught English in a Japanese junior high school and raised a German shepherd puppy to be a seeing eye dog. She has lived, studied, and traveled in thirty-eight countries on six continents, speaks Japanese and Spanish, and lives in Honolulu. She wishes she had more time for scuba diving.

koa books

Koa Books publishes works on personal transformation, progressive politics, and native cultures.

Please visit our website, www.koabooks.com, for a full list of recent and forthcoming titles.

Koa Books
P.O. Box 822
Kihei, Hawai'i 96753
www.koabooks.com